Give God a Chance:
Christian Spirituality from the Edgar Cayce Readings

by
James Kyle Brown

ISBN 0-75962-169-1

This book is printed on acid free paper.

1stBooks – rev. 03/14/01

To my friend and my wife,
Linda

Contents

PART ONE: THE EDGAR CAYCE READINGS

1   Introduction 3

2   Don't Throw the Baby Out With the Bathwater:
       Personal Experiences with the Readings 8
       **There is a River—Involvement in the Work—Personal
       Testimony—Applying the Information**

3   Faith in a Promise: Edgar Cayce and His Gift 13
       **Edgar Cayce the Man—A Gift of the Spirit—Factors
       Affecting the Readings—Cayce as an Evangelist**

4   Try the Spirits: Sources and Purposes of the Readings 23
       **Scriptural?—Supplant Individuals Relationship to
       God?—Spiritualism?—Psychic or Occult?—Eastern
       Religion?—Channeled?—Sources of Information?—
       Readings Protected from Evil?—Idolatry?—Demonic?—
       Used for Selfish Purposes?—Challenge to Religion?—
       Mistakes in Readings?—Former Members?—Cult?—
       Conclusions**

PART TWO: GOD, MANKIND AND SPIRITUAL LAWS

5   A Creation Cosmology for Today: Why Humankind and
       the Universe Exist 51
       **Secular vs. Spiritual—Back to the Source—A Plan of
       Salvation—Evolution: Physical or Spiritual?—
       History/Prehistory/Myth—Creation Cosmology—
       Conclusions—Additional Readings**

6   The Concept of Oneness from the Readings:
Monotheism 65
**God Is—Anthropomorphism—Father-Mother God—
Monotheism—Evil/Dualism—Oneness—Idolatry—The
Law of Love**

7   Manifestation in Three Dimensions—Body, Mind, Soul:
The Trinity 78
**The Temple of God—Projector Analogy—The Father—
The Son—The Holy Spirit—The Harmonious Triune**

8   Life More Abundant: Evolution of the Soul—
Reincarnation 84
**History—Prayer for the Deceased—Reaction Against
Dualism—Other Objections—The Readings—Why Don't
We Remember?—Looking for Information About Past
Lives—Schoolhouse Earth—Disadvantages vs.
Advantages—Social Implications—Sharing the Concept
of Reincarnation**

9   Spiritual Laws in a Physical World: Cause and Effect—
Karma or Grace... 105
**Church Experiences—The Man Who Was Born Blind—
Misuse of the Knowledge of the Law—Meeting
Ourselves—Spiritual Laws—God's Plan for Us—The Law
of Grace—Being Proactive—Teaching Experience—Why
Bad Things Happen to Good People—The Karma Game—
Graduation—The Pattern of Salvation—Additional
Readings**

PART THREE: CHRISTIANITY AND THE CAYCE READINGS

10   New Meaning to the Words of Old: The Bible 129
**Relevance of the Bible in Today's World—The Bible in
the Readings—Exegesis—Inerrancy—Study of the
Scriptures—Israel—A New Meaning to the Words of
Old—Behavior of Bible Characters—Challenge for the
Future**

11   The Master in All Ages and His Mission: Jesus Who
     Became the Christ.. 143
     **Picture of Jesus—Will the Real Jesus Please Stand Up—
     Jesus/Christ—Jesus Who Became the Christ—Former
     Appearances of the Christ—The Way—The
     Pattern/Example—Love Manifested—The Servant—
     Forgiveness—The Cross—Resurrection—Personal
     Relationship—Atonement—Other Biblical Names Used
     in the Readings**

12   Children of the Living God: The Early Church.............. 167
     **Birth of the Church—Sects/Heretics/Gnostics—
     Children of the Living God—Gnostic vs. Orthodox: Faith
     Watered Down—Church Councils—Conclusions**

13   From Denominationalism to Inspired Democracy: Unity
     in the Body of Christ 180
     **Church Politics—Church Membership—The True
     Church—Methods of Salvation—Denominationalism or
     Sectarianism—Church Unity—Jesus is the Church—
     Inspired Democracy—No Patent on Spirituality—
     Witness to the Readings—"Feed My Sheep"**

14   Finding Common Ideals: Other Religions...................... 205
     **Judaism—Islam—Hinduism/Buddhism—King of Kings—
     Sharing the Faith**

PART FOUR: CHRISTIAN SPIRITUALITY
APPLIED

15   A Closer Walk: Manifesting the Fruits of the Spirit........ 217

16   The Harmonious Triune: Meditation—Listening to God . 225
     **What is Meditation?—The Harmonious Triune—The
     Body is the Temple—Preparation—Protection—Be Still
     and Know—Affirmations/Scriptures—Gland Centers
     (Chakras)—Kundalini—Pineal First: The Mark of the
     Lamb—Purpose: Working Meditation—Group**

Meditation—Problems—Why Reach Out to the Churches?

17 Spiritual Growth: Safe Ways to Use Dreams and
Intuition..237
**Prayer—Fasting—Conviction/Repentance—
Dreams/Visions—Speaking in Tongues—Growth**

18 Causes and Corrections for Dis-ease: Spiritual and
Physical Healing...246
**Illness Caused by Sin—Attitudes Affect Health—All
Healing is From God—The Great Physician—Healing
From Within—Changing Old Patterns—A Person Must
Want Healing—Group Effort—Learning How to Heal—
Meditation and Prayer—Laying on of Hands—Patience
and Persistence—Give God the Glory**

19 Signs in the Heavens: Astrology—Science or
Superstition? 256
**The Zodiac—Biblical Warnings—Proper Use of
Knowledge—Interplanetary Sojourns—Free Will—Study
of History—Signs Not to Be Worshiped**

20 Mind Is the Builder: The Psychology of the Soul............263
**Mind is the Builder—Ideals—Thoughts are Things—
Personality/Individuality—Right Thinking—Shortcuts—
Mind Control—Self-Control—Learning—Attitude—
Resentment—Self-esteem vs. Guilt—Condemnation—
Mental Illness—Humor Heals the Mind—Peace:
Contentment vs. Satisfaction**

21 Applied Spirituality: Changing Old Patterns and
Lifestyles...280
**Spiritualizing Desires—Diet and Exercise—Farming and
Gardening—Sexuality—Marriage—Divorce—Home—
Children—Music—Balancing Work and Recreation**

PART FIVE: WORLD TRANSFORMATION

22   A Christ-Centered Worldview: Integrating Science and
      Religion 297
      **Positivism/Humanism—Objectivity—The Religion of
      Science—The Science of Religion—Religion and Science
      are the Same—An Integrated Worldview—Evolution vs.
      Revolution—Progress**

23   No Desire to Sin—A New Heaven and a New Earth:
      Hope for World Peace 313
      **Civilization—The Invisible Empire—Christian Witness—
      Conspiracism—The Fatherhood of God and the
      Brotherhood of Man—New World Order—Freedom—
      Equality—Technology—Environment—Leadership—
      Starling of the White House—
      Economics/Poverty/Wealth Distribution—Capitalism
      vs. Communism: Let Love Rule—Armageddon—Save the
      World Club—Second Coming—The Promised Time of
      Peace**

24   What Will You Do With This Man, Jesus? 335
      The Work—A Final Word

PART ONE

Edgar Cayce and his wife, Gertrude
©Copyright Edgar Cayce Foundation, 2001
Used with permission

The Edgar Cayce Readings

1

Introduction

For more than thirty years I have studied, and tried to test in my life, a body of information known as the Edgar Cayce readings. Even though I was a Christian before learning about the readings, some very personal experiences had left me with a commitment to seek a closer walk with the Master, Jesus the Christ. It was only after I began to read and study about Edgar Cayce and his Work that I felt confident it was possible to satisfy my deeper spiritual yearnings. Eventually, my wife and I connected with other interested people and participated in several *Search for God* study groups sponsored by the Association for Research and Enlightenment, Inc. (A.R.E.), the organization Cayce formed to carry on his Work. We became A.R.E. members as well.

Over the years I have tried to share this information with friends in church. Most of the people I talked to had little or no real knowledge of the Cayce readings, yet they often had many misperceptions and doubts about this Work. I gave various books about the Cayce Work to those who were interested. Nevertheless, I still felt a need to share my own experiences with others who might want to bridge the gap between the spiritual perspective of the readings and the beliefs of organized religious groups.

The Cayce material covers a broad range of subjects that are relevant to a Christian worldview. As I became more aware that this information could not be explained in just a few minutes, I began to write down my impressions of Cayce's Work, along with some supporting readings. This was somewhat helpful when I shared it with others. But the readings insisted that we should give only that which has been helpful to us personally. Realizing that what I had put together might sound a bit theoretical, I began to back it up with personal experiences and those things that I have seen demonstrated in real life. This effort has developed into something like a personal testimony, although it is not a personal biography. It is about what I have learned from Cayce's perspective on what it means to be a follower of Jesus the Christ. If my comments still seem to have a theological flavor, it is because theological questions have been meaningful to me in my personal relationships and also because of my desire to reach out to people in the various churches, most of whom operate to some degree within the web of historical theology.

A slight change of focus also occurred when the opportunity came to write an article for *Venture Inward* magazine, published by the A.R.E. The article, *Integrating Cayce & Church*, allowed me to share my experiences with other persons who were already involved in the Cayce Work and who might also want to work through their churches or other organizations to share the wisdom of the readings. This effort is a two-way street. Whether you are a church member, a minister, or an A.R.E. member, I hope that *Give God a Chance* will stimulate an interchange of ideas, which will allow the ideals in the readings to be tested. I believe that the results will be constructive.

Several people have asked me why those who wish to use the readings have not just formed a new church. There are already so many denominations with their various beliefs—why not one more? The readings always insisted, however, that no "ism, schism, or cult" should be formed around this Work. Such a church might answer some short-term needs for certain individuals, but it would not offer anything to those who are committed to remaining faithful to their present church family.

I once helped some friends form a local organic growers' association. I told them that our little organization was a wonderful way to help one another to improve the quality of life, but that we should also expect that these organic principles would eventually be used on a global scale by a world that was in desperate need of them. As our local efforts progressed, we actually found some support through the state university and even through the United States Department of Agriculture.

I have the same feeling about the Christian spirituality expressed in the Cayce readings. This Work has already had far-reaching positive effects on this world, but the effort has only begun. There is tremendous suffering in the world that can only be healed by a better relationship with our Creator. We need not assume that all church environments will present a closed door to the concepts in the Cayce readings. Churches often seem to be very slow-moving entities. Their inertia has the advantage of making them stable institutions in a changing world, but that stability does not have to come at the expense of spiritual growth. I have neither the advantages nor the disadvantages of being a trained minister or theologian. However, I have talked with some of both, and I have found that many church leaders are becoming more aware of the need for a deeper kind of spirituality. Some of them may not be as tradition bound as they are often stereotyped to be. They are sometimes even more open to this information than are lay people.

Jesus taught that we should judge each work by its fruits. When Christian friends express skepticism, it is not fair to assume that they are guided by selfish motives. I suspect that, in spite of some recent publicity about Edgar Cayce, most Christians don't actually know what the readings say and just how much they are in harmony with the teachings of the Christ. They are probably not aware of the good that has come from Cayce's ministry. They may never know, unless those of us who have benefited from these spiritual insights live by our ideals, not only in church but also in business, government, education, recreation, and all phases of our lives.

The main title of this book, *Give God a Chance,* is a direct quote from the Cayce readings. This phrase, found is several readings, is archetypal of the advice given throughout the readings. The subtitle, *Christian Spirituality from the Edgar Cayce Readings*, is perhaps more definitive of the focus. Edgar Cayce, both consciously and in the readings, preferred that his Work be called *spirituality*. Here are a few definitions of spirituality as I understand it in the context of the readings:

- Developing a personal relationship with God
- Making soul growth one's first priority
- Being quickened by the Spirit
- Manifesting the fruits of the Spirit
- Reliance on the biblical promises of eternal life
- Bringing constructive influences into the earth by compliance with Divine Law
- Living by the golden rule, knowing that the way you treat others is the way you treat God

Since the Edgar Cayce readings are at the heart of this Work, they are often quoted in *Give God a Chance*. I sometimes tried to express the meaning of the readings in my own words, but frequently felt compelled to let the readings speak for themselves. If these quotes seem rather lengthy at times, it is because I have followed the suggestions in the readings to avoid taking them out of context. Some background information is also given where it is relevant.

The Edgar Cayce readings, which will be explained in greater detail in later chapters, are frequently referred to simply as "the readings." The insights given in these readings are often called the "information." "This work" or "the Work" usually refers not to this book, but to the ongoing efforts of the A.R.E. and study groups around the world to apply the Christian aspects of the readings. The readings refer to Jesus the Christ with a variety of biblical names. One of the names frequently used in this book to retain the flavor of the readings is "the Master." "The Master" is never used, here or in the readings, to indicate Cayce or any person other than Jesus the Christ.

Please be patient with the readings. They often assume that the recipient is aware of information from some previous reading. They also sometimes refer to some background material or other facts in a very subtle way. They frequently use Old English even when not directly quoting the Bible. However, in spite of some unusual wording, you will probably find many of the readings crystal clear and, perhaps, even elegant.

Bible verses have usually been quoted from the Jerusalem Bible (JB) or from the King James Version (KJV). The Cayce readings themselves usually quote or paraphrase the King James Version when referring to biblical quotes. A few lengthy quotes from the Apocrypha and from the works of Josephus are included because some readers may not have ready access to these sources.

Quotes from the readings use a numeral citation such as 000-00, where the numbers before the hyphen give the code number assigned to the person receiving the reading, and the numbers after the hyphen give the number of the reading for that person. Some readings include an "R" designation, which indicates additional information placed in the Reports file after the reading was taken. In some cases several readings have been put at the end of a chapter as a reference. This does not mean that this book is intended to be a complete encyclopedia of the Cayce Work. Serious students will also look for the many other excellent books about the Work, a few of which I will mention as having been inspirational to me personally. The complete computerized body of readings and related information on CD-ROM is also available from the A.R.E.

Because some may want to use this book to find examples of what the readings say about certain topics, I have tried to organize it with that in mind. It is not essential to read them in the order they are presented. Some of the chapters are a collection of topics that almost stand alone, leaving it to you to integrate them into your own belief system. In addition to being an overview of the Christian aspects of the Cayce readings I would hope that these topics might be considered as a resource for preparing a sermon, a Sunday school lesson, or a theological discussion.

While not intended to offend Cayce students from other religious backgrounds, or to excuse the narrow-mindedness of religious bigotry, *Give God a Chance* is an effort to magnify the Christian evangelical spirit of the Edgar Cayce readings. I would hope that it might also open a door to those of other religions who seek a better understanding of the Christ.

An ordained minister of a mainline denomination once told me that, while he thought there was some truth in the readings, this material should not be given to the public at this time. Whether he was right or not, the cat is out of the bag. Many books have been written about Edgar Cayce, and his insights are widely known in the world today. I would only hope that a better understanding of this Work might clear up some misperceptions and make it more accessible to sincere seekers of all religions who would use it constructively.

The task of sharing this information is not always easy, but the mission is clear. Reading 254-106, given in May 1940 for the Association for Research and Enlightenment, Inc. regarding the "ideals and purposes" of the organization, said, "...with no desire to induce others to believe anything other than that which has proven helpful in the experiences of others; no desire to induce others to embrace or even try something other than that in which they are satisfied; but the desire to spread peace, harmony, and the love which is magnified in the life and teachings of Jesus, the Christ."

2

Don't Throw the Baby Out With the Bathwater: Personal Experiences with the Readings

Ask and it will be given to you; search, and you will find; knock and the door will be opened to you. Matthew 7:7-8 (JB)

There Is a River

One evening in the early 1960s, I was sitting at a table with several other Air Force officers in an "alert shack." We lived there for a week at a time, and sometimes the hours passed slowly. On this particular evening, we had become bored with pool, cards, and TV, so we were just talking the time away.

The conversation turned to idle speculation about the origin of the universe, the possibility of our awareness of other dimensions, and the concept of infinity. A friend quoted something from a book he had read and asked if I would be interested in it. I had nothing better to read, so I told him that I would like to see it. The book he brought to me turned out to be *There Is a River*, a story of Edgar Cayce's life by Thomas Sugrue.

I had been raised in a very orthodox Christian home and had a strong commitment to following Jesus Christ as my personal Savior. Having internally resolved many of my own questions about faith in God, I still had many questions about church dogmas and doctrines. I was particularly concerned about the multiplicity of denominations and religions that all claimed to have the exclusive truth. I had also received a secular education, which left me wondering why so many intelligent people tried so hard to discount religion. It seemed that leaders in almost all schools of thought offered scenarios based as much on imagination as on any personal demonstration of truth.

I had begun to read about religion, philosophy, and other subjects to learn more about the thoughts of others. My hope was to find some universal principles about the human experience that would help me to live in peace with my fellow human beings on this beautiful planet Earth. As I read *There Is a River*, I was immediately fascinated with Cayce's life and Work. I was impressed with his humility, and it was obvious that his Christian faith and ideals were the guiding principles behind the information given in his readings. Even though some of the concepts seemed different from my orthodox training, I was convinced that there was something there worthy of further consideration. Although I had read only part of the book when I had to return it, I remembered the title and looked for it in the local library. The book was listed in the card catalog, but it was always checked out when I tried to find it. It was several years later, after I had gotten married and transferred to another state, that I found *There Is a River* in a library. As my wife and I read it together we were very excited about what we had found.

You can imagine our disappointment when our friends and family members met our enthusiasm with doubt or suspicion. However, I knew that my faith had been deepened, and I had gained some new perspectives on life from what I had read.

I tried to apply some of the concepts found in the readings. The principles of diet and health were especially helpful to me. I lost weight and corrected some minor health problems. I felt better mentally and spiritually as well. I became more active in community and church work, even though I learned to be cautious about sharing my interest in the Cayce readings with others in the church.

Involvement in the Work

Over the years my wife and I have met many others who have had an interest in the readings. Some were only curious or they were looking for sensational phenomena or unusual experiences. Most of those moved on to other pursuits. Others found more of what they needed in some other belief system (not necessarily contrary to the readings). However, we have kept in touch with a few spiritually minded Christians who have continued to study and apply the information given in the Cayce readings.

We have also continued to be involved in church work. After moving to a small town in Middle Tennessee several years ago, we joined a Swiss Reformed church that is affiliated with the United Church of Christ. Our family has been warmly accepted into this church. And even though a few people are concerned about my interest in the Cayce readings, I have served as a deacon, as an elder, and as Sunday school superintendent. Sometimes it seems as if I live in two different worlds or cultures that could learn from

9

each other. I have searched my conscience and the readings for ways to integrate this Work with my church involvement.

Several years ago, our church was temporarily without a pastor. As the supply minister one Sunday, we had a dynamic, spirit-filled gentleman who gave an inspiring sermon. After the service, while we were having dinner at a neighbor's home, he told us how he had once been involved in giving psychic readings. He felt that he had been used by some negative force and that his Christian conversion had led him to discontinue such activities. Then someone asked him what he thought about Edgar Cayce. His reply was a quote from an earlier book about Cayce: "Let's not throw the baby out with the bathwater." He said he had seen too much healing and good come from the Cayce readings to consider them to be from any false source.

The Work of Edgar Cayce has inspired me to read the Bible through several times. His insights into the history of the Israelite people and his suggestions for application of biblical principles have made the Word come alive with a story of our relationship to a loving Creator.

Personal Testimony

I have heard many personal testimonies of how someone was changed by a religious experience. It may have come through some church experience or through reading the Scriptures or from responding to a sermon or the example of a friend. I believe that these are constructive experiences, and I am not surprised that people who have had such experiences feel compelled to share them. This is the way I feel about the Cayce readings. Wanting to share what I have found without presenting a challenge to anyone's faith or causing dissent because of the unusual nature of this Work, I searched the readings for some guidance. When Edgar Cayce was asked how one could approach strangers in relation to the Work, he replied:

> Merely give "This I know by experience. You may have same if you seek. No one may attain same for you." For thy relationships to thy Creator are personal, not group, not relations. No wife would like for the husband to love many women. No man desires that many men love the wife, in the close relationships; but all as to God. That! "If you seek you may know. For it is a personal experience." And, as

has been given, if it does not answer to that divine within, it is not yet time. For how gave He when there was the call for a separation? The day is not yet fulfilled for the Hivites nor the Hittites, but their end is in sight. So as you approach those that know not, give only your personal experience, and "Take it or leave it, as it is." 254-95

While this information is not new or necessarily different from that which can be found in other sources, it offered a perspective that allowed me to have a clearer picture of my whole relationship to God. And it allowed me to build upon what I had already found to be true. While I have applied the readings with good results, the line between that which I can claim to have demonstrated in my life and that which simply resonates with the spirit within is not always clear. I still find new gems of wisdom in the readings almost daily, and I will probably continue to study and test them as long as I live.

Recently, after a Sunday school discussion of original sin, I privately offered to a friend a perspective on that subject from the readings. He said that he had never considered the Cayce material seriously because it seemed so outlandish on the surface. Even though I questioned myself as to whether I should have shared this reading with him, I could only think of how shallow the argument between secular theories of accidental evolution and the contrived church doctrines appeared to me. I was also aware that some of the seemingly outlandish things from the readings have been verified by modern science. This is not to say that I believe the readings are infallible or that they have all of the answers. For me they have provided only an inspiration to study more of all disciplines and to integrate what little I do know into a meaningful belief system that includes God.

Applying the Information

In 1940, Cayce gave a reading for a thirty eight-year-old man who was a serious alcoholic. He outlined some of the causes of the disease and gave a comprehensive plan to correct the situation. He cautioned that to do nothing, or even to partially apply the treatments, could result in a complete loss of this individual's self-control and even bring about physical disaster. Knowing that this person could choose not to do the things that were suggested, he added:

11

Do not attempt to do one portion of the treatment without the other. If the body doesn't make up its *mind* to give God an opportunity, through an honest, sincere trial in the manners indicated, then it will be as He indicated, of those who would offend one of the little ones.

Ye have the opportunity, ye have those surroundings, ye have those opportunities for making and becoming that which has been thy desire, thy hope. Give God a chance with thy soul. For He hath not willed that any soul should perish, but hath with every temptation prepared a way, a manner. For as His promise has been, "If ye call, I will *hear!*" and will answer speedily.

Forsake not that which is set before thee. Make thy paths straight. Ye *can* in Him. 2161-1

Fortunately Mr. [2161] did follow the physical and mental suggestions given in his reading and was completely cured of his alcoholism. In reviewing the follow-up information on other readings, however, I found that some of those who had readings never followed their suggestions, thereby forfeiting any healing that might have resulted if they had.

When I study the readings, I often feel that they are speaking to those who think of themselves as the community of faith. The readings offer suggestions that might be applied to heal some of the sickness of our modern world. Even though I know that this information can be shared only with those who seek it and that it is often rejected offhand because of misinformation, I also know that there are many sincere seekers in the churches. To every person who believes in a loving Creator and who wants to have a better relationship with Him, I feel compelled to offer the opportunity to look at this information fairly and to just give God a chance to show what He can do with your soul, with your family, with your world.

As you test this information (or that from any other source) to see if it is in harmony with the Scriptures, I would suggest that you look within to the Spirit of the Christ as your guide and interpreter. The water could get a bit deep at times, but there is nothing to fear if you insist on having none other than the Master as your guide.

3

Faith in a Promise:
Edgar Cayce and His Gift

I tell you most solemnly, whoever believes in me will perform the same works as I do myself, he will perform even greater works, because I am going to the Father.   John 14:12 (JB)

Edgar Cayce the Man
Some of the first books I read about Edgar Cayce were about his life and his unusual gift. I wanted to know about his roots, his education, his connection to any group or movement, what he read, and where he went to church. Did he speak from his own experience, and what were his purposes for giving these readings? If he really had some special talent, was it a gift of the Holy Spirit or was it from some other source?

Edgar Cayce was born on a farm in Christian County, Kentucky, near Hopkinsville, on March 18, 1877. As a child, he attended the Old Liberty Christian Church, where he became the church sexton at age ten. That same year, he requested, and was given, his first Bible. He read completely through the Bible in less than six months and continued to read it through at least once a year for the rest of his life.

One day, after studying his Bible and praying in his favorite place in the woods, Cayce had a vision of an angel who told him that his prayers had been answered and asked him what he would like to have. Thinking about how Jesus had healed people, he said that he would like to be able to help others, especially children when they were sick. After telling him that this would be granted, the angel disappeared. When he later told his mother about the vision, she assured him that it had been an answer to prayer and encouraged him to continue reading his Bible. Cayce often referred to this vision as having been a defining moment in his Work.

Having completed only the eighth grade in school, Cayce worked on the farm for a while. He later moved to town, where he got a job in a bookstore. In Hopkinsville, when he was eighteen, he had an encounter with the evangelist, Dwight Moody. He told Moody about his vision and other experiences that he had had. Moody shared some of his own visions with Cayce and asked him if he had considered being an evangelist. Cayce said that it had been his ambition to be a preacher, but he could not afford the education that he needed. Moody then suggested that Cayce could use his knowledge of the Bible to teach Sunday school. Cayce followed his advice, and for many years taught Sunday school and led an outstanding Christian Endeavor group. More than forty years later, in 1942, Cayce included the following statement in a letter to a person for whom he had given a reading:

> [I] Think the man who made the greatest impression on me of all the ministers I ever met was D. L. Moody, while not of the Christian Church, was a great Evangelist, and [I] knew him very well when possibly needed some spiritual [counsel], at least from that Ass'n I began a class as a young man that possibly has had a bit to do with Foreign Missions. Dr. William Hardy was a member of that class, the first medical Missionary to Tibet. He is still there, so I hear, as well as two that went to China; another to Hawaii and to So. Africa. An interesting fact the class I try and teach now is supporting a native missionary in Africa who works under the young man, Mr. Taylor, who is in that class of mine in 1898—has been in the Congo many years, he is also of the Christian Church. Thank you for your interest in the work [I] have been doing now for more than 40 years. That its basis is in Christian living, is what appeals to me. Report 2697-1 R-3

(For more details about Cayce's encounters with Moody and many more details about his life, see *The Lost Memoirs of Edgar Cayce* by A. Robert Smith or *Edgar Cayce: An American Prophet* by Sidney D. Kirkpatrick.)

Edgar took a sales position when he was twenty-one, but he had to give it up because of a chronic loss of his voice. He eventually became a photographer, a trade he continued even after his voice had been restored. After several doctors failed to cure his illness, he allowed a traveling hypnotist to try to correct the problem. Cayce was able to speak normally under hypnosis, but the posthypnotic suggestion failed to produce any positive results.

Then a local man, Al Layne, who was studying suggestive therapeutics and osteopathy, asked if he could try an idea that he thought might help Cayce's throat.

With Cayce under hypnosis, Layne asked him to describe his own condition. He not only correctly described the problem in his own throat, but he also gave the cause and told Layne to make suggestions that would improve the circulation in the affected area. Layne followed the directions that were given, and Cayce was able to speak when he awoke. When his voice later failed several more times, he returned to Layne, and the same treatment restored his voice each time.

Layne was so impressed with Cayce's ability to diagnose his own illness that he tried asking Cayce about other people's afflictions. Encouraged with the results of this experiment, several physicians began to ask for Cayce's help on difficult cases. They even found that he did not have to be present with the patient to diagnose a disease. He merely had to be given the patient's name and address, and he could describe the physical condition and suggest the appropriate treatment. This process in which Cayce would lie down, lose consciousness, and then respond to questions about whatever information was sought, came to be known as a "reading."

Cayce continued his profession as a photographer and used his special gift somewhat reluctantly. He wanted to be sure that no one would be hurt by the suggestions that he gave while he was unconscious. He shunned publicity and was concerned about the legal implications of what he and Layne were doing.

One of the earliest cases that convinced him that his gift could help others was that of Aimee Dietrich. This five-year-old girl had deteriorated mentally since the age of two. She was having frequent convulsions and had been diagnosed as having a fatal brain disease. Cayce told her desperate parents that the condition was a result of a fall from a carriage. Her mother confirmed that the fall had occurred. Over a period of weeks, Layne administered the treatments that were suggested, and Aimee was completely cured. The only pay Edgar would accept was the train fare to the Dietrich home.

In 1903, after a six-year courtship, Edgar married Gertrude Evans. They settled in Bowling Green, Kentucky, and began to raise a family. Gertrude was reluctant to have Edgar give readings at first, because of the way he was treated by those who wanted to exploit him for personal gain. However, she later became instrumental in assisting him to use his gift to help others. When Cayce moved his family to Selma, Alabama, in 1912, he concentrated on his photography business and tried to avoid letting anyone know about his ability to diagnose illnesses. However, knowledge about his gift followed him, and he could not turn people down when they asked for his help.

A number of other individuals played an important role in helping him develop his healing ministry. One very positive change came when Gertrude began to conduct the readings. Cayce could put himself into the altered state from which he gave the readings, but he did not remember what he had said afterward. He trusted Gertrude to be sure that he would not be used for any selfish purpose.

In addition to the physical readings, many individuals sought personal or spiritual advice. Some of the sponsors of the Work requested readings for philosophical questions. One of the most interesting times for Cayce was when the readings began to suggest to people that they had lived on this earth before. Being a devout Christian, he had to do some soul searching and study of the Scriptures to reconcile this knowledge with his faith. Eventually, he began to allow more questions from others about past lives, and the information often proved to be helpful and constructive. Many such readings, now known as "life readings," were given in subsequent years.

Only when he finally decided to devote all of his time to the Work did Cayce accept a modest fee for his services. The financial rewards were never great, and he gave many readings without charge for persons who could not pay. Cayce and his family went through many turbulent times as he worked with others to try to find financial backing for his dream of building a hospital to carry on his healing Work. Eventually, following the advice given in the readings, the Cayces moved to Virginia Beach, Virginia, where a hospital was built.

During his lifetime Cayce was physically abused, jailed, and tempted with offers of fame and fortune. Nevertheless, he continued to stand firm on his ideal of service to others. More than once, Cayce was censured by other church members because of his gift, but he remained a faithful church member all of his life. For many years, all of the readings were recorded. When Edgar Cayce died on January 3, 1945, at the age of sixty-seven, he left a body of information, including more than 14,000 readings, which has yet to be fully appreciated.

There has been considerable interest in recent years in trying to look at Cayce and his gift in a historical context. When his life is considered with respect to both medical and religious trends, we can find many parallels to other persons and movements of his day. It is also interesting to speculate about the values that may have been imparted to him by the society in which he lived, as well as how his associates in the Work affected his ideas.

Some have suggested that Cayce's access to such a vast amount of knowledge resulted from his early years of working in a bookstore. I searched through the readings to find references to books that were mentioned, quoted, or recommended for people to read. Of course the Bible was the most frequent, just as it was the thing that Cayce read more than any other source. A few of the other books that were suggested for reading were: *Varieties of Religious Experience* by William James, *The Life of Christ* by Giovanni Papini, *Tertium Organum* by P.D. Ouspensky, and *The Quest of the Holy Grail* (author not given). At least two of these were written after Cayce's work in the bookstore. Henry Van Dyke was mentioned, and John Bunion was quoted. The index of the readings also contains numerous other references to *Bartlett's Familiar Quotations*. The common thread in most of these quotes and references was the implication that matter is a manifestation of Spirit rather than the other way around. They seem to have been given more as collaborative evidence with which the seeker could identify on a particular point, than as a definitive source for the overall worldview expressed in the readings. In fact, the readings are often at considerable variance with some other aspects of the sources that were quoted. In spite of his limited formal education Cayce may have read many other sources that we do not know about, but I think it would be a mistake to try to attribute everything in the readings to personal experiences that he had in this one life.

A Gift of the Spirit

Having some knowledge about Edgar Cayce's life was helpful, but what about the spiritual nature of his gift? I knew that I had to look at this source of information critically to determine if it was in harmony with the Scriptures and with my own inner guidance. The readings themselves had much to say about the source of the information given. The following discourse was given on June 20, 1941:

[Gertrude Cayce]: Considering the fact that a major portion of the information given through Edgar Cayce has dealt with bettering the physical health of individuals, and in view of the fact that the information appears to be based upon certain fundamental principles, you will give at this time a discourse on the truths of human anatomy and health upon which the analyses and suggestions for treatments are based. You will then answer any questions that may be asked.

[Edgar Cayce]: Yes, we have the question sought. Yet those analyzing and attempting to secure information have not rightly judged sources nor the conditions surrounding that which prompted the activities of the individual entity, Edgar Cayce, in seeking to be a channel to give helpful information for human ills.

First, then, in dealing with the whys and wherefores of the fact that the greater portion of that given has proved beneficial to others in correcting and in meeting the ills in their physical being—let's turn for the moment to the individual entity, Edgar Cayce.

Consider the fact that there was first the study, the meditation and prayer upon His Word, which brought that desire, that hope, that purpose to give self as a channel through which help might come to those who would in Him seek for the betterment of their physical forces and conditions.

Then consider the vision, the spoken word: *"Ask! What seekest thou? What desirest thou to do?"* Then: *"Thy prayer has been heard."*

The desire was that there might be the ability to help others who were ill,—especially children.

The results through the years speak for themselves. As to whether or not there has been the remitting of those disturbing factors in the human ills,—this has come to those who have in their seeking put God first.

As to a discourse upon the sources of the information for human ills, then, and how or why such may be helpful to others:

First, there are those influences that arise in the minds of those who hear of such. Then there is set in motion *desire, purpose, aim.*

Those that seek, then, attune themselves to that promise which was made to this entity, Edgar Cayce. Then the entity when in that state, that condition where the physical self is laid aside, becomes the channel. Then only *spirit-mind*, as may attune itself with the purpose of the seeker, may give that as may be helpful in the experience of any of those who seek to know better their relationships to their Maker.

Who knows better than the individuals themselves that which has hindered them from being physically, mentally, spiritually in accord with the divine that *is* life manifested in the body?

From whence comes that individual entity's ability to cope with the problems?

Are ye not all children of God? Are ye not co-creators with Him? Have ye not been with Him from the beginning? Is there any knowledge, wisdom or understanding withheld if ye have attuned thyself to that Creative Force which made the worlds and all the forces manifested in same? Thinkest thou that the arm of God is ever short with thee because thou hast erred? "Though ye be afar, though ye be in the uttermost parts, if ye call I will *hear!* and answer speedily." Thinkest thou that speakest of another, or to thee?

Open thy mind, thy heart, thy purpose to thy God and His purpose with thee.

As to why this or that information may be indicated oft to individuals through this channel—this may be determined by those who analyze same from a practical, material experience—as a psychiatrist, a psychoanalyst. An individual who understands the pathology of a physical body is taken where he is, and is supplied that information which if applied in that condition existent will be helpful in his relationship to that he worships!

God seeks all to be one with Him. And as all things were made by Him, that which is the creative influence in every herb, mineral, vegetable or individual activity *is* that same force ye call God—and *seeks* expression! Even as when God said, "Let there be light," and there was light. For, this is law; this is love.

Hence those who seek in sincerity, in hope, in purpose, to *know*, receive; only to the measure that they manifest their hope, their belief, their desire in a God-purpose through a promise made to a man!

Thus ye have the source. Thus ye have the manner. The seeker answers. For, know ye, all: Ye give an account unto God for every deed, for every idle word, for every purposeful hope ye have made manifest.

Then, to all:

Let not thy heart be troubled. Let it not be afraid. For ye believe in God.

Then, as His children—for thy sake, for thy Lord's sake—act like it! 294-202

Some people have said that the language of the readings is too difficult to understand, and by some literary standards that criticism may be true. However, one must keep in mind that these readings were given at a time when sentences were typically longer and more complex. Considering that Cayce was obviously having to translate abstract spiritual impressions into the English language, with all of its limitations, and that his stenographer, usually Gladys Davis, had to somehow punctuate sentences as they were given, the language is not surprisingly difficult. It is easy to forgive a few broken or incomplete sentences, knowing that there was no opportunity to rehearse or to edit the readings.

The biblical English used throughout some readings (not just in Bible quotes) may also seem a bit archaic to some. In fact many people consider the Bible itself to be quite difficult. Upon careful study, however, the message in the readings often comes through loud and clear and, at times, quite succinctly and even poetically. Anyone who has passed Literature 101 could probably learn to understand most of the readings. I believe that it is worth the effort.

In the above reading, I understood that the quality or character of information given was proportional to the faith of the person asking for help. The statement—"The seeker answers."—was most revealing and essential in understanding just what happened during a reading. As usual, there were references to Scripture and the admonition to put one's trust in God.

The readings consistently refused to be limited to a single source, saying that any source in God's universe was available to those who put their trust in God. During the readings, Cayce spoke of himself in the third person, sometimes using the editorial "we." The reason for this detached point of view may be at least partially explained by the following excerpt from another reading:

(Q) ... Is the source of this information a group source, an individual source, or a recorded source?
(A) ... *all* may be touched, *all* may be drawn upon. And, as has been given, if it were individualized by a guide, it would become limited; while if universal it is in the hands of Him that is the Maker, the Giver, the Creator. For hath He not given, "Abide in me, as I in the Father, that I in the Father may be glorified in thee!" Ye that seek self-glory know its hardships. Ye that seek the glory of the Father know its beauties. 254-95

Factors Affecting the Readings
Considering the above information, one might generalize that the character of the information received depended, to some extent, upon the following three conditions:
1. *The purposes, desires, and abilities of the individual through whom the information came.* In the Old Testament, we read about prophets of God. Then there were those, like Balaam, who had a gift of prophecy and used it for selfish purposes. Cayce may have been as unworthy as the rest of us, but I believe that his purposes were only to do good.
2. *The purposes, desires, and integrity of the person conducting the reading.* I think this is why it meant so much to Cayce to have Gertrude asking the questions. He knew that Gertrude and he were one in their faith and their trust in God.
3. *The purposes, desires, needs, and faith of the person asking for information.* It is often essential to know something about the background of the person who asked for help. It takes a little longer to study the supplementary information with the readings, but it is worth the time. The CD-ROM containing the readings includes this information and makes this much easier.

Cayce as an Evangelist

Edgar Cayce was not just a source of helpful information; he was also an evangelist.   It is this Christian orientation that attracts me the most to his Work. Of all the preachers that I have enjoyed listening to or reading, none has been more sincere, astute, well-versed in the Scriptures, or relevant to modern living than Edgar Cayce, whether he was speaking consciously or in a reading. The readings often reiterate that the answer to every problem in this world can be found within ourselves, through Him who is our advocate with the Father. The ways that this was woven into the fabric of the advice given to thousands of people over a span of about forty years is almost endless.

4

Try the Spirits:
Sources and Purposes of the Readings

It is not every spirit, my dear people, that you can trust; test them, to see if they come from God; there are many false prophets, now, in the world. You can tell the spirits that come from God by this: every spirit which acknowledges that Jesus the Christ has come in the flesh is from God; but any spirit which will not say this of Jesus is not from God, but is the spirit of Antichrist, whose coming you were warned about. 1 John 4:1-3 (JB)

The Cayce readings offered some convincing answers to my spiritual and philosophical questions. This gave me an inner peace and a resolve to apply what I had learned. I was impressed with the results, but the world around me continued to hammer away at my spiritual point of view, and the readings themselves created some new questions.

I have seen TV programs where each person in a group is given an astrology chart. After looking at their charts, a very high percentage of these people say that the chart designed for them appears to be quite accurate. Then they are surprised to find out that they all received the same chart. This says more about how people find what they expect to find than it does about the accuracy or the usefulness of astrology charts. This is also why the placebo effect has to be considered in medical research. I was familiar enough with the readings to know that they were not that simple, but without the theatrical debunking, by what standards could they be judged?

Those who observed readings as they were being given were convinced that Cayce was not consciously aware of what he was saying. After awakening from a reading, he often asked something like, "Did we get anything?" Doctors sometimes acknowledged that his diagnosis was better than their own. He correctly observed a number of incidental facts about the surroundings of persons for whom readings were given at remote sites. He even located medicines that were hard to find, gave names and addresses of many organizations and individuals, and referred patients to doctors he had never met. Once, while giving a reading for a person in Italy, Cayce spoke in Italian, which he did not consciously understand. While there are some serious questions about the accuracy of a few of the readings, the information given was generally more comprehensive than one might expect from a person with Cayce's background.

Of even greater interest, however, is the source of personal, moral, or spiritual advice given through Cayce that might be of a more universal nature and could even have a profound effect on our belief systems. The readings were not totally out of context with the conscious Edgar Cayce or with other religious and spiritual movements of the time, but they have had a more lasting appeal to thousands of people than many of the other movements.

The Bible, which Cayce probably spent more time reading than any other source of information, obviously had a major influence upon the readings. This "sleeping prophet" showed a depth, breadth, and consistency in portraying the spirit of the Christian experience that I have not found in even the most inspired scholars or preachers. It could be interpreted as blasphemy to insist that this information should always be accepted as, "Thus saith the Lord." It might also be a mistake to fail to recognize the degree to which it was inspired and therefore to not give appropriate credit to the Holy Spirit.

Church work was an important part of my life and I was puzzled as to why orthodox religion had ignored this information. The easy way out would have been to forget the readings and get involved in some other kind of activity in the church. But the questions would not go away. If there is any knowledge about the spirit that could enable us to have a closer walk with God, should this knowledge not be studied, understood, and applied? If we are going to doubt something, should we not know what it is that we are doubting, and why? If we are truly living in Christ, can we not follow the command to "prove all things," trusting that we will be guided and protected by His love?

I talked to some very sincere ministers, but most of them simply were not prepared to answer these questions. I knew that I would have to continue to study the Bible and the readings for myself. If this Work did not give glory to God, then I would leave it alone. If it did, then I would be free to use it constructively just like any other information to which I had been exposed.

All of the books that I read about Cayce were not enough to answer these questions for me. In reading 254-87, someone asked how to present the Work to someone in the orthodox faith. The reading said, "*Come* and *see!* [John 1:39] In *that* manner. Not as imposing, not as impelling, but to all, Come and see. For only those that are in need of the answering of something within will heed." My response to that reading was to do just that—come and see. My wife and I made several "pilgrimages" to the A.R.E. headquarters at Virginia Beach. While she attended a lecture or a program, I would be in the library searching through the readings and making copies. You can imagine my sense of liberation when the entire body of readings and reports was finally put on a CD that could be searched on a computer. Here is what I found in the readings in response to some of the questions that have been raised by various sources:

- *Are the readings "scriptural" and do they acknowledge that Jesus the Christ has come in the flesh?*

When I compared the information from the readings to what I read in the Bible, I wanted to know if they were compatible in purpose and source. The First Letter of John (at the beginning of this chapter) gives some standards for judging prophecy. Did the readings acknowledge Jesus as the Christ and the Son of God?

As has been so oft indicated for all, first know in what and in Whom you have believed. When you say you believe this or that, know Who is the author, Who is the finisher of same.

And unless its source is of such a nature that it is in keeping with Him that is the Author of Life itself, reject same! For these must be as the principles of Life itself!

But that you have found good, *use*—do not abuse. 254-101

Then, be one—in thy purpose. Know, as given of old, the man called Jesus is the Savior of the world. He has purchased with His own will that right for direction. And He has promised, "I will never leave thee—I will not forsake thee," save that *thou*—as an individual—cast Him out, or reject Him, for counsel from some other source. 2970-1

25

It is easy to see that Cayce and his readings are not on the same wavelength as philosophies that reject Jesus, the way of the cross, or the Bible. If the admonitions in these readings were held up as the standard, I believe many leaders in mainline, and even evangelistic, expressions would be challenged to be more "scriptural." While some suggestions in the readings might seem to differ slightly with some literal interpretations of the written Word, the Master's emphasis on the spirit of the law shines clearly through the readings.

I am acutely aware that some people feel that the philosophy of the readings challenges their concept of salvation. While I do not fully understand their position, I continue to search for ways to reconcile this dissonance. In the meantime, I have been told that it is okay for reasonable minds to differ. One hopes that being Christian does not exclude us from that category.

- *Did Cayce or his sources ever attempt to supplant an individual's personal relationship with God?*

When one person asked how he could best serve in the Association for Research and Enlightenment, he was told:

Seek rather from the source of all light and life, rather than through these channels—for why take second-*handed* orders, if it be from God? else there remains still that trust in man, who being weak is oft evil spoken of, but pray ye the Lord *that* He may *show* thee the way. 254-54

Jesus said that many false prophets would come saying, "I am the Christ." Cayce never claimed to be a messiah or leader of any kind. The readings consistently acknowledged Jesus as Lord and encouraged every individual to establish their own personal relationship with Him.

- *Was Cayce's Work related to spiritualism?*

Recent surveys indicate that a fairly high percentage of people believe they have had some kind of spiritual contact with the soul of a recently deceased person. It is only natural that people want to know more about this phenomenon. Anthropologists tell us that almost all primitive cultures have had various kinds of beliefs about contact with spirits or souls of their ancestors. This may help explain the ancient origins of the orthodox bias against such beliefs. Most monotheistic religions have had to compete with surrounding pagan cultures that had a multiplicity of gods or spirits who must be appeased. Perhaps orthodoxy has overreacted at times by denying or ignoring people's innate desire to know more about the continuity of life.

Modern spiritualism began as a religious movement in 1848 and continues its activities through several Spiritualist organizations today. Some trace the roots of this movement to the philosophy of Emanuel Swedenborg, although not all followers of Swedenborg today would call themselves Spiritualists. The fact that some Spiritualists practice distance healing and sometimes contact souls of the deceased through a medium who enters a trance would seem, on the surface, to present some striking similarities to the Work of Cayce.

Edgar Cayce was once asked during an interview in Birmingham, Alabama, if his Work involved spiritualism. He said that the term *spirituality* would be better. Being a devout member of an orthodox Christian church, it is understandable that Cayce was careful not to be identified too closely with the Spiritualist movement.

Reading 5752-5, given in response to a question about how to validate psychic sources, said, "What sought Saul? For his own satisfying of his conscience, or for the edification of that which might bring truth? Because the soul of Samuel had entered into that test inter-between did not change one iota the position that Saul bore with constructive influences. While the *channel* might be questioned, the source—and that received—was truth! For it came from the source that had already warned Saul."

The readings did not deny that souls of the departed, while they were still in what the readings called the borderland, could be contacted. They affirmed that some communications, especially near the time of death, could be constructive. Such contacts were not automatically called unclean, and the readings were sympathetic to the fact that people often need confirmation of the continuity of life. Many devout Christians tell of having had such contacts spontaneously. The real question is whether these contacts are mutually helpful (and directed by the Christ), or do they constitute an idolatrous dependence upon the departed soul who was contacted.

27

When Mrs. [1782] asked if she should continue communication with her departed husband, she was told, "Let it rather be directed by that communion with Him who has promised to be *with* thee always! and hinder not then thy companion, but—in such associations and meetings—give the direction to the Holy One." (1782-1)

Mrs. [1786] asked, "Does he know of my prayers?" The response was, "Do you wish to call him back to those disturbing forces, or do you wish the self to be poured out for him that he may be happy?...Leave him in the hands of Him who is the resurrection! Then prepare thyself for same." (1786-2)

In reading 1598-2 a sixty-seven-year-old Protestant missionary asked, "Should I follow up my psychic contacts through Dr. MacBeth with Tobe in the spirit world?..." As usual, the response was non-condemning, but it put the responsibility back on the seeker:

> If self is well founded in its purposes, very well. Do not hinder, however, the advancement of any discarnate entity by the use of its influences in material planes. You would not seek nor desire to be hindered. Neither would you ask that yourself be imposed upon others, other than that He— your Master—would direct.

In regard to being guided by others, reading 423-2 was even more to the point:

> In the realm of spirit many may seek to give that which may be of interest, and at times of aid, to individuals seeking from such realms; yet—as the promise has been unto the sons of men—He, the Lord, *is* sufficient unto thee.

Study group reading 262-89 offered this warning:

> Think how gracious has been the gift to man, that only those who have crossed the border through being glorified...have vision. For they that are on the borderland are only in that state of transition. If they were to speak to all, how terrible would be the confusion!"

- *Could this work be classified as psychic or occult?*

It is understandable that you might be concerned, as I have been, about the terminology used in connection with Cayce's gift. Cayce was consciously aware of the connotations that many persons might give to words such as *psychic, occult, esoteric,* or *mystical.* He said that while the word psychic simply means "of the soul," it would be misunderstood by some. Occult (not necessarily related to cults), esoteric, and mystical all mean hidden or concealed. It has been said that Pythagoras made his students go through spiritual training before receiving scientific knowledge to ensure that they would use such knowledge constructively. This may be the primary motivation for secrecy in most esoteric organizations. Perhaps there is also a certain egotistical enticement in knowing something that others supposedly don't know. In any case, orthodox and secular groups have often assumed that the purpose of such secrecy was to conceal something less than constructive.

While the Cayce information may be similar in some ways to that found in various esoteric traditions, there is nothing hidden about it. Reading 1592-1 says, "...that what is hidden is of God, the Father; that what is revealed is thine, to retain, to give to thy children, thy friends, that ye may *know* the law of *love*—to *do* it!" It was assumed that most students of the Work would be followers of the Christ, and there were many warnings that such knowledge should be used unselfishly. Beyond that, however, there was no effort to restrict access to this information to certain persons or to require any membership (except to obtain a personal reading) or initiation of anyone.

Then what should we call this phenomenon? Reading 254-108 answered some of my concerns about the terminology that might be applied to the process involved in a reading:

(Q) ...please give at this time a term which will best describe Edgar Cayce and his ability to give "Readings."

(A) Application of the harmonious triune; or that as may be determined by those who may "make" a word or term to designate the various phases of the activities presented through such information.

To be sure it is psychic—or of the soul. As is stated, this is confusing to many whose knowledge or awareness is only of some mediumistic seance or of some activities founded upon an experience of individuals that has led to such a train of thought.

It is the harmony of the triune—of body, mind and soul—towards the purpose of being a help, an assistance, an aid to others. 254-108

The idea of body, mind, and soul working together in harmony for a unified purpose is very powerful and avoids some of the misused terms that have become confusing. I believe that Cayce's term "harmonious triune" is very appropriate and is not just a propaganda technique used to make something more palatable.

In the New Testament, we read about "gifts of the Holy Spirit" or charismatic gifts. Within some groups today there is still a certain emphasis put on the manifestations of those gifts. I have no reason to doubt that their work is set apart from some other psychic phenomenon by their dedication to Christ. Yet, how can we know which gifts are really guided by the Holy Spirit just by the labels that have been put on them. I believe that we should be careful to judge each work by its fruits, and not by terminology that may be prejudicial.

Cayce often referred to the Holy Spirit as quickening a person from within to do God's work in the earth. In reading 281-19, for the Glad Helpers prayer group, he said that information given in a reading "from the *throne* itself" could aid the members of the group in awakening to the possibilities within their own experiences, but that to be "*awakened* from within in thine own consciousness of being in closer walk with Him is more glorious still..."

When asked in reading 2072-8 why he had such psychic abilities, Cayce replied, "Only as a gift of Him who has given, 'If ye keep my ways, I will love thee, will abide with thee, and bring to thy remembrance *all* things from the foundations of the world.'" You can call it what you wish. I believe that this is exactly the kind of spiritual gift that the apostle Paul speaks of in chapter 12 of I Corinthians.

• *Were the readings influenced by Eastern religion?*

The readings sometimes used terms from other religions such as karma and reincarnation. Does that mean that they were influenced by Eastern religion?

Before we denigrate Eastern religions we should keep in mind that Christianity originated in the area of the world that we call the Middle East. Some people, such as some Messianic Jews, believe that Christianity has been Hellenized or Westernized a bit too much. Those who sought readings from Cayce were members of a wide variety of Christian groups and even other religions, and their answers may have related to their own particular persuasion. I have found no evidence, however, that Cayce himself had any direct association with any other religion or religious movement.

I can understand how some people might be concerned by his degree of open-mindedness. In reading 262-89, Cayce said, "In seeking through all understandings, all interpretations, there may be gained something; if ye will not become confused by those who say, 'Here! This way!'" He also pointed out that most world religions have incorporated some ideas from Christianity during the last two thousand years.

Cayce assumed that all major religions try to meet the need for peace in people's lives. He said that those who earnestly seek God may find something constructive in other religions, but he carefully avoided putting any other spiritual teacher on a par with Jesus the Christ. A twenty-three-year-old man (reading 3545-1) who asked, "On which of the Masters of Wisdom should I meditate for spiritual guidance?" was told, "There's only one Master." Another reading told a thirty-one-year-old year old woman (reading 5028-1), "We find that the entity should find its spiritual ideal—and not in the mysteries of the East." While recognizing that other religions may be lights along the way, Cayce said that only the Christ has overcome the world, and that all paths lead to the cross.

- *Were the readings "channeled" from the spirit world?*

Cayce often said that we should be channels of God's blessings to those around us. In that sense, he could have been called a "channel" himself. But, channeling has taken on a slightly different meaning today. To some people, it describes the condition in which some named entity, usually supposed to be an angel, ascended master, adept, extraterrestrial, or some other highly developed being, speaks through a person to enlighten individuals or groups. To some people, however, such channeling is thought to be a form of demonic possession.

31

The Cayce readings do occasionally speak about angels. In a few cases, they mention angels of light. Usually these angels are considered to be messengers from God, much as we find in the Bible or even in popular TV programs today. In interpreting a vision for an eighty-year-old woman, Cayce said, "For the angels of light only use material things for emblems, while the angels of death use these as to lures that may carry men's souls away." (1159-1) Speaking of the color, lavender, reading 274-10 says, "Rather has it [lavender] ever been that upon which the angels of light and mercy would bear the souls of men to a place of mercy and peace..."

On the other hand, the readings do not assume that all spiritual beings are trying to help us. When Mrs. [457] asked if she would develop any spiritual gifts, Cayce's answer came back, "What dost thou desire in thine heart? That ye may play with those things that would enter in? Or, do ye seek to glorify thy Father in heaven? Would ye speak with the sons of men, or would ye speak with the angels of light?" (457-3)

St. Paul said, "...if Satan himself goes disguised as an angel of light, there is no need to be surprised when his servants, too, disguise themselves as the servants of righteousness." (2 Corinthians 11:15 JB) He did not say that Satan *is* an angel of light. I find little here or elsewhere to condone the insinuation by some religious ultraconservatives that Lucifer (because the name means "light") is still the chief angel of light and that all angels of light are out to get us. Even so, reading 1135-3 warns, "If the associations are with others, rather than the universal, then it must in itself (such activity) bring confusion; for it is contrary to the universal—or that law as of man's relationship to a Creative Force." Cayce also echoed Galatians 1:8 when he said, "...if even an angel of light proclaims other than that which thy Savior has given have none of it!" (792-1)

The group that received a series of readings to guide them in compiling the *Search for God* books, voted to reject what seemed to be an offer from a named source to clarify the readings. A later reading complimented them on their choice to depend wholly on the Christ and chided them to live up to it. However, this series of readings did contain a few brief messages, usually at the end of a reading, that were identified as being from the Archangel Michael. When, in study group reading 262-28, someone asked, "What is the relationship between Michael the lord of the way, and Christ the way?" Cayce responded:

Michael is an archangel that stands before the throne of the Father. The Christ is the Son, the way *to* the Father, and one that came into the earth as man, the Son of Man, that man might have access to the Father; hence the way. Michael is the lord or the guard of the change that comes in every soul that seeks the way, even as in those periods when His manifestations came in the earth.

Bow thine heads, O ye sons of man, would ye know the way: for I, Michael, the lord of the way, would warn thee that thou standest not in the way of thy brother nor sittest in the seats of the scornful [psalm 1:1], but rather make known that love, that glory, that power in His name, that none be afraid; for I, Michael, have spoken!

A few of the messages from Michael were stern warnings to those present to keep in the way. Study group reading 262-29 contained one of the more encouraging messages:

Hark! O ye children of men! Bow thine heads, ye sons of men: for the glory of the Lord is thine, will ye be faithful to the trust that is put in each of you! Know in whom ye have believed! Know that He is Lord of all, and His word faileth not to them that are faithful day by day: for I, Michael, would protect those that seek to know His face!

(Cayce's secretary, Gladys Davis, added this note: "Tears, silence and beautiful attunement followed above reading. EC on waking had a vision during the reading, had to leave the room a while; said he saw each of us as we should be and as we are.")

Cayce carefully avoided any attempts to identify his source as any individual or group. During reading 254-83, this question was submitted: "If Mr. Cayce is a member and a messenger of the Great White Brotherhood, how do the Masters wish him to proceed and should not his activities henceforth be presented as Their Work?" The answer was, "As the work of the *Master* of masters, that may be presented when in those lines, those accords necessary through the White Brotherhood. This—this—*this*, my friends, even but *limits;* while in Him [the Christ] is the Whole."

- *What was the source of the information that was given in the readings?*

The readings often spoke about Jesus and suggested that individuals should develop a relationship to God through the Christ. In reading 254-85 Cayce was asked if the readings should be presented as pronouncements from Jesus the Christ and God the Father. Cayce replied that this could present a barrier to some seekers and that it should be presented only as "the universality of the Father." The readings agree with the Bible that the Holy Spirit can manifest in various ways:

> To some there has been given the ability to serve as prophets; some as teachers; some as ministers; some in one manner, some in another; which are spiritual gifts, and of the same source, when applied in that manner that brings service to the fellow man... 254-31

Even so, there were still those who wanted to be sure of the source of the information. Reading 5752-6 was given at an annual A.R.E. Congress in July 1934. The suggestion given by Gertrude Cayce was, "You will give at this time a discourse on the Sources of Psychic Information." Here is part of the response:

> Hence as life is spirit, spirit is God, the true source of psychic force must come from that which is *of* that force that may make aware in the experience the individual, the soul, the fact of His presence abiding ever.
> ...look not as to who will ascend into heaven to bring him down, nor who shall go over the sea, but, lo, He is in thine own heart, and thy spirit beareth witness with His Spirit that ye are—or not—the children of God...
> Then, the source is *from* on High, if the seeking is from the soul within. If the seeking is from the carnal forces of the earth influence in thine self, that thou hast hated thy brother and begrudgest that which he hast in his hand— dost thou seek through thine inner self to gain back, dost thou seek for that which may make for the lauding of thine

own self, what be the fruits? ye bring sorrow, sickness, yea—even death; for ye have forsaken His ways, ye seek after other gods and they have beckoned His children and they have wandered astray.

If ye would know Him let thy life and thy experience be that thy deeds and thy acts are the fruits of the spirit of truth... But seekest thou that ye may lord thine self above thine brother, above thine neighbor, the answers come only from those sources, those souls that have forsaken His way.

...Seek to know Him, and that thou receivest in thine experiences—as ye approach through all those channels that may attune themselves to the throne of grace—will be the knowledge and understanding that, "As ye do it unto the least of these, my little ones, ye do it unto me."

What seekest thou? The Spirit of Truth, or that thou may justify thyself in thine own carnal self? Each may be found. Yea, the way is broad—and many there be that wander therein, but ye that love the light, ye that would find a helping hand, give a helping hand to thy brother; and as ye give, so shall it be measured to thee in that thou seekest in thine inner self. For *there* the Spirit of *Truth* may indeed *only*—to thee—*first* be found. For that which makes thee aware is that *God* in His love, in His mercy, has *opened* the way for thee. Flesh and blood may not reveal... Hence whether ye receive through this, that or the other channel that may open itself for the pouring of the spirit, *as ye seek* so shall ye find.

What are the sources of psychic information? What seekest thou? What art *thou* willing to give for thine own soul? Pleasure in the earth for the moment?...

They that love His coming will only approach in such a way and manner that though the heavens fall, though the earth may pass away, His word, His promise in them shall *not* pass away. Only in such an attitude, such an understanding, may the Spirit of Truth come in unto thee. Seek ye not lower, if ye would *find* that which will bring rest unto thy soul!

The apostles knew that we would have to make choices. Mark 13:22 (JB) warns that false prophets will "produce signs and portents to deceive the elect, if that were possible." In the following reading, Cayce said that the real test of the information is not signs and wonders, but lasting changes in lifestyles:

> These are determined by what you have seen the information from such a source produce in the life of individuals, in your own self, in your neighbor, in those with whom you have come in contact in one manner or another; and not through that of any nature that is to startle any group. The startling thing to every soul is to awaken to the realization that it is indeed a child of God! That is startling enough for any man, any woman, any being, in this sin-sick world!...
>
> For what was the judgment, what *is* judgment, what will ever be the judgment? They that deny that He hath come in the flesh are not worthy of acceptation. They that give thee that which is not helpful, hopeful, and patient and humble, and not condemning any, are not worthy!
>
> ...But "Try ye the spirits." Know those that know Him are in accord with that which is His purpose, His desire, with men. 254-95

- *How were the readings protected from evil forces?*

Once, my two teenage sons asked if they could use the car and go to a party at a friend's house. When I sounded a bit skeptical, one of them said, "But Dad, what could happen?" I explained to them how that response almost caused them to lose all credibility.

They knew as well as I did that the kind of social activity they wanted to attend could statistically be accompanied by an increase in the rate of drug abuse, sexual promiscuity, and automobile accidents. Perhaps if they had sincerely expressed an awareness of all of the dangers and assured me that their future and my happiness meant too much to them to allow them to take any chances, then I might have gotten fewer gray hairs over the incident.

I have heard people say the same thing about meditation. What could happen? Cayce did not go into the readings with that kind of attitude. He assumed that any tool that was powerful enough to be helpful could also be harmful if used without the proper precautions. Speaking of an electrical appliance that was suggested for use by many people, reading 1179-4 said, "For there's no such thing that if an application can't help, it can't hurt! Because if it is helpful, mis-applied it must be harmful—this is natural!" Should we not use the same standards to judge psychic phenomenon as we do to judge worldly sources such as books or TV?

This is not to say that we should become so paranoid about imagined dangers as to be paralyzed by fear and avoid using our God-given spiritual abilities. In a life reading, Ms. [1928] was told, "...there is nothing outside of self half so fearful as that that may be builded or brewed within self's own mental and material being." Reading 1928-1 went on to say that these fears could be forgotten by focusing on the good that could be done for others.

When Mr. [5392] asked in his life reading if he had any psychic powers and how he could develop them constructively, his answer was, "Each one who has a soul has a psychic power—but remember, brother, there are no shortcuts to God! Ye are there— but self must be eliminated." (5392-1)

Time and time again, the readings call upon individuals to surround themselves with the Spirit of the Christ before opening themselves up to any influence. Here are some typical examples:

...no influence without or within may be of a detrimental force to self; so long as self will surround self with the thought and the ability of the Christ Consciousness, and then practice same in its dealings with its fellow man. 2081-2

Those influences that are about thee are for good [this does not say that they are demons], but rather *ever* let that which thou would gain through thy writing be inspired by the best in self as magnified through the Christ, than *any entity* or spirit or soul! While these seek for expression ever, they be seekers as thyself. And as He gave, if the blind lead the blind *both* shall fall into the ditch. Be thou led rather by that which comes from thine own soul, which thou meetest in the temple of thy body, thy God in thee. And if He uses other influences, He will *direct* same. Be not thou *directed* save by the spirit of the Christ that *is* thy heritage. Faint not. Be not overcome. But use that thou hast begun to develop *in* thyself; letting thy Master, thy God, be thy director ever. *Woe* to he that would harken to the voice that would turn thee aside. For as the prophet of old has said, if even an angel of light proclaims other than that which thy Savior has given have none of it! In thy meditations, then, much hast thou grown in thy closeness with Him... Write, yea—but let it be prompted by the spirit of the *Christ* with thine *own spirit.* 792-1

- *Did the readings involve any kind of idolatry?*

This is perhaps one of the most important questions that can be asked of any work. All sin or error can be traced back to our failure to put our relationship to God first in our lives. We must each personally guard and develop this relationship. Rules and regulations, even the Bible itself, can only point the way. Groups and organizations, as helpful or even necessary as they might be, cannot do it all for us.

The following reading, 3548-1, was given for a fifty-two-year-old man who asked for advice about how to develop his own spiritual talents. It is typical of such advice and is complementary to that found in the Bible:

The true God-forces meet within, not without self. For when there are altars builded outside, which individuals approach for the interpretation of law, whether it be physical, mental or spiritual, these are temptations. It is concerning such that warnings were given to the peoples. Though the entity or others may say, "Oh, that's the old Jewish conception of it," but be ye Jew, Gentile, Greek, Parthenian or what, the law is one—as God is one. And the first command is "Thou shalt have no other gods before me."

Then those influences without—know of whom they give evidence. It is true that ye have been warned, "Try ye the spirits." But this [Cayce readings] is also that that is questioned.

Rather then as we would give, so live in thine own life, in thine own application of the divine law, that there may be no question within self. And if ye live with the divine law, who may question. To be sure, there may be questions by some who have interpreted the law to their own understanding or their own undoing. Yet there is ever the

38

answer "My spirit beareth witness with thy spirit as to whether ye be the child of God or not."

...For as He gave, who was, who is, who ever will be the manifestation of the Spirit—which is true psychic force—he that will be the greatest will be the servant of all. Not necessarily being as a doormat, but ever willing, ever helpful—but to the glory of God, to the honor of self. Not to the glory of self in any manner or way, but in humbleness preferring one another.

...Thy body is the temple. ...keep it as a place worthy of thy Father-God, and thy Savior, the Christ, meeting with thee in that body, that mind, that soul.

Then, know in what ye believe—and know who is the author of same. His purpose has been "If ye love me, keep my commandments and if ye keep my commandments I and the Father will come and abide with thee.".

Then, are ye looking for some other? These should be questions. Remember, those who had familiar spirits were classified as wizards. They are classified with the liars, the adulterers, and those of that class—which as ye know is not in keeping with patience, love, kindness, brotherly love and the like.

Then be consistent in thy choices of that which will be thy source, thy understanding. For if the Lord thy God be with thee, who may be against thee?   3548-1

- *Was there a demonic influence in the readings?*

When we think of demons, we think of that power we call Satan. Cayce said that Satan is merely the personification of selfishness or rebellion. Study group reading 262-52 states: "Evil is rebellion. Good is the Son of Life, of Light, of Truth... As there is, then, a personal savior, there is the personal devil." Some religious pundits react to anything not approved by their group as if it were from a demon. Perhaps there are such things as demons. I suspect that some of the worst of them come from within our own minds, but I will leave it up to the experts to define and categorize them.

It is my perception that many of the phenomena that are called demons are from other souls (whether in the flesh or in the borderland). They are not necessarily fallen angels, or even consciously serving the forces of evil. Still, there is no reason to think that they are any more qualified to give advice than if they were visible in the flesh, and, we still have to have some standards by which to test them.

A few years ago, some of my students were discussing the question of "backtracking," or supposedly hidden messages on some musical records and tapes, that were believed to reveal themselves when the song was played in reverse. They asked me if I thought they contained "satanic" influences. I told them that I could not be sure about the reality of such messages, but that, if they did exist, anything that glorified rebellion or self-indulgence was satanic, and that we didn't have to play the tapes backwards to check for that.

Jesus said that some who questioned Him were sons of the devil. Does that not apply to all of us when we do something selfish or unkind? Wouldn't it be simple if we had a picture of the devil so that we would know what to avoid? Here are some readings that might be helpful in separating the wheat from the chaff:

> Did He not—the Christ, the Maker—say this over and over again? that so long as spite, selfishness, evil desires, evil communications were manifested, they would give the channels through which *that* spirit called satan, devil, Lucifer, Evil One, might work? 262-119

> There are those two principles, two conflicting forces in the earth today: the prince of this world, and that principle that says to every soul, "Fear not, I have overcome the world and the prince of the world hath nothing in me."
> Can ye say that? Ye must! That is thy hope; "That the prince of this world, satan that old serpent, hath no part in any desire of my mind, my heart, my body that I do not control in the direction it shall take." 3976-29

In the light of these readings, to accuse Cayce of being influenced by demons might be similar to the time when Jesus was accused of casting out demons by Beelzebub, the prince of demons.

- *Could Cayce's gift have been used for selfish purposes?*

There were times when those around Cayce attempted to use his talents for personal gain. Being aware of the temptations associated with his gift, he often struggled with the moral issues of giving readings. With the exception of certain A.R.E. conferences, he usually refused to give readings before groups of people, even for the purpose of promoting the Work. Although consistently non-condemning, he, or his Source, often saw through the many self-serving questions he was asked, sometimes bluntly refusing to answer. Even when he did go along with efforts to raise money to further the Work, the results were often disappointing.

When asked if it would be acceptable to use information gained from the readings to bet on sporting events so the proceeds could be used to further the Work, Cayce responded:

As has been given, only that information may be used as does not give one individual the advantage over another. It is never right to do that which is evil that good may come, and with the foundation of work as classified under that of spiritual understanding of the soul and physical forces in an individual would only mean such institution or work was founded upon shifting sands...

Let that mind be in you as was in the Master, and cleave only to the good that may be done to others, without the expense and the questioning of the intent, and in all keep thyself unspotted from the world.

It would not be in keeping or in accord with that being attempted... 254-7

- *Does this work challenge the turf of organized religion?*

Since becoming a member of my present church congregation, I have spoken to at least four of our regular pastors about my interest in Cayce and asked for their opinion of his Work. The first pastor, a kindly, older gentleman, admitted to knowing little about this Work, but was interested in further discussion. Unfortunately, he left soon thereafter. The next minister said that he had heard of Edgar Cayce and that his only criticism was that he thought Cayce was somehow against the church. I gave him a book to read, which he returned, saying only that it was well written. The third minister knew little of the Work, but was not critical of it. He allowed me to do an evening study program about the Work, but was unable to attend. The fourth said that he had heard of Edgar Cayce and did not think too highly of him.

I felt that the source of the less than warm response by two of these pastors had something to do with what might be called turf—not necessarily on their part, but on the part of those from whom they had heard something about Cayce. If you take a few comments out of context from the readings (as religionists often do with the Scriptures) you might think that the Church is being threatened. Here are some examples:

> Even as He gave, the day is at hand when neither in this mountain nor in the temple in Jerusalem but in thine own heart will He speak—to those who love His ways and His coming! 1598-1

> The Church is never a body, never an assembly. An *individual* soul becomes aware that it has taken that Head, that Son, that Man even, to be the intermediator. *That* is the Church; that is what is spoken of as the Holy Church. 262-87

> Then it is not by this or that tenet, this or that creed, this or that group. For remember, as given to many, think not to attain because of thy...connection with some individual group. 5007-1

On the other hand, the readings do encourage church participation:

> Do not get away from the church! In the church keep these activities, that there may be surety in self that has to do or to deal with only the use of such insight, such vision, to the glory of the Father as manifested in the Son. 4087-1

Insisting that God is not a respecter of persons, the readings refuse to set any particular group above the others:

> (Q) Which person, or group, today, has the nearest to the correct teachings of Jesus?

(A)   This would depend upon who is the judge.   The teaching, the consciousness of the Christ-life is a *personal* thing.   And hence they that are aware of His abiding presence are the nearer.

Who? They that walk with Him and do not, *cannot, will* not, force themselves on others—even as He! 1703-3

This information may present some constructive criticism to the churches, but from my perspective, Cayce was the greatest lover of the Church since the Master was with us in the flesh.

- *Were there any mistakes or failures in the readings?*

Even if we believe that the readings' source is in harmony with our ideal, we must realize that there are some aspects of the readings that are less than perfect. The physical readings are not that different from what you would find in the medical profession. Sometimes, when results were not as hoped for, people would ask for another reading. Some were told that they had not applied the treatments exactly as given or that they must be more patient. Some were told to try something different. The recipients of the readings and their doctors did not always agree with the diagnosis. Even though there were some spectacular cures, it is important to remember that they came through a person who was just as human as the rest of us. In the following reading, Cayce gave a spontaneous dissertation on the reliability of the readings:

EC: Yes we have the body here, [531]—11:47—he has just laid aside his paper he was reading:

In giving information concerning this body, [531], it would be well that the body understand or have an idea of how such information may be given that there may be credence put in that which may be supplied as helpful information in the experience of this body, entity, soul, at the present...

Then, in seeking information there are certain factors in the experience of the seeker and in the channel through which such information might come. Desire on the part of the seeker to be shown. And, as an honest seeker, such will not be too gullible; neither will such be so encased in prejudices as to doubt that which is applicable in the experience of such seeker. Hence the information must not only be practical, but it must be rather in accord with the desires of the seeker also.

This desire, then, is such that it must not only take hold on that which is primarily the basis of all material manifestation of spiritual things, but must also have its inception in a well-balanced desire for the use of such information not only for self but for others...

On the part of that channel through whom such information may come, there must be the unselfish desire to be of aid to a fellow man...

What, then, is the hypothesis of the activity that takes place during such an experience? Not merely that word telepathy, that has been coined by some untutored individuals; neither that a beneficent spirit seeking to do a service seeks out those ones and in an unseeming manner gives that from its sphere which makes for those experiences in the mind of the seeker, as some have suggested. For, if such were true at all times, there would never be a fault—if real developed spirits were in control. But rather in *this* instance is *this* the case:

The soul of the seeker being passive, and the soul of the individual through whom information comes being positive (as the physical is subjugated into unconsciousness) goes out on the forces that are in activity by being guided by suggestion to that individual place of the seeker. And the souls commune one with another.

Then, it is asked, what prevents the information from always being accurate, or being wholly of unquestionable nature? The fact that such information must be interpreted in material things. And that then depends upon how well the training of the physical-mental self is in such picturing. 531-2

Edgar Cayce's two sons, Hugh Lynn Cayce and Edgar Evans Cayce, wrote *The Outer Limits of Edgar Cayce's Power.* In this book, they discussed some of the readings that seemed to give erroneous information or to contradict other readings. There are some possible explanations for these discrepancies, but this might be a good book to read if you are ever tempted to think that the readings are infallible.

- *Have any persons who were formerly interested in the readings written about why they have changed their mind about them?*

Since most of the ministers and scholars whom I questioned about the readings simply avoided the question, I looked for writings that questioned or challenged the readings. Most of the negative comments that I read or heard on the radio reflected complete ignorance, or at best a dangerous smattering of less than accurate information. I did find one booklet, *Edgar Cayce and Christianity* by James Morrison, that seemed, at first, to present a more coherent "expose" of the readings. Morrison had been an attorney for the U.S. government for about twenty years. He and his wife had been very active members of the A.R.E. for thirteen years. The booklet, copyrighted in 1983, delineates their reasons for extricating themselves from the Cayce Work and offers to serve as a warning to others who might be deceived by the Work's logic. Morrison admitted that, before joining his present church and embracing a different set of beliefs, the physical and medical readings had brought much help to himself and his family. He feels, however, that he has found some major flaws in both the source of the readings' information and in the spiritual ideas expressed in them. He also takes exception to the notion that good can come only from God. He strongly differs with Cayce's "individual approach" to religion and the emphasis on reincarnation, and he concludes that the readings are not in harmony with the Bible.

Edgar Cayce and Christianity is thoughtful and well documented, although Morrison's selective use of Scripture seems typical of some fundamentalist sects. He also said that the readings tend to ignore evil or the devil. A quick search of the readings on CD-ROM shows otherwise. He said that Cayce seldom talked about obedience to God. Again, I find that Cayce often quoted Hebrews 5:5, which says that Jesus learned obedience through the things He suffered, and encouraged people to follow that example. Cayce also frequently equated rebellion to evil or sin.

Morrison's booklet often criticizes statements made by other students of the readings or the actions of other A.R.E. members, rather than focusing on the actual readings. Morrison also is concerned that some people seem to revere the readings above the Bible. I agree with him that this can be a problem for some people. However, I believe that anyone who really studies the readings will be directed back, through the Holy Scriptures, to a relationship with God.

I must add that I talked to James Morrison. He and his wife were very friendly and sincere, and I believe that they are involved in a new ministry that is also serving God. Criticism of Cayce's Work from Morrison and other sincere Christians has caused me to do some soul searching about my own interest in the readings. In the long run, however, I do not find any idolatry in this Work, and I believe that it has produced good fruits in my life and in the world.

The underlying cause of much of the criticism of Cayce's Work seems to be questions of church authority. This is essentially the same contention that has existed among various sects and denominations from the beginning. I cannot give up hope that all such injury in the Body of Christ will someday be healed. In the meantime, it would be well to remember that our areas of agreement are much greater than the things on which we differ. I pray that we will be able to work together in love without letting the evil one find a toehold of resentment in our hearts.

- *Has this work become a cult?*

In the broader sense of the word, "cult" could apply to any religious practice. However, most people think of a cult as some kind of fringe group that has excessive control over one's life. The readings stressed that this Work should never become an "ism, schism, or cult," and that it should not replace one's activities in a church. It has never been suggested to me that membership in the A.R.E. could impart salvation or that it was not compatible with membership in any other constructive organization. I have known a few A.R.E. members who were also members of various other societies or groups such as Rosicrucianism, I AM, Urantia, Unity, A Course in Miracles, Subud, Sufi, Spiritualism, Transcendental Meditation, or Freemasonry. I have known an even larger number of A.R.E. members who are Catholic, Episcopal, Methodist, Baptist, Pentecostal, Evangelical, or are even from other religions. Still, it would not be fair to judge the A.R.E. by association with any of these groups.

46

Since the A.R.E. is a research organization with open membership, a wide degree of diversity is to be expected. Its excellent library includes resources on almost any spiritual or religious topic. Workshops, conferences, and books sold in the bookstore disseminate ideas about a variety of subjects and opinions. As in a university or a library, it is up to individuals to use only that which is compatible with their own spiritual convictions.

When I read the literature of many churches, religions, or spiritual organizations, I often sense a subtle (and sometimes not so subtle) condemnation of other groups. Very often, newer groups have an adolescent reaction toward other groups that they perceive to be the corrupt establishment. We often believe that we are seeking the freedom to be different. When we always take the opposite stand from those whom we challenge, however, we are still governed by that which we resist, and we relinquish the right to agree about anything. This is why the Cayce readings insist that the Work should not become even as much as a tenet. These readings are somewhat unique in their refusal to condemn anyone or even to insinuate any authority to Cayce or to the A.R.E. As reading 1468-1 says:

> ...these do not become as tenets do not become as edicts, but as *opportunities* in the experience of self to make each association, each contact, more and more aware of the love the Father hath shown to the children of men—if they seek to know His face.

Conclusions

These tests or comparisons of the spirit of the Cayce Work could be useful for analyzing any other spiritual teaching as well. The above cautions, however, should never be used to criticize any expression of the Holy Spirit in this Work or any other. St. Paul expressed this concern when he wrote, "Never try to suppress the Spirit or treat the gift of prophecy with contempt..." (I Thessalonians 5:19-20 JB)

A friend in the A.R.E., for whom I have tremendous respect, suggested that the points discussed in this chapter might put doubt into the mind of someone who might otherwise have no reason to question the readings. I would rather take that risk than to leave a seeker unaware of little surprises that may pop up along the way. I can only say that I have included in this chapter the things that I wish I had known thirty years ago.

Those who understand warfare know that the man with the bazooka draws fire from the enemy. It is to be expected that any useful work will be challenged. This discussion will not answer every question that might arise, but it has helped me to see Edgar Cayce as having more in common with Billy Sunday or Father Damien than with Cagliostro or Rasputin.

More than causing you to identify with Elijah as he single-handedly stood against the perverted world, I hope that the Cayce Work will challenge you to emphasize the areas where you agree with others. Speaking of political, religious, and economic factions, reading 1226-1 says, "...looking for rather that in which the thoughts agree, rather than their differences, may there be brought peace and harmony and greater understanding..." I know in my heart that this works because I have tried it. If the readings said nothing else, this one concept would be worth the time and effort I have expended in studying them. Without that kind of inner confirmation, arguments about sources of authority have little significance.

When telling about a person's past during a life reading, Cayce often began by saying that he would "magnify the virtues and minimize the faults." Cayce did not necessarily have instant access to all absolute facts in the universe. He did have the spirit of Christian service and some unusual talents with which to implement his calling. If manifesting the love of God is our measuring stick, then I believe that this Work is uncommonly useful. Assuming that you will take responsibility for safeguarding your own relationship to God, I hope to do for Cayce what he would have done for you or for me—magnify his virtues and minimize his faults.

PART TWO

God, Mankind and Spiritual Laws

5

A Creation Cosmology for Today:
Why Humankind and the Universe Exist

It is by faith that we understand that the world was created by one word from God, so that no apparent cause can account for the things we can see. (Hebrews 11:3 JB)

Ever since God created the world his everlasting power and deity—however invisible—have been there for the mind to see in the things he has made. (Romans 1:20 JB)

Do not starve either of these phases of thy unfoldment, for all that is in mind and body first appears in spirit. 3652-1

Although reading about various worldly philosophers left me with unanswered questions, it did help to prepare me for what I found in the Cayce readings. For example, Plato and others talked about how physical objects are conceived in mind before taking form in matter. Reading 3424-1 says, "For all is born first in spirit, then in mind, then it may become manifested in the material plane." Reading 262-78 also says, "... for matter is an expression of spirit in motion to such a degree as to give the expressions in materiality."

The Christian faith in which I was raised taught about eternal life. In addition to stories about saints and mystics, I saw real people who lived by faith and demonstrated the fruits of the spirit, but the world was also out there, and many who ignored or even scoffed at religion seemed to be getting by pretty well. However, for me, secular science created more questions than it answered.

Secular vs. Spiritual

Is the physical world all that exists in the universe? Did mankind evolve from lower animals? If physical birth is the beginning of a soul's existence, will death not be the end of it? Does the competition among species justify competition among individuals? If there is no reward or retribution beyond the grave, what is the incentive for moral behavior?

Secular philosophies are not new. In my Jerusalem Bible the introductory comment to the Apocryphal Book of Wisdom (assumed to have been written in the first century BC) says:

> The author is writing for his fellow Jews whose faith is shaken by the attraction of the cultural life of Alexandria, its imposing philosophical systems, its advance in the physical sciences, its fascinating mystery religions, astrology, Hermetic doctrines, its seductive popular cults. Nevertheless, he has the pagans in mind, too, hoping to lead them to God the lover of all men...

Because most modern Bibles do not include the Book of Wisdom, the following passages are also included here:

> Death was not God's doing, he takes no pleasure in the extinction of the living...the world's created things have health in them, in them no fatal poison can be found, and Hades holds no power on earth; for virtue is undying.
>
> But the godless call with deed and word for Death, counting him friend, they wear themselves out for him, with him they make a pact, and are fit to be his partners. For they say to themselves, with their misguided reasoning:
>
> "Our life is short and dreary, nor is there any relief when man's end comes, nor is anyone known who can give release from Hades. By chance we came to birth, and after this life we shall be as if we had never been. The breath in our nostrils is a puff of smoke, reason a spark from the beating of our hearts; put this out and our body turns to ashes, and the spirit melts away like idle air. In time, our name will be forgotten, nobody will remember what we have done...the seal is set: no one returns.
>
> "Come then, let us enjoy what good things there are, use this creation with the zest of youth: take our fill of the dearest wines and perfumes, let not one flower of springtime pass us by, before they wither crown ourselves with roses. Let none of us forgo his part in our orgy, let us leave the signs of our revelry everywhere, this is our portion, this the lot assigned us." (Wisdom 1:13 - 2:9)

They do not know the hidden things of God...they can see no reward for blameless souls. Yet God did make man imperishable, he made him in the image of his own nature; it was the devil's envy that brought death into the world, as those who are his partners will discover. (Wisdom 2:22-24)

The tendency to develop a rationalistic WYSIWYG (what you see is what you get) philosophy may seem to be an honest effort to accept things the way they are. However, the author of Wisdom recognized such materialism as an attempt to avoid facing the long-term consequences of one's actions. There are choices to be made by each of us every day, and our beliefs affect those choices. Whatever your beliefs are, they are likely to be challenged in the academic world with some of the same old secular logic.

Back to the Source

There were times when such questions tempted me to stop trying to understand religious matters. There was one experience, however, that always brought me back to a search for spiritual truth. In my early teens, I would often stay awake after going to bed at night and ponder various questions about life. I was already being tempted to do things that were against the values that my religious training had emphasized, and I struggled with the inconsistency between my faith and my relationship to my peers. One particular night, I decided that if there were a living God, then only He could answer my questions. And answer He did! Even if only for a moment, I seemed to be aware that God was not only present with me then, but that He had been with me, or I with Him, since the beginning of time. I knew that no matter how far I might stray, I only had to look within my own memory to find the way back to God. Years later, when I read the following reading, my earlier experience was confirmed in a way that I had not found elsewhere:

For no soul hath wandered so far that when it calls He will not hear. For as the Psalmist has given, "Though I take the wings of the morning and fly to the utmost parts of the earth, He is there. Though I ascend into heaven, He is there. Though I make my bed in hell, He is there."

Hence the purposes for each soul's experience in materiality are that the Book of Remembrance may be

53

opened that the soul may know its relationship to its Maker.

Thus we find, as in this entity's experiences, those influences that bring again, again, again, the opportunity to know the Lord that He *is* good. 1215-4

A Plan of Salvation

As far as the existence of God and His standards were concerned, I knew that my religious training had been essentially correct. Still, I had not acquired the understanding of how to change my own habits and attitudes to live according to my Christian values. The following reading is an example of one that suggested to me that growth in that direction was possible. While somewhat lengthy and difficult, it is not only a dissertation on the nature of man, but it is also a beautiful sermon. It challenges a soul to analyze its relationship to God, to accept the spiritual conviction that can result, and to apply a plan of salvation that promises constructive results:

As given in the Scripture, there was breathed into man the soul. Biologically, man makes himself as an animal of the physical; with the desires that are as the instinct in animal for the preservation of life, for the development of species, and for food. These three are those forces that are instinct in the animal and in man. If by that force of will man uses these within self for the aggrandizement of such elements in his nature, these then become the material desires—or are the basis of carnal influences, and belittle the spiritual or soul body of such an individual.

So, the basis of physical desire is adding to, contributing to, or gathering together in forces that which makes for the abilities for such a soul, such an individual, to rebel in those forces that are of the animal nature of that individual. Hence he becomes, through carnal or physical desire, one who has no recourse through other than spirit; though he is given the soul that it may be everlasting, that it may be a companion with the Creator, that it may be aware of itself yet one with those influences that make for the spiritualizing of that force which is creative in itself—that makes for god-likeness in the individual soul or activity.

Then, what is the basis of mental desire? The mental as an attribute is also of the animal, yet in man —with his intellect—the ability to make comparisons, to reason, to have the reactions through the senses; that are raised to the forces of activity such that they create for man the environs about him and make for change in hereditary influences in the experience of such a soul. These are the gifts with that free-will agent, or attributes of same; or mind is a development of the application of will respecting desire that has become—in its essence—used as a grace, the gift to give praise for that which it has applied in its experience.

Then, the mental desire that is to laud self, to appraise self above its fellows, or to use that gift in its application to the various activities in the experiences of self or others, makes for that channel through which the carnal desires only become the stumbling blocks in the experiences of those who dwell on same.

For, as has been given as one of the immutable laws, that which the mind of a *soul*—a *soul*—dwells upon it becomes; for mind is the builder. And if the mind is in attune with the law of the force that brought the soul into being, it becomes spiritualized in its activity. If the mind is dwelling upon or directed in that desire towards the activities of the carnal influences, then it becomes destructive in such a force.

Hence, as it has been given, "Let Thy will, O, God, be my desire! Let the desire of my heart, my body, my mind, be Thy will, O Father, in the experiences that I may have in the earth!"

Where there is the consideration within self, through the self-analysis of self in the light *truly* of that which has been given, how oft must thine own acts condemn thee! And, as the Master has given, "I do not condemn, for thou art condemned already" in the manner thou hast applied thyself, thy abilities, thy birthrights, in the light of that thou knowest, that thou seest manifested in thy life day by day!

And when ye consider what disappointments ye have had in individual associations, think how thy God must have been disappointed in thee when thou hast spoken lightly of thy brother, when thou hast condemned him in thine own conscience, when thou has questioned as to the purpose of those hearts that sought in the light of the best that *they* understood—or that even used their abilities for the aggrandizing of their own selfish motives. Hast thou prayed with them? Hast thou spoken kindly of them? Might not their path have been shown in *thine* life that desire as He manifested when He thought it not robbery to be equal with God and to offer Himself, His life, His body, His desires, as a sacrifice for thee that thou in thine own self-glory, in thine own understanding, might come to a knowledge that the desires of the heart—if they are spiritualized in that thou livest the life He has shown thee— thou may have in thine experience that He has promised, "What ye ask in my name, believing, that may the Father give thee?" Why art thou impatient? For the carnal forces are soon given over to the lusts thereof, but the spirit is alive through eternity! Be not impatient, but love ye the Lord! 262-63

Evolution: Physical or Spiritual?

While trying to understand myself and apply patience in my own spiritual growth, I was also still searching for a better understanding of the "big picture" that would reconcile my belief in eternal life to my scientific understanding of the world. Here, again, the readings seemed to ring true. There was no question that Cayce rejected the materialistic evolutionist's point of view in the following excerpts:

(Q) Is the Darwinian theory of evolution of man right or wrong? Give such an answer as will enlighten the people on this subject of evolution.

(A) Man was made in the beginning, as the ruler over those elements...man appeared not from that already created, but as the Lord over all that was created...the *soul of man* is that making him above all animal, vegetable, mineral kingdom of the earth plane.

Man *did not* descend from the monkey, but man has evolved... from time to time... 3744-5

[Survival of the fittest] Applies in the *animal* kingdom— not in man!...

56

Let all read history! Which has survived—the brute strength, or the development towards that of God? Which survives—the man that studies God and seeks to emulate His forces and powers, or the man that emulates the forces of earth or flesh? 900-340

But Cayce did acknowledge that the earth had been around for millions or billions of years and that mankind had changed or evolved over the several million years that souls had been in the earth. While confirming that the stories of Noah and the flood, the exodus from Egypt, and even the virgin birth of the Christ, were actual facts, the information put the allegorical aspects of the Genesis creation story in a perspective that left no excuse for fabricating a conflict between the Bible and science.

When we consider the evolution of the soul, the evolution of the body seems much less of a determining factor. Mr. [1233], who asked during his life reading, "From which side of my family do I inherit most?" was told, "You have inherited most from yourself, not from family! The family is only a river through which it (the entity, soul) flows!" (1233-1)

...we find the evolution of the soul...as is manifest in the material world, took place before man's appearance, the evolution of the soul in the mind of the Creator, not in the material world. 900-19

...there is the evolution of the soul, evolution of the mind, but not evolution of matter—save through mind, and that which builds same. 262-56

Cayce says that it is our soul that is made in the image of the Creator. Evolution means to unfold or roll out like a scroll. This implies that the pattern is implanted in the soul at the time of its creation. Like a flower when it blossoms, the pattern for our lives is within our soul. The body is only a vehicle for the soul and a manifestation of it in the physical world.

History/Prehistory/Myth

Almost all societies on earth have had some kind of story that goes beyond recorded history to explain from where the earth and all life on it came. Most of these stories are obviously mythical or

57

allegorical. They may or may not contain elements of literal truth, but they do say something important about that society's perception of the purposes for creation and their relationship to the Creator.

At some point in the story of mankind, myth blends with prehistory and recorded history. Archaeologists differ as to where that point is. For example, there is still much lively discussion among biblical archaeologists as to whether the patriarchs actually lived as real people. Yet, there is general agreement that at least some of the later historical accounts in the Bible are based on verifiable facts.

Scholars also differ about the degree to which Plato's account of the legendary continent of Atlantis is based on truth or fiction. A lot of effort has been expended in recent years to try to rediscover this ancient lost continent. This quest has resulted in some interesting TV programs about various parts of the world that might fit the legends.

The Cayce readings sometimes mention Atlantis as if it actually existed. They also say that many other civilizations have risen and fallen before what we know as recorded history, and that their fall was often due to misuse of their knowledge. The readings tell of souls who experienced life in the earth, first as thought forms and then taking on physical form with some of the attributes of the surrounding creation. Then God created Adam in a more perfect form as the first of the present race.

While Cayce affirmed that the story of Adam refers to a real human being, he also saw the story of Adam as archetypal of all of us. The pattern, from Adam to Christ, is within each soul, waiting to be activated so that we can grow to become the children of God that we were created to be. This can be realized only by following the example of Jesus who became the Christ.

The readings also speak of a time in ancient Egypt when there were efforts to accelerate the physical evolution of humankind. This was somewhat helpful physically, but they did not fully understand that the physical body is a manifestation of the Spirit, rather than the other way around. History seems to be repeating itself as scientists search for genetic causes and cures for almost every human ill. The readings, however, go on to suggest that perfecting the body alone will not produce soul growth. They also say that if we could understand how spiritualizing our desires would produce soul growth, which would then affect the physical, we could be on the verge of a new plateau in human evolution that would be the natural result of spiritual growth.

As you probably know, the readings are not the only source of metaphysical accounts of the history of the earth and mankind. Since the beginning of recorded history, there have been those who studied the esoteric sciences and emphasized the superiority of spirit over matter. Some esoteric or even reincarnationist points of view, however, often seem to say that matter is bad and spirit is good and all that souls need do to be saved is to free themselves from their entanglement in matter. The readings, on the other hand, suggest that the advent of sin, error, or selfishness is a spiritual event that occurred before the earth was created and that the creation of the material plane was a merciful act of God to provide a place where we could learn about spiritual laws. It is our spiritual tendency to selfishness that expresses itself in our desire to use material opportunities for self-indulgence or self-glorification:

> In the beginning was the word, and the word was God. He said, Let there be *light*—and there was light. Like begets like. It *is* both cause and effect, and they that choose some other way become the children of darkness; and they are these: Envying, strife, hate; and the children of these are sedition, rebellion, and the like.
>
> The children of light first love, for "Though I may have the gift of prophecy, though I may speak in unknown tongues, though I give my body to be burned and have not the spirit of the Son of man, the Christ Consciousness, the Christ Spirit, I am nothing." For, the children of light *know* Him; He calleth each by name. 262-46

Preoccupation with the material, or carnal, world may cause a soul to lose its true purpose and even deny its own spiritual nature. Overcoming such tendencies may be our ticket to graduation from this material school. To blame our mistakes on the physical world, however, does not seem to me to be an enlightened or mature attitude. The physical world, temporal as it may be, is just as real as God's love, of which it is a manifestation. Only by using these merciful opportunities constructively can we hope to grow toward heaven. The readings confirm over and over again that man has free will and must choose between that which is constructive or that which is destructive physically, mentally, and spiritually. Reading 3003-1 says, "For, as a corpuscle in the body of God, ye are free-willed—and thus a co-creator with God." Reading 5749-14 even says, "...it is only when the soul that is a portion of God *chooses* that God knows the end thereof."

Creation Cosmology

The following three points sum up the Cayce cosmology of creation as I understand it:

- *God created all souls in the beginning, in his likeness, to become his companions.*

I still appreciate the old catechism answer to the question of why God created us. It was something like this: "To know, love, and serve Him in this world and to be happy with Him in the next." Jesus even called His disciples "friends." Here are a few excerpts from readings that support this belief:

All souls were created in the beginning, and are finding their way back to whence they came. 3744-4

First, the entering of *every* soul is that it, the soul, may become more and more aware or conscious of the divine within, that the soul-body may be purged that it may be a fit companion for the *glory* of the Creative Forces in its activity. 518-2

For, the Creative Force made or brought into being *souls* to be equal with, and one with, Him; even as is manifested in the Way, the Truth, the Light. 2830-2

For the image in which man was created is spiritual, as He thy Maker is spiritual. 1257-1

- *Selfishness (sin, error, or rebellion) came into the consciousness of souls before the material universe was created, and this has separated us from the awareness of God's presence.*

The Genesis story, even though it is a story of Adam or physical man, is allegorical of this separation. The readings agree with the Bible that we have all erred:

As has been given, error or separation began before there appeared what we know as the Earth, the Heavens; or before Space was manifested.

This becomes hard to conceive in the finite mind; as does the finite mind fail to grasp the lack of or *no* time. Yet out of Time, Space, Patience, is it possible for the consciousness of the finite to *know* the infinite.

Hence, then, the interpretations of Spirit as it manifests to the sons of men must follow closely what we have chosen as Holy Writ. 262-115

Self-glory, self-exaltation, self-indulgence becometh those influences that become as abominations to the divinity in each soul; and *separate* them from a knowledge of Him. 1293-1

Hence that force which rebelled in the unseen forces (or in spirit) that came into activity, was that influence which has been called Satan, the Devil, the Serpent; they are One. That of *rebellion!* 262-52

- *The Christ Spirit, God's active desire that no soul should perish, brought the physical universe into being and eventually manifested itself as the savior of mankind, even Jesus the Christ.*

The Cayce information suggests that the creation of the Earth was the act of a merciful Creator so that souls who entered, even for selfish reasons, might become aware of their own individuality. As souls experience physical laws, which are a reflection of spiritual laws, they learn of their need to depend upon God and be one with Him. God has not left us alone in this condition, but actively pursues us, though without coercion. He has sent angels, prophets, and even the Christ to win us over, and he continues to speak to us individually whenever we will listen:

How readest thou? As given from the beginning, by becoming aware in a material world *is*—or was—the only manner or way through which spiritual forces might become aware of their separation from the spiritual atmosphere, the spiritual surroundings, of the Maker.

What has been given as the truest of all that has ever been written in Scripture? "God does not will that any soul should perish!" But man, in his headstrongness, harkens oft to that which would separate him from his maker! 262-56

For the spirit of God moved and that which is in matter came into being, for the opportunities of...His sons, His daughters. These are ever spoken of as One.

Then there came that as sought for self-indulgence, self-glorification; and there was the beginning of warring among themselves for activity—*still* in Spirit.

Then those that had made selfish movements moved into that which was and is *opportunity*, and there came life into same. 262-114

Do study creation, man's relationship to God. What is light, that came into the earth, as described in the third verse of Genesis 1? Find that light in self. It isn't the light of the noonday sun, nor the moon, but rather of the Son of man. 3491-1

Conclusions

The picture of creation given in the readings offers a real opportunity for healing between evolutionist and creationist theories. By drawing a clear distinction between the development of animals and of man, the readings allow us to study the fossil records with an open mind while retaining our spiritual identity as children of the Creator. These ideas have challenged me to learn to correlate or integrate the extremes in thought in other areas as well.

The cosmology expressed through the Cayce readings has gradually become central to my way of thinking and looking at the world. Not that I pretend to know exactly how it all happened, but this perspective offers possible solutions that do not destroy my faith in God. I have no doubt that some people find the same inner peace by applying what we sometimes call blind faith, and I do not fault that. Still, the Bible exhorts us to prove all things, and I needed what I found in the readings.

These readings present a great deal of interesting information about history, prehistory, creation, and ancient writings. I hope that scholars will not reject the historical aspects of the readings just because they do not appear to fit their present models of history.

Additional Readings

- *Spiritual Creation*

The soul of man is the greatest, then, of all creation, for it may be one with the Father... Ye, then, are not aliens—rather the *sons* of the Holy One. 262-24

For, the entity finds itself body-physical, body-mind, body-soul. The body-soul is a citizen of that realm we call heaven, as much as the body-physical is a citizen of the land we call home. 2823-1

- *Physical Creation*

...the worlds [were] created—and are still in creation in this heterogeneous mass as is called the outer sphere, or those portions as man looks up to in space...

...yet man [was] given that to be lord over all, and the *only* survivor of that creation. 900-340

That in the material world is a shadow of that in the celestial or spiritual world. 524-2

- *Error*

...for being afraid is the first consciousness of sin's entering in, for he that is made afraid has lost consciousness of self's own heritage... 243-10

..."*Subdue* the earth." For all therein has been given for man's purpose...for man's interpreting of God's relationship to man. And when man makes same only a gratifying, a satisfying of self, whether in appetite, in desire, in selfish motives for self-aggrandizement, self-exaltation, these become—as from old—stumblingblocks. But he that hath put off the old and put on the new is regenerated in the new Adam, in the last Adam, in the Christ. 262-99

• *Growth Toward the Light*

The *Spirit* moved—or soul moved—and there was Light (Mind). The Light became the light of men—Mind made aware of conscious existence in spiritual aspects or relationships as one to another. 1947-3

For each entity in the earth is what it is because of what it has been! And each moment is dependent upon another moment. So a sojourn in the earth, as indicated, is as a lesson in the school of life and experience. Just as it may be illustrated in that each entity, each soul-entity, is as a corpuscle in the body of God—if such an entity has applied itself in such a manner as to be a helpful force and not a rebellious force. 2823-3

6

The Concept of Oneness from the Readings:
Monotheism

Jesus replied, "This is the first: Listen, Israel, the Lord our God is the one Lord, and you must love the Lord your God with all your heart, with all your soul, with all your mind and with all your strength." (Mark 12:29-30 JB)

For, "Know, O ye people, the Lord thy God is *one!*" Of Him ye came, to Him ye owe all that thou art, thou canst be or ever *will* be! For in Him ye live and move and have thy being. Ye *are* indeed gods in the making! Then quit yourselves as the sons of a merciful Father; and as ye would have mercy and find grace and have peace, so must ye show mercy, so must ye be peaceful, that ye may become aware of the indwelling of His presence in thine inner self. 816-3

Through my high school years, I seldom questioned the existence of God or the concept of monotheism. While many people around me showed contempt for Christian values by their actions, I rarely heard even the most irreverent or amoral of my acquaintances actually question the existence of God. I had known about Darwinism, of course, and how these ideas about evolution had created considerable controversy, but I thought of that as just a technical question about which we were still learning. I could even identify with some of the feelings of earlier humanists until I became more aware of the anti-Christian influences of some of the works of persons such as Freud and Marx and Nietzsche and was exposed firsthand to the hard-core atheism of some who might be called secular humanists. I did not perceive all of them to be intentionally destructive or without any redeeming value, but I was stunned by the tremendous impact that these thought patterns had on the beliefs and attitudes expressed in our educational institutions.

Before finishing college, I entered the Aviation Cadet program in the Air Force. This presented less of a challenge to my faith and less time to worry about it than I had had in the academic environment. After completing officer training, navigation training, and electronics warfare training, I was assigned to a permanent station as a B-52 combat crew member. Then I started making an effort, at first informally, to continue my education.

I found myself grappling again with the challenges presented to a traditional belief in God. While I still attended church, formal religion seemed to provide little intellectual support. A friend had introduced me to some of his favorite philosophers, and I developed a very enjoyable habit of reading philosophy. This broadened my view of history but did little to enlighten me about the nature of God.

I once attended a lecture by a gentleman who classified himself as a philosopher. He defined philosophers as, "blind persons in dark rooms looking for black cats that aren't there." He considered himself one notch above theologians, whom he defined as, "blind persons in dark rooms looking for black cats that aren't there—and they find them." Fortunately my status in each of these fields was amateur at best, so I was free to follow Cayce's advice to expect a personal encounter with God. In a mental/spiritual reading Mr. [440] asked, "What is the highest possible psychic realization...?" The answer was, "That God, the Father, speaks directly to the sons of men—even as He has promised." (440-4)

God Is

Most religious and spiritual belief systems acknowledge that the existence of God is self-evident in all that we see of the universe. Yet, unbelief and skepticism often press in on us like an ominous storm cloud. With scientific knowledge abounding, we often feel that spirituality will be eclipsed. For me, the Cayce readings helped to dissipate those clouds of doubt.

Hebrews 11:6 (JB) says, "Now it is impossible to please God without faith, since anyone who comes to him must believe that he exists and rewards those who try to find him." The readings echo this verse time and again. They say that even God will not impose Himself upon a person who refuses to believe that He exists:

First we begin with the fact that God *is;* and that the heavens and the earth, and all nature, declare this. Just as there is a longing within *every* heart for the continuity of life.

What then is life? As it has been given, in Him we live and move and have our being. Then He, God, *is!* 1567-2

The following reading makes me wonder if Edgar Cayce was a Boy Scout. When asked how to explain God to a child, Cayce said:

In nature. As the unfolding of that that is seen *about* the child itself, whether in the grasses, the flowers, the birds, or what; for each are an expression of the Creative Energies in its activity, and the sooner *every soul* would learn that they themselves are a portion of everything about same, with the ability within self to make one's self one *with* that that brought *all* into being, the change is as that of service in its *naturalness.* 5747-1

Anthropomorphism

Anthropomorphism is the belief that God exists in human form with a body and the feelings and emotions that humans have. The Greeks worshiped Zeus, with his many human characteristics, as the highest of their many gods. The Romans called him Jupiter or Jove and added some myths and legends of their own.

Most Christians would not think of the idea of God having human form as being literally correct, but they understand that our mental images of God are useful analogies in understanding our relationship to Him. Jesus said, "God is spirit, and those who worship must worship in spirit and truth." (John 4:24 JB) This is not a simple concept to articulate. Perhaps our materialistic view of the human condition does make it difficult for us to conceive of thought, companionship, and love existing outside of the physical realm. Even though most of us think of God as being pure Spirit, we often understand spiritual things best by using images and analogies with which we can identify.

The Old Testament used numerous names for God to depict His relationship to us. Jehovah-Hoseenu (The Lord Our Maker), Jehovah-Rophi (The Lord, The Physician), Jehovah-Rohi (The Lord My Shepherd), Adonai (My Ruler), El Elyon (God Most High) are a few of many titles that convey the ancient Hebrew awareness of the Creator. In the New Testament, both Jesus (Mark 14:36) and Paul (Romans 8:15, Galatians 4:6) call God "Abba, Father."

In his fascinating historical work, *Jews, God and History*, Max I. Dimont suggests that the genius of the Jews, and one of the driving forces behind Western civilization, is that they "invented" Jehovah, their universal and monopolistic God. He also suggests that they have refined their concept of God throughout the centuries, to meet human needs. I would agree with Dimont that prophets such as Isaiah foresaw a developing brotherhood of man. I can also agree that our understanding of God is a growth process. However, I believe that these prophets were inspired by an encounter with a real, universal, unchangeable, living, spiritual Being and not just by a humanistic desire for a better worldly society. The Cayce readings say that the Israelites were chosen to spread the knowledge of God because they alone responded to God's call.

Some modern philosophers such as Spinoza, believing that we have created the Judeo-Christian god, Jehovah, in our own image, reject our anthropomorphic view of God. Spinoza was a pantheist, equating God with nature. This can be a really confusing topic because some people think of nature as the same Creative Force that we call God, while others think of nature as only the physical phenomena that can be apprehended with the five senses.

Even though Spinoza, who was born Jewish, believed that we should love God, he was thoughtful enough to know that his kind of pantheism, which perhaps leaned slightly toward the physical, was not compatible with belief in either man's free will or God's divine providence. While this type of thinking may be a sincere outgrowth of one's understanding of physical science, it has little to say about soul growth or eternal life.

Cayce's ideas of companionship with God are consistent with mainline Christian concepts of fellowship. If we think of God as personal, however, how do we reconcile this with His universal and transcendent nature? Even small children often wonder how God can personally answer prayer and yet interact with millions of other people at the same time. Cayce dealt with similar questions in the readings:

(Q) If God is impersonal force or energy –
(A) (Interrupting) He *is* impersonal; but as has just been given, so *very* personal! It is not that ye deal only with *impersonal*—it is *within and without!* It is *in* and *without*, and only as God *quickeneth* the spirit within, by the use, by

the application of the God-force within to mete it out to others. Else *how, why,* did that material experience of a man hanging on a Cross bring—*bring*—redemption to a world?

In this:

Though ye know He had the power within Himself to come down from the Cross, though He had the power to heal, though He had power to rid the very taking *hold* upon death, it had no claims upon Him. Why? *quickened* by the Father because the life *lived* among men, the dealings among *men,* brought *only* hope, *only* patience, *only* love, *only* longsuffering!

This then being the law of God made manifest, He *becomes* the law by manifesting same before man; and thus—as man, even as ye—becomes as one with the Father.

For until ye become in purpose, in activity, a savior— yea, a god—unto thy fellow man, ye do not take hold upon that *personality,* the *individuality* of *God*—that is the life, that is the being of life, eternity, hope and love!

These then become not only as impersonal but personal, in that ye know thyself, even as He—thy brother in the flesh—made manifest that ye are aware of thyself *being* thyself, yet one with Him; and thus able to enter into the joys, *wholly,* that are prepared since—yea, before—the very foundations of materiality, for those that keep His ways. 1158-12

What *is* thy God? Let each answer that within self. What *is* thy God? Where is He, what is He? Then ye may find yourselves lacking in much. How personal is He? Not as Moses painted a God of wrath; not as David painted a God that would fight thine enemies; but as the Christ—the Father of love, of mercy, of justice. 262-100

Father-Mother God

Genesis says that we are created in the image of God. The readings frequently remind us of this fact, but say that it is our souls that are made in God's image. We do not have to reinvent our concept of God to see that this is just as true for women as it is for men.

GIVE GOD A CHANCE

Perhaps our Judeo-Christian tradition does reflect some evidence of having been developed during times when male-dominated societies were prevalent. However, that did not keep Old Testament writers from using the name *Shaddai,* meaning "breasted one," when referring to Jehovah as providing perfect supply of our spiritual needs and perfect comfort. Neither did it prevent Jesus, as He looked out over Jerusalem, from using the analogy of Himself as a mother hen wanting to gather her chicks.

In my own church denomination, as in many others, there has been an effort in recent years to use inclusive language. In some even more liberal movements, feminine pronouns are used almost exclusively to refer to God. I found nothing in Cayce's Work to support this, but the readings did use some inclusive language long before the present trend in our churches.

While the readings often refer to God as "He" and use the term "Father," just as Jesus did in His time, I do not sense even the slightest intent of sexism in the readings. Not only do they confirm the biblical concept that there is no such thing as gender in the spirit and frequently avoid using-gender specific terms, the readings also sometimes balance the use of "Father" with the "Mother" image. Cayce referred to God as "Father-Mother God" in several readings that span the time period from 1937 to 1944. These are almost equally divided among readings given for males, for females, or for a group. The reading categories under which this occurred include life, philosophy, physical, and prayer group readings. They usually relate to healing or to attunement to God and were often given as part of an affirmation. Here are a couple of examples:

For man and woman in their manifestations are given— by the All-Wise, All-Merciful Father, the First Cause, the Mother-God, the Father-God—the opportunity to be one with Him. 945-1

(Q) Please give a prayer for meditation to be used while writing the pamphlets, the book, and the poem.
(A) *Father-mother-god! In thy mercy, in thy love, be thou the guide just now, as I seek in humility and in earnestness to present that which may give my fellow man a better and a more perfect insight into the love which was manifested by*

Jesus, my Lord and my God. Help, thou, O God, my every effort. 849-76

In addition to using inclusive language, Cayce also made it clear that men and women were equal before God, and he gave credit to Christianity for raising women's status in society. Speaking of a woman who was said to have been Judy, the leader of the Essenes at the time of Jesus, reading 1472-3 said:

> Hence we find the entity in those periods soon after the Crucifixion not only giving comfort but a better interpretation to the Twelve, to the Holy Women; an understanding as to how Woman was redeemed from a place of obscurity to her place in the activities of the affairs of the race, of the world, of the empire—yea, of the home itself.

In another reading for a woman, who was commended for her desire to make a home for those who had erred, Cayce said:

> ...many of those whom ye would aid may come to know, too, the blessings of the Holy One, who honored woman that she might, too, be equal with man in the redemption of man from the wiles of the devil, or the wiles of him who would cause man or woman to err in any manner. 5231-1

Monotheism

The readings sometimes equate the idea of One God with the concept of all souls having "the One Father" or "the One Purpose." Reading 696-3 says:

> For, as the Teacher of teachers gave, as all who have pointed a service to their fellowmen, there is *one* God; or "The Lord thy God is *One*"—and the expression should be, "My Spirit (not spirits, but *my* Spirit) beareth witness with *thy* spirit (not spirits) as to whether ye be the child of God or not."

Some scholars suggest that monotheism in ancient Israel was an idea that developed over a period of hundreds of years. According to Cayce, the concept of one God is much older than even Israel. There are numerous readings that refer to the children of "the law of One" in the legendary civilization known as Atlantis:

> In that experience [Atlantis] the entity gained; for as in the present, it held to the Law of One,—as one wife, one home, one state, one religion, one God, one purpose. *Hold* to these in their proper relationship one to another in the present. 2437-1

This belief in the one God was widely accepted in Atlantis, he said, until those with selfish purposes rebelled:

> The sons of Belial were of one group, or those that sought more the gratifying, the satisfying, the use of material things for self, *without* thought or consideration as to the sources of such nor the hardships in the experiences of others. Or, in other words, as we would term it today, they were those without a standard of morality. 877-26

The Cayce readings are very consistent about monotheism. They frequently say that individually, in corporate worship, and in public life we should have one God. Reading 2279-1 quotes Deuteronomy 6:4, "Know, O Israel, the Lord thy God is one!" I found 123 references to this Bible passage in the readings index. The readings elaborate on this theme to say that, within ourselves, we should worship only the one Holy Spirit and not entertain other purposes.

We also recognize a kinship with all other souls when we believe in the one God. This is why Jesus taught us to pray, "Our Father." When World War II was beginning, world affairs reading 3976-26 said, "Let each and every soul call on not their God but the *one* God!" Reading 1438-1 adds, "For know that *God* is not a respecter of persons nor of races..." Reading 1599-1 also says, "...there cannot be one relation with thy fellow man and another with thy Maker, not one expressed in words and another lived in the inner life."

Evil/Dualism

Some beliefs, possibly related to Persian forms of mysticism, such as Manichaeism, are thought of as teaching that everything in the universe is a manifestation of two opposing forces, good and evil, light and darkness. This philosophy is called dualism by those who think of it as idolatry. The imagery of light and darkness corresponding to good and evil is not unique, however, to this part of the world nor to this time period. It occurs many times in the Old and New Testaments.

Various sects that have come and gone over the centuries have believed that matter is evil and spirit is good. Some of them even associated Jehovah of the Old Testament with darkness (the material world), and the Father that Jesus speaks of with light (Spirit). I have even heard vestiges of this theory suggested by many sincere Christians and new age seekers today. Some of the church fathers thought of this as idolatry, which is one of the reasons that these sects have been resisted by most orthodox factions within the church.

While there are some parallels between the readings and certain beliefs that are sometimes called Gnostic, there is no question in my mind that the readings are closer to the orthodox beliefs in this respect. The readings frequently used *I Am, The Great I Am, Abba, Father, Yah, Yahweh, Lord, God, and The God Of Abraham, Isaac And Jacob,* saying that these all refer to one and the same God. Jesus certainly gave a better concept of God's spirit to the world than even that found in the Old Testament, but that does not mean that He worshiped a different God. I have found no hint in the Cayce readings of even the smallest excuse for making a distinction between the God of the Old Testament and the God of the New Testament.

On the other hand, it seems to me that orthodox thinkers have sometimes reacted too strongly to the idea of dualism—or at least painted their heretics with too broad a brush. For example, some of the early sects believed in the preexistence of the soul, a belief that I find no legitimate reason to condemn. I fail to see how the belief that we existed before we were born in the flesh has caused any real problems. Yet some modern theologians, believing that they must resist the heresy of dualism, still oppose any ideas that suggest that the soul can in any way exist without the body. Any belief in angels, the personification of evil as Satan, or any form life after death also would be seen by some as dualism. It does not seem to bother them that their denial of evil tends to negate the possibility of free will.

73

While they do not dwell on evil, the Cayce readings do put it into a perspective that is consistent with biblical teachings. Reading 5752-3 says, "...Fellowship, kindness, gentleness, patience, long-suffering, love; these be the fruits of the spirit. Against such there is no law. Doubt, fear, avarice, greed, selfishness, self-will; these are the fruits of the evil forces. Against such there *is* a law." The readings assert that, while there is only one God who is all good, when souls separate from the spiritual realm to enter into material manifestation, we must then choose between good and evil. Reading 262-52 says:

Hence, will is given to man as he comes into this manifested form that we see in material forces, for the choice. As given, "There is set before thee (man) good and evil."

Evil is rebellion. Good is the Son of Life, of Light, of Truth; and the Son of Light, of Life, of Truth, came into physical being to demonstrate and show and lead the way for man's ascent to the power of good over evil in a material world.

As there is, then, a personal savior, there is the personal devil.

Another rationalization that seems to me worse than dualism is the idea that evil just happens to us even though neither we nor God have done anything to cause it. Evil, however, is not something that just happens to us. It might be better to think of evil as something that we allow to manifest through us by conscious choice or by default. We may choose to call anything uncomfortable that happens to us "evil." But, according to study group reading 262-94, Jesus did not see things that way:

No one could speak evil of Him, yet *we* say, *ye* say, evil was done Him. Yet He said, "for that purpose came I into the world, that I might overcome the world," and thus that the Glory of the Father, of the Creator—yea, of thy Elder Brother—might be manifest.

There is never any question in the readings that Christ has overcome the forces of evil and that, in Him, we can do the same. In other words we can no longer externalize the blame for our mistakes by saying, "The devil made me do it." As reading 1293-1 says:

> ...the soul may find its way through the vicissitudes of experience in materiality, that it may know its God. For He manifested in flesh that the evil forces, as manifest in the relationships of individuals as one to another, may be eradicated from the experiences of man.

The readings also made several statements to the effect that evil cannot manifest in the world in a fleshly body. People are not totally good or evil in themselves, but they allow one or the other to manifest through them in various situations. Reading 689-1 told a person who was dealing with family problems:

> For *good* alone may wholly, materially manifest in an earthly world; for so came thy Lord into flesh. *Evil* only hath its appearance in the mind, in the shadows, in the fears of those that know not the light in its entirety.

Oneness

The first lesson for *six months* should be *One*—One—One—*One*; Oneness of God, oneness of man's relation, oneness of force, oneness of time, oneness of purpose, *oneness* in every effort—Oneness—Oneness! 900-429

While I think of monotheism as a theological concept that affects our belief systems, I tend to see oneness as an attitude or a lifestyle that affects our relationship with all of God's creation. These are not separate ideas, just two sides of the same coin. We expresses oneness when we say that we strive for a win/win situation in our dealing with others. At some level of spirituality it becomes apparent that what is best for our own soul is also best for every other soul. In a sense the following reading is saying that there is "one good" in all things:

> In every form of good, all element, all power in the material, all the chemical, or the mechanical world, there is the manifestation of the good which is God. 3143-1

Most of us are somewhat familiar with the ethnic forces that have brought fighting and consternation in the area of the world we call the Balkans. When our efforts to work together are destroyed by each group or individual grasping for some ethnic, local or provincial interest we now say that we have been Balkanized. Cayce often told people to try to be agreeable and to emphasize the common ground between beliefs rather than exaggerating the differences. This is not to suggest that we should compromise our ideals just to appear to be agreeable. We should, however, constantly analyze our own motives. To think that the spiritual needs of the individual could conflict with the spiritual needs of society is to lack faith in a loving God.

Idolatry

The idea of worshiping idols may seem like something done in ancient times by ignorant peoples and not something that happens in the modern world. The readings do speak of historical and even prehistoric modes of idol worship. Reading 339-1 told a young woman that she had lived, "in the Atlantean period when there were those contentions between those of the one faith and those that were of Bel-Ra—or the idol worshippers." Reading 5756-11 gives some additional insight into idolatry: "But rather some became worshippers of that the sun produced, rather than of that which had produced the sun: There's a difference!"

While the carved images of Old Testament days may be simpler to identify, anything that we put before our relationship to God becomes an idol. Speaking of constructive activities, reading 1437-1 says:

> ...they become mental and soul building, bringing with same a joy, a peace not found in unconstructive experience, nor in the gratifying alone of selfish interests. For these oft turn and rend those that make of themselves or their appetites idols in their daily experience.

Cayce was not alone in expressing the idea that idolatry is most often seen in the form of self-indulgence. In *Peace of Soul,* Bishop Fulton J. Sheen said:

> There is no surer formula for discontent than to try to satisfy our cravings for the ocean of Infinite Love from the

teacup of finite satisfactions. Nothing material, physical, or carnal can ever satisfy man completely; he has an immortal soul which needs an Eternal Love.

The Law of Love

If there is one thing on which most adherents of all of the world religions could agree, it might be that God is Love. We have observed that the universe in which we live operates according to certain laws. Cayce said that the spiritual universe also is subject to laws. The highest of these laws is the Law of Love. In reading 3574-2 we find:

What is truth? Law! What is Law? Love. What is Love? God. What is God? Law and love. These are the circle of truth itself. And wherever ye are, in whatever clime. For, as it is said of him, He is ever the same, yesterday, today and forever—unalterable!

When we speak of the love that God has for us, we are not just speaking of a desire or a feeling. Rather we think of love as an active, creative, constructive force for good. God calls on us to be channels of that love and, thereby, to become co-creators with Him:

What is the will of the Father? That all men should know Him, through the acts of the ones that claim to be, or who are by their natural heritage, the brethren; by the deeds done in the body. Through *faith* are ye healed, through love are ye made free, in that ye do unto thy neighbor, thy brother, as ye would have them do unto you. 254-71

God is love. An individual entity, each soul, each entity, each body, finds the need of expressing that called love in the material experience; from its first awareness until its last call through God's other door... 2174-2

7

Manifestation in Three Dimensions—Body, Mind, Soul:
The Trinity

The Christian doctrine of the Trinity is mentioned in several other chapters, and this discussion could have been included in one of them. However, the unusual way in which Cayce understood the Trinity deserves a brief chapter of its own.

Even though references to Father, Son, and Holy Ghost are found in the Bible and early church writings, the use of the term *Trinity* (*trinitas*) was not found in the early church until it was used by Tertullian in the second century. Much of the terminology used by theologians today concerning the Trinity was developed in the fourth century.

During the development of this doctrine in the early church councils, there was much discussion of its biblical, metaphysical, and numerological merits. The church fathers even saw in the use of the common Hebrew name for God (in the plural form Elohim) in Genesis 1:26, a suggestion of the Trinity. Augustine thought of the Trinity as relating to different phases of the human mind. The idea of persons comes from *persona,* meaning masks. These are seen not as hiding God, but as ways in which God can manifest or reveal Himself to us in the material world, where the idea of pure Spirit is difficult for humans to grasp.

Cayce never questioned the belief in the Trinity. In fact, he used it extensively to explain spirituality in a three-dimensional world. The unique concepts of the Trinity found in the Cayce readings have been helpful to me in talking with persons of other religions. Both Muslims and Jews are strong believers in monotheism, and some of them have traditionally viewed the Christian belief in the divinity of Jesus as a form of idolatry. Even though Christians know that they believe in one God, it is not always easy to convince others of that fact. I have found the concept of the Trinity to be easier to understand by others when we emphasize that we perceive the one Creative Force or God in this way because of our own nature in this three-dimensional world. Cayce's suggestion, that the concept of the Trinity is a pattern for us to attune ourselves—body, mind, and soul—to one single purpose of a loving relationship with God, may facilitate an understanding of the Trinity by those of other religions who are taught to avoid idolatry.

This understanding does not eliminate the need to clear up the confusion caused by the early church arguments about the divinity of Christ and beliefs about His mother, Mary. The early councils did their best to balance conflicting ideas and deal with what they saw as heresy, but I believe that they were not infallible and that we still have much to learn. There is no doubt, however, that the belief that Jesus was the Son of God is found in the Gospels and in early church writings. This is the basis of the Trinitarian beliefs that have been generally accepted. Here are some readings that reflect Cayce's beliefs about the Trinity:

In giving for this entity a mental and spiritual reading, it is well that the premise be given from which such information is drawn.

We accept the fact that there is the one God and that Jesus the Christ is His manifested messenger in the earth; and that the gift of the Holy Spirit by and through the Christ is ever to be the comforter to those who seek to know the Lord, the Father-God, through Him.

Through the revelations of holy men—as recorded in the Bible—there have been those things oft in man's experience that have caused some confusion, in man's attempt to apply such precepts as indicated there in the daily relationships.

We find that such confusions arise primarily from man's inability to coordinate in his personal experience those precepts that are related to the various phases of man's consciousness in the material plane.

Man finds himself a body, a mind, a soul. The body is self-evident. The mind also is at times understood. The soul or the spiritual portion is hoped for, and one may only discern same from a spiritual consciousness.

The body, the mind and the soul are as the Father, the Son and the Holy Spirit,—just as infinity in its expression to the finite mind is expressed in time, space and patience. 2879-1

Thus may we, as individuals—as we apply ourselves—become aware of that abiding presence as He promised—yea, as He maintained—"If I go away I will send the spirit of truth, the spirit of righteousness, and he shall *abide* with you. And I and the Father will come." 2879-1

But man being a creative nature, man being endowed with divinity within self, may work that to his own undoing or to his own glory in the Father, the Son and the Holy Spirit that worketh in and through these according to that purposed in their hearts. 3976-17

The Temple of God
Reading 2067-1 compares the human condition to the holy temple:

The entity finds self a body, a mind, a soul... These are as the shadows which were indicated in the mount by the outer court (the body), the inner court (the mind), and the still more holy of holies (the soul). These are but shadows, and yet indicate the trend of the development...

Projector Analogy
One of Cayce's associates made an interesting analogy by comparing soul, mind, and body to the phenomenon that is seen when watching a movie. This excerpt could be helpful to anyone who understands how a movie projector works:

(Q) Let the light represent the Spiritual, the film the physical faculties of senses (mind), and the moving picture on the screen this physical life—talking, feeling, tasting, thinking, emotion, etc., and one has a good comparison. Changing pictures, but One Fixed Light.
(A) Correct. 900-156

The Father
Jesus referred to God as the Father, and the Cayce readings frequently do the same. When speaking of the Trinity, the readings also often refer to God as the Creator:

God, the Father, then, is the Creator—the beginning and the end. In *Him* is the understanding, *by* and through those influences that have taken form—in universes—to meet the needs of each soul—that we might find our way to Him. 5755-2

But let thy light so shine that others, seeing thy good work, may be constrained to glorify the Father,—not an individual, not a group nor an organization, but the Father, the Maker, the Creator of the heavens and the earth. 2982-1

The Son

The idea that the mind is the builder is expressed throughout the readings. Here are a few readings that express the idea that, in the Trinity, the Christ is represented as the mind:

Now we have seen, we have heard, we know that the Son represents or signifies the Mind.

He, the Son, was in the earth-earthy even as we—and yet is of the Godhead.

Hence the Mind is both material and spiritual, and taketh hold on that which is its environ, its want, in our experiences.

Then Mind, as He, was the Word—and dwelt among men; and we beheld Him as the face of the Father.

So is our mind made, so does our mind conceive—even as He; and *is* the Builder.

Then that our mind dwells upon, that our mind feeds upon, that do we supply to our body—yes, to our soul! 1567-2

Hence mind is ever the builder, the way; as *He*, the ideal—in mind, in materiality, yea in spirit—is the way, the truth, the light. 2326-1

Then the Master—as the mind—is the way, is the how, that one becomes aware through application, through administration of the hopes, the desires, the faith of the soul itself. For, mind is of body and of soul, and when purified in the Christ-Consciousness it lives on and on as such. 3292-1

For materially He says, "Come unto me, ye that are weak and heavyladen, and ye shall find rest unto your souls."

To the mental He says, "In my father's house are the many mansions, the many phases, the many stages of activities."

To thy spirit He says, "Be ye *one* —even as I and my Father are one!" 1598-1

The Holy Spirit

Many people, not all of them Pentecostals, have felt that the Holy Spirit has been somewhat ignored in some churches. As a result, there are charismatic groups even in most mainline denominations today. While not necessarily putting exactly the same emphasis on certain gifts, the readings do encourage everyone to be open to the action of the Holy Spirit.

When one person asked how to overcome little annoyances in daily life, reading 262-24 said, "As was given of Him, as ye seek, know there is that Comforter present that will speak for thee under *every* condition..."

In study group reading 262-15, Cayce suggested that those writing about their experiences could test them as to whether they are from human confidence or from faith by analyzing "whether it partakes of the physical conscious sense or that of the spiritual intuitive forces as comes from close communion with the Holy Spirit, the promised Comforter, the consciousness of the Christ." Reading 262-29 says:

Then, the Christ Consciousness is the Holy Spirit, or that as the promise of His presence made aware of His activity in the earth. The spirit is as the Christ in action with the Spirit of the Father.

For a thirty-five-year-old man with a serious health problem, Cayce recommended an electrical appliance. Then the reading added:

All of the mechanical appliances that ye may muster will not aid to complete recovery *unless* thy purpose, unless thy soul has been baptized with the Holy Spirit. 3124-2

The Harmonious Triune

The concept of the harmonious triune is discussed in other chapters, but if there are any questions about Cayce's belief in the triune God, then perhaps these readings will state it once again:

...even as the Father, the Son and the Holy Spirit are one. So must body, mind and soul be one in purpose and in aim, and as ye ask, believing, so is it done unto thee. 5246-1

Do stay close to the Ark of the Covenant which is within thee; knowing the Father, the Son, the Holy Ghost must move within and through thee if ye would bring thyself closer to the fullness of thy purposes in the earth. 5177-1

8

Life More Abundant:
Evolution of the Soul—Reincarnation

"Do not let your hearts be troubled.
Trust in God still, and trust in me.
There are many rooms in my Father's house;
if there were not, I should have told you.
I am going now to prepare a place for you,
and after I have gone and prepared you a place,
I shall return to take you with me;
so that where I am you may be too.
You know the way to the place where I am going."
(John 14:1-4 JB)

When I was in high school, I read an article about the religion in Japan called Shintoism. The article, which I had found in a news magazine, discussed the Shinto belief in reincarnation. My first reaction was that belief in reincarnation was motivated by an attachment to the world. One could come back in an endless series of incarnations and never have to give up worldly desires. I thought about the millions of years that the earth could last if it did not meet with some catastrophe sooner than that, but I had been promised eternal life. A million years, or even a billion years, was not good enough. My perception was that reincarnationists did not really believe in a spiritual God, so I rejected or ignored reincarnation, viewing it as wishful thinking. Only later did I realize that a belief in reincarnation was almost synonymous in many cultures with a belief in survival of the soul or eternal life. I did not realize that so much of Christian theology had turned toward either a humanistic philosophy that emphasizes only the "now," or some kind of "resurrection" theory where the world, and the bodies of the saved, will be reconstructed and last forever.

Later, when I learned about the Cayce readings, I realized that they spoke of a series of lives as a growth experience that eventually could lead to eternal companionship with God. The readings never failed to acknowledge Jesus the Christ as the example or pattern or the Way to eternal life. He was spoken of as an elder brother and a personal Savior. I could find no idolatry or false religion in these concepts. They settled into my mind with a joy and peace that could only be compared to finding an old friend.

As I began to experience some negative reactions when I tried to share the idea of rebirth with others, I searched through the Bible for answers. Although it was not really explicit one way or the other, there were some interesting passages. There could be no question that Jesus himself said that John the Baptist was the fulfillment of Malachi's prophecy that Elijah would return (Malachi 4:6, Matthew 11:14, 17:9-13, Mark 9:12-13). Even though John answered "No" when the priests asked him if he was Elijah (John 1:21), we cannot assume that he would have known who he was in a past experience, nor that it would have been safe for him to answer in the affirmative, even if he did know.

In any case, this question, along with those in Matthew 16:14 and John 9:1, could indicate that the people of that time believed in reincarnation. An even more striking example of the belief in the preexistence of the soul is found in the apocryphal book of Wisdom. The speaker says, "I was a boy of happy disposition, I had received a good soul as my lot, or rather, being good, I had entered an undefiled body..." (Wisdom 8:19-20 JB) Another example is Jeremiah 1:5, which implies that God knew Jeremiah before he was conceived.

When Cayce was asked where in the Bible reincarnation could be found, he suggested that a person study the fourteenth through the seventeenth chapters of John. He also said that the term *resurrection* meant much the same then as reincarnation does today. Of course, I often heard Hebrews 9:27 ("...it is appointed unto men once to die" KJV) quoted as an argument against rebirth. For some people, that settled the issue. I did not have a canned answer for that passage, nor did I feel compelled to rationalize one. The author of Hebrews was speaking of the return of the Christ, emphasizing that Jesus would not have to deal with sin again when He returns. In my mind, that one quote, often taken out of context, did not outweigh all the other evidence. The book of Hebrews (2:15) also says that Jesus the Christ has set free those who have been kept in slavery by their fear of death. If reincarnation, or the immortality of the soul, is a fact, would its denial not have the same effect as denying that liberation?

I read several books about reincarnation and was surprised to find that so much had been written on the subject. Of course, there are many different ideas about how rebirth occurs. There are Hindu and Buddhist philosophies, with their beliefs about karma. There are Theosophist and Rosicrucian ideas, with some unusual beliefs about Christianity. Many primitive societies have beliefs about reincarnation. There are and have been many famous writers and other notable persons, many of them Christians, who believe in reincarnation. There are hypnotists and psychologists who have studied the subject from a more objective point of view, some with some interesting statistics and case histories. There are even psychologists who treat patients by hypnotic regression to deal with past life-trauma. Those who have propounded theories about reincarnation are no more in exact agreement with each other than the various churches or sects are in agreement with each other about the Gospel.

History

Some who believe in reincarnation say that one of the early church fathers, Origen, believed in reincarnation and was condemned for this belief by one of the ecumenical councils. There are some written anathemas against Origen in some manuscripts of the Second Ecumenical Council of Constantinople (AD 553), but scholars differ on whether they originated within the Council itself.

It may be true that Origen believed in the preexistence of the soul and the other metaphysical concepts for which he was anathematized. His own writing from around 225-250 AD (long before the anathemas against him) indicate, however, that he did not believe in reincarnation. In fact, he argued strongly against it. Some of his arguments were primarily against transmigration, the belief that humans come back as animals, but he definitely argued against reincarnation as well, as did several other early church writers. Just for the record, reading 2464-2 clearly indicates that Cayce might agree with them about transmigration when it says, "This is not intended to indicate that there is transmigration or transmutation of the soul from animal to human..."

Even though Origen and some other early Christians wrote against reincarnation, there is little evidence to back up the traditional argument that the church councils removed reincarnation from the Scriptures. In fact, many of the orthodox arguments that I have found against reincarnation date from 150 years or fewer after the Crucifixion of the Christ, long before the councils were convened. It must also be remembered, however, that most of these arguments were directed toward "heresies" that existed within the church. Therefore, it is clear that some of the factions within the early church did believe in reincarnation. Perhaps some sacred writings were left out of the Bible in order to exclude reincarnation, but I have found no proof of that either, except for the recent practice of leaving the apocryphal books out of most versions. Even if someone did try to edit reincarnation out of the Bible, they did a poor job of it.

What we would really like to know is whether Jesus believed in reincarnation. Since the Gospels are not quite explicit enough to be taken literally on that point, it would be helpful to know what the prevailing beliefs of the Jews were at that time. Some of the most concrete evidence of Jewish belief in reincarnation at the time of Jesus is found in the works of Josephus, a historian and Jewish priest in Jerusalem in the first century. The works of Josephus seem to be gaining in respect among scholars in recent years (See the articles about Josephus in the September/October 1990 issue of *Biblical Archaeology Review*).

Here is some of what Josephus had to say:

[Speaking of the Pharisees:] "They also believe that souls have an immortal vigor in them, and that under the earth there will be rewards or punishments, according as they have lived virtuously or viciously in this life; and the latter are to be detained in an everlasting prison, but that the former shall have power to revive and live again; on account of which doctrines, they are able greatly to persuade the body of the people; ..."

"But the doctrine of the Sadducees is this: That souls die with the bodies; nor do they regard the observation of anything besides what the law enjoins them..."

"The doctrine of the Essenes is this: That all things are best ascribed to God. They teach the immortality of souls, and esteem that the rewards of righteousness are to be earnestly striven for..." Josephus—*Antiquities of the Jews* 18.1.3-5

[Speaking of the Essenes:] "For their doctrine is this:—That bodies are corruptible, and that the matter they are made of is not permanent; but that the souls are immortal, and continue for ever; and that they come out of the most subtle air, and are united to their bodies as in prisons, into which they are drawn by a certain natural enticement; but that when they are set free from the bonds of the flesh, they then as released from a long bondage, rejoice and mount upward... whereby good men are bettered in the conduct of their life, by the hope they have of reward after their death, and whereby the vehement inclinations of bad men to vice are restrained, by the fear and expectation they are in, that although they should lie concealed in this life, they should suffer immortal punishment after death..."

"...the Pharisees...ascribe all to fate, and to God, and yet allow, that to act what is right, or the contrary, is principally in the power of men, although fate does co-operate in every action. They say that all souls are incorruptible; but that the souls of good men are only removed into other bodies,—but that the souls of bad men are subject to eternal punishment. But the Sadducees are those that compose the second order, and take away fate entirely, and suppose that God is not concerned in our doing or not doing what is evil; and they say, that to act what is good, or what is evil is at men's own choice, and that the one or the other belongs to every one, that they may act as they please. They also take away the belief of the immortal duration of the soul, and the punishments and rewards in Hades. Moreover, the Pharisees are friendly to one another...But the behaviour of the Sadducees one towards another is in some degrees wild..." Josephus—*Wars of the Jews* 2.8.11-14

Apparently, the belief of the Pharisees and Essenes in reincarnation was not considered to be strange or occult (except possibly by the Sadducees) at the time of Jesus. There is no reason to believe that Jesus took exception to this point of view. Some would ask why these beliefs were not spelled out more clearly in the Scriptures if they were known to the Master. My guess would be that the return of souls was simply taken for granted by most people of that time, so there was no reason to spell it out. Jesus took the Sadducees to task for their lack of faith in resurrection (Matthew 22:23-33, Mark 12:18-27, Luke 20:27-38). That the belief in resurrection and in the spirit was well established among non-Christian Pharisees is seen in the way Paul caused them to argue with the Sadducees in the Sanhedrin, thereby saving his own life (Acts 23:6-10).

The idea that the ancient Jews did not believe in the survival of the soul, or any concept of eternal life, is certainly contrary to the writings of Josephus as well as to the teachings of the Master. While the Mosaic Law may not speak specifically of reward or punishment in an afterlife, it could be implied. In his book, *Judaism*, Rabbi Dr. Isidore Epstein, speaking of the Torah, says, "Scripture, nevertheless, found it necessary to cast a veil over the whole question of survival beyond the grave, in order to wean people away from the idolatrous cult of the dead with which this belief was at that time associated." Anyone who reads the apocryphal books of Wisdom or II Maccabees can see that the idea of resurrection was well developed long before the time of Jesus. Some scholars might suggest that this was due to Greek influence. Perhaps some Greeks did believe in the survival of the soul, but the Jews tended to reject Greek religious beliefs because of what they perceived to be idolatry and immoral behavior.

Early Christianity did not come into a religious vacuum, nor had the Jewish tradition existed in such. Judaism was one of the oldest known religions to teach the belief in one God, but it was not the only one. During the Jewish exile in Babylon, that land was conquered by the Persians. Many Persians of that day were adherents of Zoroastrianism. The Zoroastrians may have had an even stronger sense of moral responsibility than the Jews of that time, and this may have had a very positive effect on Judaism. They taught that people have a free will and that they will be judged after this life and rewarded or punished in heaven or hell, depending on what they deserve. It would appear to me that Jewish interpretation of these Zoroastrian beliefs had a strong influence on the "one life, then heaven or hell" scenario which dominated much of Western Christian thinking prior to modern secularism.

Once the orthodox forces in the church had effectively outlawed belief in reincarnation, it was primarily only those outside of the church who maintained that belief or even consider it as a possibility. No wonder there is the tendency to condemn the concept as being occult.

Within the various other systems of thought that have taught reincarnation in one form or another, rebirth is not always thought of as a doctrine or a dogma. Rebirth is simply a fact that is perceived (and perhaps even exploited) by various disciplines in various ways. Just because some religions have incorporated the concept of reincarnation into systems of thought that, within a Christian value reference, are idolatrous and exploitative, it does not follow that a knowledge of reincarnation is the cause of these errors, nor that concealing the fact will somehow help Christianity to be above such mistakes.

Some who have been missionaries to India or China in recent years are quick to point out that knowledge of reincarnation has not solved those countries' problems nor ushered in a new age. Some missionaries blame belief in reincarnation for the caste system in India. It seems more likely, however, that the Hindu concept of reincarnation has simply been used as a rationalization for maintaining the caste system. Being born into a certain societal level (or caste) may very well be a way of meeting conditions that were begun in some previous lifetime, but that does not justify the stratification of society or taking advantage of others who are less fortunate than ourselves. If Cayce's concepts of karma are correct, then exploiting those of another group is the best way to find oneself in that same position in the future. If we truly believe that we might have to return to this environment, then it would be to our benefit to work toward a more equitable society.

Believing that one has had a prior physical appearance in the earth does not necessarily mean that a person has become a Hindu or that he or she has rejected Jesus as Lord and Savior. In *Edgar Cayce and Christian Faith,* Lynn Sparrow says, "I want first to point out that there is nothing inherently Christian (or non-Christian, for that matter) in the reincarnationist philosophy..."

Prayer for the Deceased

Another subtle factor in the modern lack of belief in the survival of the soul, or the continuity of life, is the Reformation ban on praying for the dead. (This ban was also a factor in the Apocryphal books of the Old Testament having been left out of most modern bibles.) While the readings do not exactly confirm all Roman Catholic beliefs about purgatory, nor do they condone the selling of "indulgences" to raise money, their frequent use of the term "borderland" is quite parallel to the idea of purgatory. Several readings clearly recommend prayers for the dead. One reading actually uses the term purgatory:

> Hence there has been given that the Master preached to those in purgatory, ...[I Peter 3:19] and that the passing through same was for their understanding, and again there is seen the prayer made even in the law of Moses for one passing into that land in between, and again is prayer made by him who would intercede for the soul passing into the borderland [Luke 23:43; I Peter 4:6], see? 900-311

In addition to Roman Catholics, some Episcopalians, Orthodox Christians, Orthodox Jews, Muslims, Buddhists, and those of many other faiths also pray for those who have recently died. Some Protestants believe that it is acceptable to pray for their deceased loved ones privately, but not in corporate worship. Opposition to the practice of praying for the dead did not begin with Luther or Calvin. It was part of the anti-Catholic beliefs of the Waldensians of the 12th Century. It was probably also opposed by the Sadducees, who did not believe in the survival of the soul, and perhaps by many other groups in ages past. As with many other issues, I believe that the Cayce readings offer a balanced approach that might help us move toward a better understanding of the truth.

Reaction Against Dualism

A few years ago, I attended an evening seminar at a local seminary. One of the professors, warning against dualism, said that the notion that the soul can in any way live independently of the body was "heresy." I wonder what creative explanation he might have had for the passage in I Kings 17:22 (JB), where it is written, "Yahweh heard the prayer of Elijah and the soul of the child returned to him again and he revived." If Cayce's quote of Jesus as saying, "For as He gave again, what profit it a man though he gain the whole world and has lost sight of being a soul?" (853-9), can be accepted, then denying the continuity of the life of the soul is the real heresy, if there is such a thing as heresy.

Dualism (also discussed in other chapters) is not the only way that the knowledge of reincarnation can be interpreted. The Cayce readings do not see matter as evil, but as a merciful creation where souls can grow to become companions to God. It is seen as a gift of the Creator that we can have various opportunities to enter the earth plane. Souls are expected to overcome selfishness in successive incarnations designed by a loving Creator to foster growth. Accepting the Christ as example, guide, and friend is in no way contrary to a belief in reincarnation. Nor does the idea that we must struggle continually in successive lives without experiencing forgiveness, necessarily follow from the acceptance of reincarnation.

Other Objections

Over the years, I have read other opinions and asked individuals why they object to the concept of rebirth. Here are some of the reasons I have found:

- *Positivistic science.*

This objection is used not just by scientists, nor even those who call themselves atheists, but also by many theological liberals. It is also conveniently adopted by many who do not want to be bound by any moral codes that they believe have been imposed upon them by religion. Adherents of this kind of thinking accept only what can be observed with the five senses. There is no such thing as spirit that transcends matter. When you are dead, you are dead. Many of these types of thinkers are also found in churches, either living a dual life or honestly struggling with the concept of immortality, but afraid that they will have egg on their "scientific" faces if they believe.

Would-be rationalists often express the belief that a very high percentage of all the people who have ever lived are alive today. This implies that there have not been enough human bodies in the history of the earth for each soul to have incarnated multiple times in the past. Several plausible rationalizations could be offered to counter this theory. The readings assume that mankind has been in the earth for several million years and spawned lost civilizations of which we have no record. There may also be many souls who have rarely if ever incarnated before. There may even be some here who have transferred from some other planet in the universe. Admittedly, these answers are just as speculative as the belief that prompted them. In any case, these speculations are much less relevant since an article by Carl Haub was published in the February 1995 issue of *Population Today*. Haub stated that approximately 99.7 billion people have died since 50,000 BC, when Homo sapiens are assumed to have appeared on Earth. This would allow for at least seventeen former lives for each of the 5.7 billion persons who are alive today. Haub asserts that an unknown author in the 1970s published the erroneous guess that 75 percent of all the people who had ever lived were alive then. This error has since been repeated and magnified many times.

- *Conservative Christians.*

I believe that the skepticism that many Christians have about reincarnation is simply a lack of knowledge about beliefs such as those expressed in the Cayce readings. To them the concept of reincarnation seems to remove the pressure to make a choice now. Some insist that it only takes a moment to be saved, not many lifetimes. Reincarnation seems to them too much like a self-help course where we work ourselves to perfection. They often ask, "Are we not saved by faith, not just by working out our karma? If we have done what our religion requires, why should we have to come back?" They might refer to the good thief on the cross as an example of instant salvation (Others might say that this is proof that church membership and rituals are not necessary for salvation.). They fail to see the working of grace when God allows a sinner another opportunity, or lifetime, to outgrow old patterns. They do not have an answer for those who never had a chance to hear the Gospel. If their theory is correct, then why not limit life to one year or one hour or one minute.

An even more serious problem for some Christians is the question of resurrection. Some take resurrection to imply that we will always have the same physical body and personality that we have now, even though our bodies and our personalities often change, even during this one lifetime. Some theologians, in order to justify their definition of resurrection, believe that the earth itself is eternal. The readings don't have simple answers for such beliefs, but they do contain many interesting perspectives about resurrection.

- *Liberal Christians.*

While they may seem to be open minded about some things, many liberals tend to reject anything supernatural as "mythology." Extreme liberals often do not even believe in resurrection in any form. In addition to the scientific aspect, there is also a social component to such unbelief. Some believe that any concept of an afterlife competes with the urgency of their social agenda. I have even known some persons who study Eastern religions and other esoteric philosophies and practice various types of meditation and yet still have sincere doubts about reincarnation for similar reasons.

- *Orthodox Christians.*

While researching the subject of reincarnation at a seminary library, I found a Russian Orthodox publication that mentioned that "spiritism" had been something of a fad in Moscow some years earlier. It implied that, because of the belief in reincarnation, many divorces had occurred when people believed that they had found their "soul mate" to be someone other than their spouse. This may have occurred, but it has little to do with anything that is in any way condoned in the Cayce readings. There are only nine readings that mention soul mates, and then the term most often appears in the question rather than in the answer. The readings do acknowledge that there are some souls who have had a strong affinity for some other soul from the beginning of time, and that these souls do often incarnate in the earth at the same time and place, sometimes ending up married to each other, at other times as relatives or co-workers. It was not suggested, however, that these relationships should interfere with either individual's marriage to some other person.

Cayce usually discouraged divorce, challenging people to live up to the promises that they had made. He said that most people had to grow toward being the right mate for whomever they chose to marry and that having a common ideal was the place to start. Reading 275-38 says that marriages are not made in heaven but happen only when "each do His biddings. For His sons, His daughters, His mothers, His fathers, are they that do His will in the earth." Another person's reading said, "Yet the entity finds self rather questioning self as to its choice of a mate. But know, the soul is rather the soul-mate of the universal consciousness than of an individual entity." (2988-2)

- *Spiritualists.*

These are persons who believe that they contact deceased persons (or some kind of angelic beings) through mediums or channels. Some Spiritualists, even some who are interested in the Cayce readings, may assume that these concepts are in harmony with their understanding of reincarnation. Others believe that all persons who have ever died are eternally available in the spiritual realm for them to communicate with. For this reason, they find the idea of reincarnation unacceptable. At least they do believe in the survival of the soul. However, while acknowledging that prayer for, and even communication with, our deceased loved ones could be constructive, the readings warn that departed souls should not be held back from continued spiritual growth by our attachments. The readings also caution that there could be an element of confusion and even idolatry in seeking advice from those in the borderland.

The Readings

Many of the references to reincarnation found in the readings were given for individuals who sought spiritual advice. This advice was often presented in Biblical terms. Following are some examples that deal with rebirth and spiritual laws:

..."In my Father's house are many mansions—"—many consciousnesses, many stages of enfoldment, of unfoldment, of blessings, of sources. 2879-1

For, each soul enters that it may make its paths straight. For they alone who walk the straight and narrow way may know themselves to be themselves, and yet one with the Creative Forces.
Hence the purpose for each entrance is that the opportunities may be embraced by the entity for living, being, that which is creative and in keeping with the Way. 2021-1

For Life and its expressions are one. Each soul or entity will and does return, or cycle, as does nature in its manifestations about man; thus leaving, making or presenting—as it were—those infallible, indelible truths that it—Life—is continuous. And though there may be a few short years in this or that experience, they are one; the soul, the inner self being purified, being lifted up, that it may be one with that first cause, that first purpose for its coming into existence. 938-1

Know that life is a river or a stream which is constant and each appearance is as a pool that may refresh, in which others may be refreshed... make the world a better place because ye have lived in it. 5392-1

First we begin with the fact that God *is*; and that the heavens and the earth, and all nature, declare this. Just as there is the longing within *every* heart for the continuity of life...

Then we say, when our loved ones, our heart's desires are taken from us, in what are we to believe?

This we find is only answered in that which has been given as His promise, that God hath not willed that any soul should perish but hath with every temptation, every trial, every disappointment made a way of escape or for correcting same. It is not a way of justification only, as by faith, but a way to know, to realize that in these disappointments, separations, there comes the assurance that He cares! 1567-2

(Q) Where are the dead until Christ comes? Do they go direct to Him when they die?

(A) As visioned by the beloved, there are those of the saints making intercession always before the throne for those that are passing in and out of the inter-between; even as He, the Christ, is ever in the consciousness of those that are redeemed in Him.

The passing in, the passing out, is as but the summer, the fall, the spring; the birth into the interim, the birth into the material. 281-16

There is no death, only the transition from the physical to the spiritual plane. Then, as the birth into the physical is given as the time of the new life, just so, then, in physical is the birth into the spiritual. 136-33

This, then, is the purpose of the entity in the earth: To be a channel of blessing to someone today, now; to be a living example of that He gave, "Come unto me, all that are weak and heavy laden—take my Cross upon you and learn of me."

These are thy purposes in the earth. These ye will manifest beautifully, or make a miserable failure again as ye did in Atlantis, as many another soul in this particular era is doing.

Which will it be? 2794-3

It isn't the great things. No great deeds of valor are accomplished without *ages* of preparation in the *soul* of one that accomplishes same. 416-7

Cayce saw reincarnation as an opportunity, given through the grace of God, to rectify past mistakes. Strangely enough, those who question reincarnation often insinuate that it denies the operation of grace, saying that we are saved by grace. Is it not only through His grace and mercy that God allows us to live another day, another year, or another lifetime, even after we have abused our previous opportunities?

A life reading for a person who had lived in the Holy Land and had shared the disappointment of others when the Savior was crucified, says:

Yet, through the teachings of those close in the household of Peter, as well as the friends of the nephew of Peter (Mark), the entity came to know much of the beauty and the love and the joy that comes with finding peace in the knowledge of the risen Lord. For in same He becomes the resurrection, the symbol of life, and the fulfilling of that as He gave, "I came that ye might have life and that more abundant." What can be more abundant than more experiences of life in the earth, and these the manifestations through which opportunities of body, mind and soul may express self, in giving glory and praise ever to the sources of life, light and truth. 3418-1

Why Don't We Remember?

There are many theories about why we usually don't remember past lives. It was asked, in reading 294-189 for Cayce himself, when he would return and if records could be left that he would be able to find at that time. After being told that the time, place, sex, or race of his next incarnation could not be given and that these things would depend upon what Cayce needed for soul growth, the following question was asked:

(Q) Would you suggest any way that a record may be left by an entity?

(A) By *living* the record! For when the purposes of an entity or soul are the more and more in accord with that for which the entity has entered, then the soul-entity may take *hold* upon that which may bring to its remembrance that it was, where, when and how. Thinkest thou that the grain of corn has forgotten what manner of expression it has given? Think thou that *any* of the influences in nature that you see about you—the acorn, the oak, the elm, or the vine, or *anything*—has forgotten what manner of expression? Only man forgets! And it is only in His mercy that such was brought about. For what was the first cause? Knowledge—knowledge! What then is that cut off in the beginnings of the Sons of God? Becoming entangled with the daughters of men, and the Daughters of God becoming entangled with the sons of men! As in Adam they forgot what manner of men they were! Only when he lives, he manifests that life that *is* the expression of the divine, may man *begin* to know *who*, where, what and when he was!

That there may be read from the records of God's Book of Remembrance, as from here, in the keepers of the records, is true—if thy purpose, thy desire, in heart, in soul, is for the love of God as may be manifested among the sons of men; but these may read only by those in the shadows of His love.

When asked why people do not usually remember previous lives, Cayce answered:

The same may be asked of why there is not the remembering of the time when two and two to the entity became four, or when C A T spelled cat. It always did! Ye only became aware of same as it became necessary for its practical application in the experience! 2301-4

The following are a couple of excerpts from readings that touch upon the nature of the records in time and space and the difficulties of translating them into human language:

...From what source, or how, is such a record read of the activities in the past? How may self know that there is being given a *true* record of the activities in a period of which there is no written *word* history? Yet, the entity itself...is studying the records that are written in nature, in the rocks, in the hills, in the trees, in that termed the genealogical log of nature itself. Just as true, then, is the record that the mind makes upon the film of time and space by the activities of a body with its soul that is made in the image of the Maker; being then spirit, in its form... 487-17

Hence these [Akashic] records are *not* as pictures on a screen, not as written words, but are as active forces in the life of an entity, and are *often*—as may be surmised—*indescribable* in words... 288-27

Looking for Information About Past Lives

Many people who learn about the possibility of reincarnation want to know more about their past lives. Those who got life readings from Edgar Cayce usually expected some information about these prior experiences in the earth. In the many life readings that Cayce gave, he often said that he would tell the seeker only about other experiences that could help them live a better life today. There were even times that he declined to answer some questions:

(Q) Altogether, how many incarnations have I had?
(A) Rather use the ones you know of and have need for, rather than knowing numbers! Know, as there has been

indicated, there is a wisdom as concerning incarnations or activities that cometh not from above. Use that thou hast in hand, that more may be given thee in its proper place and sphere. Remember Moses and his doubts when he took hold of the serpent. Would you take hold?

These become not as criticisms, but are the attempt to have the individual entity attain to that consciousness of "using that I have in hand." For, know, as He hath given, "I will bring to thy remembrance *all* things, since the foundation of the world." Where has He promised to meet thee? In thine own tabernacle. For thine body—thine body—is the temple of the living God. There ye may ascertain thy needs. These become eventually the consciousness of all who attain complete righteousness in purpose, in hope, in desire. These may be given as ye apply self in making those adjustments, those corrections in that ye have in hand. 1861-12

As to the experiences in the earth—not all may be given here; neither are they all applicable under the present stress. These are indicated merely that there may be gathered how, and in what manner, the continuity of life has been, and is, in the experiences of each soul through its search for that home not built with hands, but eternal— in the heart of God Himself. 2401-1

It would be reasonable to assume that others could do what Cayce did if they prepared themselves properly. In fact, there are many today who claim to give information about past lives, by one method or another. I would want to know something about a person's faith before I would ask that person for help with past lives, however.

Some psychologists use hypnotic regression to past-life traumas to help patients overcome psychosomatic illnesses. There have been some episodes about this phenomenon on TV in recent years. Because of the power of suggestion, however, many psychologists consider hypnosis to be unreliable as far as facts are concerned. As a result, there seems to be a trend for these psychologists to assume that the stories that patients tell are relevant to the patients' psychological well-being, whether or not the past-life recall is historically factual.

There are those who prefer, through their own spiritual development, to receive such information from within, in God's good time. The Cayce readings offer many suggestions on how to do just that through meditation, dreams, or visions.

Schoolhouse Earth

If it is true that our spiritual progress is evolutionary or that it is an unfolding toward the pattern imprinted in our souls, then it might be useful to think of earth as a schoolhouse for souls. Our souls' evolution is quite parallel to the process that takes place in our educational institutions.

One model in education is a system in which the student is exposed to a given body of information through various organized activities, after which a test is administered. The individual is then given a grade that will be a long-term record of proficiency in that subject.

Another model is one in which the student participates in various learning activities and then is tested to a very high standard. Then the student is shown the areas in which improvement is still needed and is allowed to participate in more learning activities that relate to those areas. The student is retested with a similar but different test. Study and retests continue until a certain level of proficiency is achieved in all areas of that subject, at which point the student progresses to the next subject.

As a teacher, I have used both of these methods in the classroom, and the second method has worked far better for my students and me. It is easier for students to move at their own pace. Many who would otherwise not have mastered the subject do much better, even if it takes them a little longer. Students seldom learn less just because they will have another chance. In fact, once they build confidence that they can learn with less fear of failure, they are usually challenged to learn faster. The difference between the two methods is that the second method allows more time for those who need it rather than lowering standards.

Of course, neither system works very well without encouragement, support, and high expectations from parents and teachers. I believe, however, that the second system is much more like the real-life operation of reincarnation, karma, and grace. Most educators also know that some lessons have to be relearned several times at different levels before they become an integral part of the individually. This concept also parallels reincarnation and the development of character or virtue.

Life, like school, may seem unbearable at times, but we can trust that God knows what He is doing and that He wants things to be well with us. What could be better than having our Elder Brother, the first graduate of the school, as example and mentor? His example proves that it is possible to overcome the world. Not that He could ever lower the standards for us, but with infinite patience He lets us keep trying and challenges us to do better, as long as we are sincerely making our best effort.

Disadvantages vs. Advantages

It is difficult to imagine how reincarnation could be proved to a skeptical mind. Just to summarize some of the arguments, let us assume that we are the pundits who are designing a new religion and we have secret knowledge of the fact of reincarnation. What might be a few of the advantages or disadvantages of teaching this doctrine to our new devotees?

Some disadvantages of believing in reincarnation might be:

- Believers might dwell too much on past experiences with which they are not equipped to deal.
- They might tend to look on others' suffering as something that is deserved and not try to help the sufferers or even treat them fairly.
- They might seek for knowledge of past lives in ways that are false or not constructive.
- Thoughts about reincarnation could create more problems for a person who is already unstable or delusional.

Some advantages of believing in reincarnation might include:

- Each person would become responsible for his or her own problems without blaming others.
- They would never feel too old to learn. Present talents may have been developed in other lives. What they learn now might be used in later experiences.

- People might be more patient and consistent with themselves and others, knowing that old patterns and attitudes may be deeper than they appear. They also could choose to change.
- They would have a better understanding of history. Old patterns reemerge as groups of souls return in different circumstances.
- They would see others as fellow souls, with color, sex, social status, etc. stripped away.
- They would be less likely to doubt the continuity of life and the ultimate justice of God's universe.

Weighing the advantages of such a system of thought against its disadvantages does not prove or disprove its truth. If reincarnation is not a fact of life, then the advantages of such a belief are just an illusion. If rebirth is a fact, then the dangers of such knowledge are probably not as real as perceived, and suppression of it will not succeed in the long run.

Social Implications

More and more people are becoming aware of the concept of reincarnation. Surveys have recently indicated that as many as twenty-five to thirty percent of the people in this country believe they have lived before. Those people probably manifest some of the advantages and disadvantages listed above and, perhaps, others that I have not thought of.

Still, I believe that the awareness of reincarnation is needed today to shed light on some of the limitations of much of modern-day theology, sociology, and psychology. With this knowledge, it may be possible for us to begin to heal our relationships with other individuals and groups by forgiving and laying aside some of these ancient forms of contention and strife. People are hungry for knowledge about the continuity of life. The study of beliefs about reincarnation probably will not go away any time soon. It might be better to focus on responsible ways to use such information.

Sharing the Concept of Reincarnation

...ye *grow* to heaven, rather than going to heaven. Ye grow in grace, in knowledge, in understanding. 1436-1

Considering the possible truth of reincarnation does not, in itself, require any kind of idolatry or indulgence in any selfish or self-indulgent act. Church leaders should be aware of that which many of their members already believe. Perhaps they could also help provide some guidance about which avenues are safe and constructive for exploring such beliefs. Even if reincarnation is openly discussed and studied, it does not have to eclipse the central message of Christianity. The following reading was given for a sixty-six-year-old woman who was planning a move to Virginia Beach so that she could write about the work of the A.R.E:

> (Q) Is it [the purpose for her writing] to spread the message of reincarnation as interpreted through the Life Readings?
>
> (A) That is merely a part. Remember, the real purpose as should be for each soul is the message of the love of the Savior, Jesus the Christ, for the children of men. That phase of Christian experience (reincarnation) is questioned by many, yet there is this period when the fact needs stressing to answer many questions. But that this is to be the primary fact—reincarnation, no. *That* is merely the plan as He demonstrated. 1152-12

9

Spiritual Laws in a Physical World: Cause and Effect—Karma or Grace

Don't delude yourself into thinking God can be cheated: where a man sows, there he reaps: if he sows in the field of self-indulgence he will get a harvest of corruption out of it; if he sows in the field of the Spirit he will get from it a harvest of eternal life. We must never get tired of doing good because if we don't give up the struggle we shall get our harvest at the proper time. While we have the chance, we must do good to all, and especially to our brothers in the faith. (Galatians 6:7-10 JB)

Originally a Sanskrit or Hindu word, *karma* is now so commonly used that it is considered part of the English language. I mention this to make the point that its use in the Cayce readings does not necessarily indicate that Cayce was espousing any particular Eastern religion. In my thesaurus, destiny, fate, and fortune are listed as synonyms for karma. It is also usually implied that this destiny is a result of our own actions, perhaps even from other lifetimes. Karma in personal relations is roughly equal to Newton's third law of motion in physics. In fact, it is often called the law of cause and effect.

Folk wisdom is full of proverbs about the law of karma. You may have heard it said that, "Your sins will find you out," or "What goes around comes around," or "Your chickens come home to roost," or "The sword cuts both ways."

In one sense, karma can be thought of as being either positive or negative, but it is most often used to indicate some problem or negative condition with which one must deal. Cayce reading 903-23 uses karma in this way when it says, "Destiny is within, or is as of faith, or is as the gift of the Creative Forces. Karmic influence is, then, rebellious influence against such."

In the readings, karma (or karmic) was also sometimes used to indicate that some of our relationships with other people are influenced by former relationships in other lives. However, this idea was often misunderstood. When a twenty-seven-year old woman (1436-3) asked if she had some karmic debt to be worked out with other individuals, she was told:

> This ye have made a bugaboo!... What is thy life but the gift of thy Maker that ye may be wholly one with Him?... And whether it be as individual activities to those who have individualized as thy father, thy mother, thy brother or the like, or others, it is merely self being *met*, in relationships to that they *themselves* are working out and not a karmic debt *between* but a karmic debt of *self* that may be worked out *between* the associations that exist in the present! And this is true for every soul.

The following reading contains one of the most definitive statements about karma that I could find in the readings:

> Well that karma be understood, and how it is to be met. For, in various thought—whether considered philosophy or religion, or whether from the more scientific manner of cause and effect—karma is all of these and more.
>
> Rather it may be likened unto a piece of food, whether fish or bread, taken into the system; it is assimilated by the organs of digestion, and then those elements that are gathered from same are, made into the forces that flow through the body, giving the strength and vitality to an animate object, or being, or body.
>
> So, in experiences of a soul, in a body, in an experience in the earth. Its thoughts make for that upon which the soul feeds, as do the activities that are carried on from the thought of the period make for the ability, of retaining or maintaining the active force or active principle of the thought *through* the experience.
>
> Then, the soul re-entering into a body under a different environ either makes for the expending of that it has made through the experience in the sojourn in a form that is called in some religions as destiny of the soul, in another philosophy that which has been builded must be met in some way or manner, or in the more scientific manner that a certain cause produces a certain effect.
>
> Hence we see that karma is *all* of these and more. What more? Ever since the entering of spirit and soul into matter

there has been a way of redemption for the soul, to make an association and a connection with the Creator, *through* the love *for* the Creator that is in its experience. Hence *this*, too, must be taken into consideration; that karma may mean the development *for self*—and must be met in that way and manner, or it may mean that which has been acted upon by the cleansing influences of the way and manner through which the soul, the mind-soul, or the soul-mind is purified, or to be purified, or purifies itself, and hence those changes come about—and some people term it "Lady Luck" or "The body is born under a lucky star." It's what the soul-mind has done *about* the source of redemption of the soul! Or it may be yet that of cause and effect, as related to the soul, the mind, the spirit, the body. 440-5

Once in a study group, we were discussing karma. One gentleman asked, "Does that mean that if I punch someone in the nose, that something similar will happen to me sometime in the future?" His wife said, "That's right." To which he responded, "That's not fair!" Of course this person was only joking. But how often do we actually respond this way to the things that we are dealt in life? The fact that God's justice will ultimately prevail is not always easy to accept.

Church Experience
I recently remarked in a Sunday school class that we would each eventually get what we deserve. Our minister and another retired minister who was in the class took me to task for suggesting such a ridiculous thing. One brought up a cruel statement that he had heard from a "Calvinist" minister who had told a young couple that their child's illness was due to their sin of divorce. He also wanted to know if the Jews who were killed in the Holocaust had deserved what they got. When I quoted the book of Job, the other minister implied that God's castigation of Job (Job 38:2), and Job's repentance (Job 42:6) were added at a later time to satisfy some kind of Greek mentality. I later told a friend about this conversation, and he said, "Do they think that if I paint their house, that I will not send them a bill?"

I mention this story not to criticize the two ministers, but to illustrate the reality of a serious problem in modern theology.

Both of these persons are sincere workers for the church. To some extent, they are only being true what they were taught in the seminary. It is my impression that both they and their teachers believe themselves to be strong defenders of the faith. They truly want to comfort and heal those who are oppressed or hurting. My guess is that some of their rationalizations also stem from an attempt to reconcile the Scriptures with modern science. However, all of this has necessitated the concoction of a strange theory of "evil" that somehow just happens to people without God's approval. I am thankful to them for pointing out to me just how difficult it is to share the truth of cause and effect with those who are committed to some other philosophy of life. This also makes me appreciate Edgar Cayce's ministry all the more.

When I got home from church that Sunday, I looked up references in the Bible to the law of cause and effect, which I had marked earlier. Here are just a few of the more direct passages I found:

He who sheds man's blood, shall have his blood shed by man, for in the image of God man was made. Genesis 9:6 (JB)

...yet he lets nothing go unchecked... Exodus 34:7 (JB)

Choose life... Deuteronomy 30:20 (JB)

And the woman said to Elijah, "...Have you come here to bring my sins home to me and to kill my son?" 1 Kings 17:18 (JB)

Avoid any tendency to wrong-doing, for such has been the true cause of your trials. Job 36:21 (JB)

...he has trapped the wicked in the work of their own hands. Psalms 9:16 (JB)

The man who digs a pit falls into it, the stone comes back on him that rolls it. Proverbs 26:27 (JB)

The man who throws a stone in the air,
throws it on to his own head;

a treacherous blow cuts both ways.
The man who digs a pit falls into it,
he who sets a snare will be caught by it.
On the man who does evil, evil will recoil,
though where it came from he will not know.
Ecclesiasticus 27:25-27 (JB)
[Do we sometimes think these things only happen to the coyote in the Roadrunner cartoon?]

I, Yahweh, search to the heart, I probe the loins, to give each man what his conduct and his actions deserve. Jeremiah 17:10 (JB)

For the Son of Man is going to come in the glory of his Father with his angels, and, when he does, he will reward each one according to his behaviour. Matthew 16:27 (JB)

Jesus then said, "Put your sword back, for all who draw the sword will die by the sword." Matthew 26:52 (JB)

The amount you measure out is the amount you will be given... Mark 4:24 (JB)

Do not judge, and you will not be judged yourselves; do not condemn, and you will not be condemned yourselves; grant pardon, and you will be pardoned. Luke 6:36-37 (JB)

"Now you are well again, be sure not to sin any more, or something worse may happen to you." John 5:14 (JB)

Vengeance is mine—I will pay them back, the Lord promises. Romans 12:19 (JB)

For the truth about us will be brought out in the law court of Christ, and each of us will get what he deserves for the things he did in the body, good or bad. II Corinthians 5:10 (JB)

...because there will be judgement without mercy for those who have not been merciful themselves; but the merciful need have no fear of judgment. James 2:13 (JB)

> ...so that all the churches realise that it is I who search heart and loins and give each one of you what your behaviour deserves. Revelation 2:23 (JB)

From beginning to end, from Adam and Eve to the last chapter of Revelation, the law of cause and effect is a central theme of the Holy Bible. In addition to the above passages, I also noted passages too numerous to mention that teach of God's justice. Jesus went even further and holds us accountable even for our thoughts. I wondered what my Bible would look like if I were to blank out every reference to justice or to the law of cause and effect. Then what if I marked out the virgin birth of the Christ, the Resurrection, all miracles, and everything else with which some modern theologians do not agree. There would not be much left of the Good Book.

Some people are more comfortable with the idea that our difficult experiences are the natural result of our own actions, rather than viewing them as God's anger and wrath. It makes no sense to me to quarrel about which is correct. The readings say, "And law is love. Law is God. God is love. God is law." (1942-3) I am comfortable with the idea that I am meeting myself, but I also appreciate being chastised by a loving Creator if it will turn me around before I cause more negative karma for myself.

The Man Who Was Born Blind

Having made the case for cause and effect in the Scriptures, I must mention the one passage which is most often brought up by those who wish to believe that there is no correlation between our thoughts and actions and what happens to us in the future. In this story, Jesus' disciples asked Him if it was a blind man's sins or his parents' sins that caused him to be born blind. "Neither he nor his parents sinned," Jesus answered "he was born blind so that the works of God might be displayed in him." (John 9:3 JB) Even though it is hard to see how this one statement, attributed to the Master, could outweigh all of the Scriptures quoted above, I will not try to tell you that it was added just to suit the purposes of the author of the Gospel. In fact, there are seven Cayce readings in which this same Gospel story is used to make a point.

To a woman who was being advised to be a speaker to various groups, a reading said:

110

He *alone* is each soul pattern! *He* is thy *karma*, if ye put thy trust *wholly* in Him! See?

Not that every soul shall not give account for the deeds done in the body, and in the body meet them! but in each meeting, in *each* activity, let the pattern... be the guide...

When questioned as to political, economic or social order, what were His answers? Did He condemn the man who was born blind? Did He condemn the woman taken in adultery? ...Did He condemn any? Rather did He point out that in *Him* each meets that karmic condition found in self, and that the pattern is in Him; doing good, being kind, being patient, being loving in *every* experience of man's activity.

Do thou likewise. 2067-2

The parents of a slowly developing child (4140-1) asked why their child had this condition. They were told that this was to meet conditions created by the child and for the necessary learning of the parents. Cayce quoted the question asked of Jesus as to who sinned for the man to be born blind, then said, "Neither, in that sense..." The reading goes on to say that in "the meeting of that condition merited" the parents might manifest their concept of the glory of the Father in the earth.

We all know that the meaning of the word *sin* is simply error or missing the mark. However, even in Jesus' day, the concept of sin probably included an element of condemnation. The person asking the above question may have even implied that the man did not deserve to be healed. I believe that it was this sense of the word that Jesus wanted to avoid. Even if the man and his parents had built something into their experience that required the learning of patience, Jesus knew that the lesson could best be learned only by manifesting the love of God. We might also keep in mind that Jesus had the power to forgive sins, as he often did when healing someone. Thus, He was demonstrating that, in Him, our sins or karma become of no importance.

The mother (2746) of a blind girl (2436), asked Cayce what "karmic tie-up" had caused her little daughter to be born blind. The reading responded, "That the glory of the Father might be made manifest in thee and in [2436]. (2796-1)

Fifty-one-year-old Ms. [3582] was told in her life reading:

For as the entity realizes, there is little or nothing that happens by chance, but ever after a pattern, a law. And that the entity may build in the mind from the spiritual, that it accepts as its director alters results that may be had in the experience of the individual—in the same measure as was asked "Master, who sinned—this man or his parents, that he was born blind?" 3582-2

In this story, Jesus does not deny the action of karma, but chooses rather to focus on the opportunity presented by the situation rather than to condemn anyone for their past mistakes. Some say that karma is the same as fate, but Jesus refused to see it in a "fatalistic" way. Likewise, Cayce was saying that we don't overcome karma just by trying to correct our past mistakes, but rather by living each day with Jesus as our pattern, having the desire to manifest God's love as He did.

Misuse of the Knowledge of the Law

There is nothing Christ-like about an attitude that chooses to ignore the suffering of others on the assumption that they have caused their own problems. We may not always be able to protect others from the consequences of their actions by just picking up the tab for them. We must, however, learn to show mercy if we would have mercy. Otherwise we may be like Job before his testing, thinking that we have no need of mercy.

The following prayer group reading deals with this problem and suggests answers that we have seen manifested in Christian people such as Mother Teresa:

(Q) When one is working out a karma, is it right to try to help that one?

(A) This may be answered, even as was that "Who sinned, this man or his parents? That the works of God might be manifest before you!" When there are karmic conditions in the experience of an individual, that as designates those that have the Christ-like spirit is not only in praying for them, holding meditation for them, but aiding, helping, in every manner that the works of God may be manifest in their lives, and *every* meditation or prayer: *Thy will, O God, be done in that body as Thou seest best.*

Would that this cup might pass from me, not my will but Thine be done!

(Q) How do we know when to help an individual?

(A) Do with thy might what thine hands, hearts, minds, souls, find to do, leaving the increase, the benefits, in *His* hands, who is the Giver of all good and perfect gifts. Be not faint hearted because, as thou seest, that is not accomplished in the moment. What is eternity to a single experience? 281-4

Meeting Ourselves

Reading 1204-3 says, "For, know that each soul constantly meets its own self. No problem may be run away from. *Meet* it *now!*" The following readings brought this truth home to various individuals, along with some advice on how to deal with these problems:

(Q) What has been the reason for the experiences I have had for the past 25 years?

(A) You are just meeting yourself. As ye meted it to someone else, it is being meted to you. What do you think of it? ...Be patient, and in patience ye will find your soul. 3486-1

For it is self that one has to meet. And what ye sow—mentally, spiritually, physically—that ye *will* eventually reap. ...that effort, that purpose for which ye as an entity plan, consider, has already brought in eternity its own shadow of things to be. 257-249

In the present the entity finds self meeting many of those same problems. For it is not what someone else has done to thee, but what thou hast done to thy neighbor. For what is the law? "As ye sow, so shall ye reap!"

Be not—*be not* deceived—do not misunderstand—God is not mocked! For what man soweth, man reapeth; and he constantly meets himself!

For what ye have done, that ye must meet.

If ye attempt to meet it alone in thyself *then* it becomes karma. But *who* stands—*who* will stand in thy stead?

Do good, as He gave, to those that despitefully use thee, and ye overcome then—in thyself—that ye *have* done to thy fellow man! 1650-1

Is it any wonder that Jesus challenged us to do unto others as we would have them do unto us? He was saying that what we do to others, we are doing to God and, ultimately, back to ourselves. What a powerful way to learn how it feels to walk in the other person's shoes!

Spiritual Laws

When we think of laws, we sometimes think of rules that are made by a legislative body or enacted by the decree of someone in authority. Spiritually, we might think of Moses as the Lawgiver. But, these laws are not just something that Moses invented, and they are not just rules to live by. Some of these laws, like the laws of physics, are based on immutable truths about how the universe works. These divine laws can be applied by anyone, and will yield consistent results.

When I did a computer search of the readings for the word *immutable,* most of the readings I found had something to do with the law of cause and effect. Here are a few of the ideas that were connected with the word immutable. They are not mutually exclusive, but are just worded in different ways:

- There is only one God. We must not seek others.
- Seek and you shall find (if you plan to apply such knowledge constructively).
- The way you treat your fellow man is the way you treat your Maker.
- All that you can know of the divine, you must manifest in your dealings with your fellow man.
- The fruits of the spirit are manifested in patience, love, fellowship, and kindness. These cost nothing, but give dividends of peace.
- Peace is not something that just happens to you. To have peace, you must have created peace in the experiences of others.
- You reap what you sow. God is not mocked. Like begets like.

According to the readings our choices have consequences:

For it is in Him that each soul lives, moves and has its being. And while a man may defy the laws of nature, defy even the laws of his Creator, he must pay and *pay* and *pay!* 830-2

For it has ever been and is, even in materiality, a reciprocal world. "If ye will be my people, I will be thy God." If ye would know *Good*, do Good. If ye would have life, give life. If ye would know Jesus, the Christ, then be like Him... 1158-9

Justice, or cause and effect, was the basis of much of the Old Testament law. This is why Jesus said, "Do not imagine that I have come to abolish the Law or the Prophets. I have come not to abolish but to complete them [to bring to perfection]." Matthew 5:17 (JB). Jesus went on to say that our righteousness must go deeper than that of the Pharisees (based solely on external performance of the law). Understanding that hatred is equal to murder and lust equal to adultery frees us from rules, regulations, and rituals, but makes spiritual healing all the more imperative.

God's Plan for Us

I have heard many preachers say, "God has a plan for you." I could not agree more. He has had a plan for us from the beginning, and when we fall, he has a plan of renewal. I cannot summarize it better than these readings:

For, it is not by chance that each entity enters, but that the entity—as a part of the whole—may fill that place which no other soul may fill so well. 2533-1

...know that the experiences of a life in the varied consciousnesses are a portion of the divine plan for each soul to find its closer relationships to the Maker. 1257-1

(Q) What is God's plan for me...?
(A) Brighten the corner where thou art from day to day. 3357-1

[For a forty-year-old writer who asked if her talents could be used for good:] ...Do not inject self or self's development, but God's way and God's plans—and they may be utilized! 954-5

For, each soul enters that it may make its paths straight. For they alone who walk the straight and narrow way may know themselves to be themselves, and yet one with the Creative Forces...

For, the Father has not willed that any soul should perish, and is thus mindful that each soul has again and again—and yet again—the opportunity for making its paths straight. 2021-1

For the entity came not merely by chance. For, the earth is a causation world, for in the earth, cause and effect are as the natural law. And as each soul enters this material plane, it is to meet or to give those lessons or truths that others, too, may gain the more knowledge of the purpose for which each soul enters. 3645-1

The Law of Grace

When discussing karma, questions usually arise about the part God's grace plays in our redemption. I find it difficult to understand grace without assuming there is some kind of system of accountability underlying it. Imagine that you lived in a time when people were put into prison if they could not pay their debts. The spirit or purpose of the law was reciprocity: you were expected, to repay only what you owed. To prevent lenders from being cheated it was deemed that there had to be some penalty for failure to repay a loan. If you had problems meeting your payments and a kind lender gave you more time to earn the money, then you could call it a grace period. If you still could not pay, you were thrown into prison, and you had no means of redeeming yourself. Now, imagine that a shipping merchant came and paid your debt if you agreed to work for him for a time, after which you would have your freedom in the new world, where you could own land and prosper. The purpose of the law was not violated, but you experienced grace, and mercy, and redemption.

In Romans 6:23 (JB) Paul says, "For the wage paid by sin is death; the present given by God is eternal life in Christ Jesus our

Lord." Without the law of cause and effect there would be no need for grace. Reading 5001-1 says:

> For the law of the Lord is perfect, and whatsoever an entity, an individual sows, that must he reap. That as law cannot be changed. As to whether one meets it in the letter of the law or in mercy, in grace, becomes the choice of the entity.

The parents of a five-year-old girl were warned to take some precautions to avoid accidents. This reading went on to say: "These are a part of the karma, unless there is kept that law of grace through which karma is *not* an actual experience. (1635-3)

Then how do we activate the law of Grace? The following readings give several perspectives on choosing God's grace:

> *Karma* is rather the lack of living to that *known* to do! As ye would be forgiven, so forgive in others. *That* is the manner to meet karma. 2271-1

> Thus does He—as in His promise, "Lo, I am with thee always, unto the end"—*become* thy way, and become that termed by some thy karma.
>
> What is karma but giving way to impulse? Just as has been experienced by this entity, when the entity has sung Halleuliah it was much harder to say "dammit." 622-6

> ...in the compliance of the laws of the Giver of all good and perfect gifts, grace is commuted unto him who would seek to do His biddings, and place self in the hands of Him that gives life abundant. 900-253

> Thus we may through those administrations of that which is the spirit of truth made manifest, turn this karma, or law, to grace and mercy. For the pattern hath been given those who seek to know His face. 5209-1

> ...meeting those things which have been called karmic, yet remembering that under the law of grace this may not be other than an urge, and that making the will of self one with the Way may prevent, may overcome, may take the

choice that makes for life, love, joy, happiness—rather than the law that makes, causes the meeting of everything the hard way. 1771-2

> Karma may be lost in Him, if ye will but seek, if ye will but have Him guide, if ye will but believe! For all power hath been given unto Him. For He *alone* hath overcome!
> And doth He forgive, doth He stand by? Only when ye individually or personally put Him from thee, and turn *thy* face away, is He from thee at all!
> For His great promise has been in these:
> "Be my child—I will be thy God. Though ye wander far afield, though ye may be discouraged, disheartened, if ye call I will *hear*—and will answer speedily."
> O Child, put Him in thy heart and try Him! 954-5

This is one of the beautiful things about the readings. They assume that anyone can change for the better and overcome old tendencies by following Jesus as the pattern. He forgave those who persecuted Him, and He continued to have faith in the apostles when they failed Him.

Being Proactive

Belief in cause and effect is a major component of what psychologists and motivational speakers call being proactive. On a TV program, I recently saw Warren Bennis, who wrote *Managing People is Like Herding Cats*, talking to a group of city managers. He said that one common trait that he had observed in all successful leaders is that they believe that their efforts will be rewarded. Without this kind of faith, we constantly see ourselves as victims of circumstances. Reading 5203-1 expresses the inner motivation for being proactive when it says:

> He who doubts that the best will come to him with doing of that which is correct is already defeated. Don't blame others for what has happened or may happen. Do right yourself, physically, mentally and spiritually, and the best will come to you.

Faith in God's justice frees us from the kind of pessimism that causes us to helplessly blame others for our problems. It also relieves us from wasting energy on resenting those who do wrong to us or to others, and it spurs us on to do good to everyone, with the assurance that our behavior will eventually bear fruit (See Galatians 6:9).

Teaching Experience

Having taught high school electronics for the last twenty years, I have tried to learn a little about what motivates young people. Since electronics is a branch of physics, other laws of physics are also dealt with in this course. Because this is a vocational course, work habits and personal relations are also part of the curriculum. When we deal with Newton's third law of motion, we often also read the thirtieth chapter of Deuteronomy and Galatians 6:7 and then discuss whether the students believe in cause and effect in personal relationships.

Most of the students do believe in cause and effect, but have never given much thought to applying this in their attitudes toward others on a daily basis. I can see the growth and improvement in attitude that takes place in some of them as they begin to be more proactive and feel less like victims in a world over which they have no control.

Why Bad Things Happen to Good People

How often have you heard people complain that a just God could not allow so many bad things to happen to innocent people? Reading 2528-3 says:

> Apparently, there are often experiences in which individuals reap that which they have not sown, but this is only the short self-vision of the entity or the one analyzing or studying purposes and ideals in relationship to those particular individuals.

When I have discussed Biblical concepts of God's justice in groups such as a Sunday school class, I know that many of those present have had loved ones who have suffered greatly from various misfortunes. As long as we have a physical body we may be subject to illness and pain from time to time. The book of Wisdom puts our trials in perspective with the hope of eternal life:

But the souls of the virtuous are in the hands of God,

no torment shall ever touch them.
In the eyes of the unwise, they did appear to die,
their going looked like a disaster,
their leaving us like annihilation;
but they are in peace.
If they experienced punishment as men see it,
their hope was rich with immortality;
slight was their affliction, great will their blessings be.
God has put them to the test
and proved them worthy to be with him;
Wisdom 3:1-5 (JB)

Still, it is understandable that the atrocities of war and crime cause some people to doubt, even though we hear some amazing stories of those who have helped victims of such events and those who have survived adversity through their faith in God. We cannot judge anyone to be guilty or innocent, but we can reach out to help those who suffer, and we can try to make the world a place where things such as the Holocaust will never happen again.

The Karma Game
The law of cause and effect works like the computer programs that teach typing. These programs give you a lesson, measure your progress, and then tailor the next lesson to emphasize the keys on which you need the most improvement. Life works the same way. Even though we are frequently evaluated by the highest standards, we do not have to look backwards to stew over past mistakes. We can be assured that, as we do our best to meet each moment of each day by applying Christian love, we have been presented with the lessons that have been tailored by a loving Creator to meet our needs, no matter how difficult or inappropriate they may seem at the time. Each moment, each day, each year, and each lifetime is another chance, given to us by the grace of God, to get the lesson right.
Winning the karma game is not an end it itself, just as achieving great speed and accuracy is not the final purpose of the typing program. Both are only training tools, and the end result is the long-range good that we can accomplish by improving our abilities as we grow toward fellowship with God. The Master said that when we do good in small things, we will be given greater responsibilities (Matthew 25:21). What is wrong with the belief

that we are being prepared for even greater service in other realms? The final test is whether we have become more Godlike in our actions and habits.

Graduation

Violet M. Shelley's book, *Reincarnation Unnecessary,* is a study of the Cayce readings for eighteen persons (out of about 1,200 who had life readings) who were told that, after this life, they might have the choice of not reincarnating in the earth. The following excerpt from reading 322-2 is a good example of these:

> Quite an enviable position, may it be said, that the entity occupies; in the matter of truth, veracity, clean *living,* that the entity has made in this experience! and there will be little need, unless desired, for a return to this earth's experience.
> For, there may be those cleansings that will make for, "Come thou and enjoy rather the glory of thy Lord, for it may be said thou hast truly shown that thou preferest thy brother to thine own gratification!" 322-2

These people were not necessarily very impressive from a worldly point of view. They were not all doing some great thing to save the world. Some did not even appear to have their own spiritual act together yet and were given advice on how to overcome present problems. Some were told to avoid self-indulgence and self-aggrandizement. Most were encouraged to continue to follow Him who is the Light. Some were praised for the good qualities that they had applied in their lives, both present and past. Giving to others and preferring others above self were probably the most frequently mentioned virtues of these people. One person, 5366-1, was told:

> Who would tell the rose how to be beautiful; who would give to the morning sun, glory; who would tell the stars how to be beautiful? Keep that faith! which has prompted thee. Many will gain much from thy patience, thy consistence, thy brotherly love.

Ms. [5366] was also told that she had been a close friend of a Roman leader and that she had laughed at the Christians who

121

were being injured in the arena because of the pleasures she gained by befriending this leader. Such behavior had resulted in considerable physical suffering in this life. She was told, nevertheless, to hold to the ideals of those at whom she had once scoffed and that she might not have to incarnate in the earth again.

This kind of hopeful reading may make us wonder when we might be ready to move on to a higher calling. Here are two readings in which individuals asked how they could complete their earthly lessons:

(Q) Can I finish my purpose in this incarnation, so that I will not need to return to the earth?
(A) As may any; if they will but put *off* the old and on the new—that is in Him... Yes. 1037-1

(Q) If possible, what can I do to finish my earth's experience in this life?
(A) It is ever possible. Studying to show forth the Lord's death till He comes again!!
What meaneth this?
Just living those that are the fruits of the spirit; namely: peace, harmony, longsuffering, brotherly love, patience. *These*, if ye show them forth in thy life, in thy dealings with thy fellow man, grow to be what? *Truth!* In Truth ye are *free*, from what? *Earthly* toil, *earthly* cares! 987-4

When people tell me that Christianity does not work because there are still wars and suffering in the world, I am reminded of the words of Admiral Richard Byrd: "Christianity has not failed. It is simply that nations have failed to try it. There would be no war in a God-directed world." The Cayce readings suggest to us that some individuals have already tried Christianity and that it has worked for them.

When we are saddened and frustrated to see physical, moral, and spiritual degradation in a world that seems to recklessly follow every temptation, it is comforting to have hope that at least some souls may be learning the lessons they came here to learn. This kind of belief in eternal life does not leave us just singing about the "sweet by and by" while ignoring the problems of the here and now. The readings about the people who were within reach of completing their earthly labors spoke of their giving, forgiving, and caring about others. Admiral Byrd was right. If more people were aware of the continuity of life and were striving for that closer relationship with God, the world would become a much better place in which to live.

The Pattern of Salvation

Believing in the law of karma might suggest to some a belief that we can work our own way to salvation without God's help. This may be true for some teachings about karma, but it is not a fair criticism of the Cayce readings. Reading 5758-1 says:

...God alone can prepare the heart. For eternal life is never earned—it is the gift of God, by the grace of God— through the giving of the life of the Master, Jesus, who became the Christ by overcoming death, hell and the grave, overcoming the world.

Understanding a little about spiritual laws should not make us become like Job's friends who thought they could speak for God as they tried to explain the causes of his suffering. Perhaps true humility is in accepting God's justice even when we can't understand it, and acknowledging our need for the power of the Christ to help us to meet ourselves when life seems impossible. Knowing that our thoughts and actions have consequences does give us the power to do something about our future, but it also opens up the possibility that we may have patterns from the past that we are not prepared to deal with. Once we recognize responsibility for our actions, real peace of mind also comes from the promise that God will give us the strength to bear whatever we must face, whether we can relate it to our own actions or not (see I Corinthians 10:13). The Cayce readings make reference to this passage more than 150 times.

...knowing that He doeth all things *well,* and that no one is tempted or tried beyond that which they are *able* to bear, or that is *best* for their *soul* and *spiritual* development; ...That conditions arise that are hard to be understood from *man's* own view of reasoning, know that, that which comes to pass is that builded, and that necessary for the proper building of the soul that may be one with the Creator. 5696-1

...and He will not let thy loved ones—nor those with and for whom ye pray—be tempted beyond that they are able to bear. 5758-1

Additional Readings

- *You Are What You Were*

Ye are what ye are because of what ye have been. So is everyone else! 2823-1

Thus we find this entity—as each entity—is in the present the result of that the entity has applied of Creative influences and forces in every phase of its experience. Thus it makes for that called by some karma, by others racial hereditary forces.
And thus environment and hereditary forces (as are accepted) are in their reality the activities of the *mind* of the entity in its choices through the experiences in the material, in the mental, in the spiritual planes. 1796-1

- *Leave Vengeance to God*

The entity swore vengeance. Hence the entity needs to be mindful of itself in regard to such conditions in the present; holding to those things that are ideal, and not to prejudices that would cause the entity to attempt in any manner to get even... This ye cannot do. For remember that ye sow ye must also reap. 3704-1

- *Get It Right This Time*

[Given to a person who was encouraged to develop a talent for writing and music.] ...do not let this experience, when ye meet thine self from thy throwing away of thine opportunities in the Atlantean sojourn, repeat itself in the present. Rather, as the opportunities are presented, be aware of them and in the position to make not merely amends but to meet thyself; choosing rather to be the doorkeeper in the house of God than a prince in those palaces of the unjust and wicked.

...Remember, ye cannot run away from thyself. 1776-1

- *Spiritual Renewal*

...rather put thy ideal in those things that bespeak of the continuity of life; the regeneration of the spiritual body, the revivifying of the temporal body for *spiritual* purposes, that the seed may go forth even as the Teacher gave, "Sin no more, but present thy body as a living sacrifice; holy, acceptable unto Him, for it is a reasonable service." 969-1

PART THREE

Christianity and the Cayce Readings

10

New Meaning to the Words of Old:
The Bible

Then thy body is indeed the temple of the living God. *there* He has promised to meet thee, to commune with thee. *There* is the psychic development, the psychic phenomena that ye seek! For as ye read, as ye study, only that which answers to that being sought within thine *own* self answers to thy prayer, to thy seeking. Then, it is well to write about these.

For the book of Books *is* the greater source of psychic experiences of individuals, and as to *what* they did *about* such! even from Adam to John—or from Genesis to Revelation. These are living examples that are thine. For each day is thy Eden; yea, each evening is the call, "Whosoever *will* let him come and take of the water of life freely." 1598-1

Soon after I started working with the Cayce material, I began to have a desire to know more about the Bible. I was challenged by Edgar's method of reading the Bible through once each year. The readings also made me aware that twenty-five years of churchgoing had introduced me to only a smattering of what Cayce often called "Holy Writ."

I remembered how my mother had handed me a Bible several times and suggested that I start at the beginning and read it through. After a few pages, it would seem like an impossible task, and I would give up. This time, however, I knew more about what to look for. Cayce said that the Bible was the story of mankind from beginning to end, and I wanted to know the whole story.

I first read the Book of Job, which introduced me to a person who insisted on a personal relationship with God and whose faith transcended his limited understanding of righteousness and suffering. After reading Job, I started at the beginning and read the whole Bible through. I looked for things such as what God expects of us, the law of cause and effect, the purpose of Israel, and prophecies about the Messiah and the promised time of peace. I made up my mind not to get hung up on things I did not understand. I kept on reading, trusting that there was value in what I was doing. I think it was my second time through the Bible that things started to make sense. This time, I underlined passages that had particular meaning to me. I still have that old Jerusalem Bible (now rebound), and there are only a few pages that don't have some underlined passages or notes on them. Later, my wife and I read through the Bible together and, still later, we read a chapter or two almost every day, along with our children, over a period of several years. I have not matched Edgar Cayce's record of reading it through every year, but the Bible has become like an old friend.

Another level of appreciation for the Bible came when I read *Edgar Cayce's Story of the Old Testament* by Robert W. Krajenke. I also enjoyed Jeffrey Furst's *Edgar Cayce's Story of Jesus*. These fascinating stories introduce details from the readings that confirm and embellish the history and meaning of the Old and New Testaments.

Relevance of the Bible in Today's World

There is such a plethora of spiritual works in the world today that some seekers spend little time studying the ancient Scriptures. On the other hand, there are sects who justify their dogmas and rituals by the written Word alone, and some almost seem to worship the Bible in place of an interactive relationship with a living God. Both extremes may have contributed to the lack of appreciation for the Bible in what has been called the post-Christian era.

The Bible is a collection of works, written by many different authors, which has been passed down to us over a period of thousands of years. Cayce indirectly attributed much of its authorship to the Master. Unlike some modern scholars, however, he insisted that the Bible was a record of real people and their relationships to God:

> For as has been given from the beginning, the deluge was not a myth (as many would have you believe) but a period when man had so belittled himself with the cares of the world, with the deceitfulness of his own knowledge and power, as to require that there be a return to his

dependence wholly—physically and mentally—upon the Creative Forces. 3653-1

As I try to share the power of the readings with those in the churches, I see their love of the Scriptures as an asset, not a liability. Jesus said to the Jews, "Search the scriptures; for in them ye think ye have eternal life: and they are they which testify of me." (John 5:39 KJV) He used their love of Scripture to introduce himself, the author and finisher of the written Word. In various readings that quote John 5:39, Cayce challenged individuals to find God's promises, purer ideals, better health, a relationship to the Christ, and eternal life through studying and applying the advice in the Scriptures. The following Cayce reading is one that emphasizes this verse:

> For from the very first of the Old Testament to the very last even of Revelation, He is not merely the subject of the book, He is the author in the greater part, having given to man the mind and the purpose for its having been put in print. For it is in Him ye live and move and have thy being and as He gave, "Search ye the scriptures, for they be they that testify of me, and in them ye *think* ye have eternal life."
> If ye know Him, ye know that in Him ye have eternal life. For He is the beginning and the end of all things. 5322-1

Sometimes we are tempted to ignore the Bible in reaction to our friends who interpret and apply it in a legalistic manner. A more proactive approach might be to try to persuade these friends to seek a closer walk with the Master by better understanding the Scriptures. His light and healing can put rituals and dogmas in a perspective that leaves little reason for traditional contentions.

The Bible in the Readings

Many people who knew him considered Cayce to be a Bible scholar. This knowledge must have influenced his ability to apply Scriptures in such an appropriate manner to almost any situation. In one study group that I attended, someone suggested that the readings only agreed so much with the Bible because of Edgar Cayce's own Christian background. Perhaps they were colored by that rich heritage, and that seems to me to be fortunate, but

Cayce never hesitated to offer insights that disclosed unknown historical facts or unusual interpretations to biblical passages.

The readings quote or paraphrase the Bible many thousands of times. They also frequently recommend the Bible in general, as well as various books or chapters in particular, for study by certain individuals. Passages from nearly fifty individual books of the Bible are quoted or mentioned specifically for study.

Biblical Treasures, compiled by Dick Daily, lists 473 verses, which include all of those quoted in the readings three times or more and some of those quoted only once or twice. The most frequently quoted Bible verse is II Timothy 2:15, which appears 651 times. About half of the time, this passage is followed by James 1:27. Reading 3384-3 contains a typical example:

> As indicated, analyze self, know thy relationships to thy Maker, then study to show thyself approved unto God, a workman not ashamed, rightly dividing the words of truth; condemning none, keeping self unspotted from the world.

Exegesis

In their attempt to understand what the Scriptures have to say to us, scholars have devised many different approaches and methods of interpretation. At times in history, some have used allegorical speculations to the extent that others have reacted with literal or humanistic methods. Some see in the Bible a mixture of prophecy, history, and conventional wisdom. Others see a literal mandate to re-create the first century community of faith. Some say that the Bible is the sole source of spiritual guidance, while others place tradition on an equal basis with the written Word. Some condone or encourage individual interpretation, while others insist that only certain church leaders are qualified to interpret the Bible.

The readings offer a more balanced approach that avoids polarizing people on such issues. In response to a question about the symbolic meaning of the book of Revelation, Cayce said:

> ... there is that as may be said to be the literal and the spiritual and the metaphysical interpretation of almost all portions of the Scripture. ...

Yet all of these to be true, to be practical, to be applicable in the experience of individuals, *must* coordinate:

132

or be as one, even as the Father, the Son and the Holy Spirit. 281-31

Inerrancy

There has been a trend in modern thinking to play down or question the validity of the Bible as a guide to spirituality. Whether this stance is coming from a humanistic view that denies the continuity of life, from an esoteric perspective that thinks its beliefs have been edited out of the Scriptures, from a social view that would magnify the Bible's differences with the other great Scriptures of the world, or from an erudite theological mentality that is afraid of appearing unsophisticated, it does not square with the Edgar Cayce readings.

Without falling into the trap of "inerrancy," the readings recognize in the Scriptures the distilled wisdom of thousands of years of experience and the pattern for soul growth that was demonstrated by the Christ. The Bible is seen as a tuning fork for the spirit. The Scriptures become not something to be worshiped, but an instrument that points to the Holy of Holies within each person.

It seems to me that the inerrancy concept makes it easier for some people to feel justified in rejecting the Bible because of what they see as inconsistencies. It is like saying that no one could have come to Christ through the preaching of Dwight Moody unless Moody were perfect. Reading 262-60 challenges us to analyze our motives when we make claims about the meaning of the Scriptures:

> For, much might be given respecting that ye have that ye call the Bible. This has passed through many hands. Many that would turn that which was written into the meanings that would suit their own purposes, as ye yourselves oft do. But if ye will get the spirit of that written there ye may find it will lead thee to the gates of heaven. For, it tells of God, of your home, of His dealings with His people in many environs, in many lands. Read it to be wise. Study it to understand. *Live* it to know that the Christ walks through same with thee.

Expecting perfection in the Bible also leads to the question of which translation is the best or correct one. In response to a question that asked which version of the Bible was nearest to the true meaning, reading 2072-14 said:

> The nearest true version for the entity is that ye apply of whatever version ye read, in your life. It isn't that ye learn from anyone. Ye only may have the direction. The teaching is within self. For where hath He promised to meet thee? Within the temple! Where is that temple? Within! Where is heaven or earth? Within! Meet thy Savior there...
>
> ...but remember that the whole gospel of Jesus Christ is: "Thou shalt love the Lord thy God with all thy mind, thy heart and thy body; and thy neighbor as thyself."
>
> Do this and thou shalt have eternal life. The rest of the book is trying to describe that. It is the same in any language, in any version.

Several years ago I met a charming ninety-five-year-old lady named Ruby. Ruby played a tune for us on the piano, that she had written at the age of nineteen. She had written this music to go with the words from the seventy-first Psalm, which she also sang. I was so impressed with her faith that I asked Ruby about her church. She told me some moving stories about her spiritual journey but added that, in her present church, they were arguing about the inerrancy of the Bible. She said, without any bitterness, "Why don't they form a separate church if they can't agree?" Then she added, "Even if we agree that the Bible is without error, we will not agree on the meaning of every word."

While the Dead Sea Scrolls and other archaeological evidence affirm much of the history and integrity of the Bible, even some students of the Cayce information still suspect that it has been edited to exclude certain concepts such as reincarnation. I find little evidence of such editing except, perhaps, in the choice of which books to use. We are free to read the many other writings that were not included in the canonical books of the Bible. I especially enjoy some of those in the Apocrypha, which were included with most Bibles until about the turn of the 20th century. Even if some of the individuals who chose which books to include had their own agenda, that should not be an excuse for not using what we have. As reading 281-20 says, "For, there be many misinterpretations, poor translations, but to find fault with that thou hast and not use same is to make excuses that you haven't it as it was given." Or is there something better? Reading 1966-1 says, "But study to know thy relationship to thy Creator. No better handbook may be used than the Scripture itself."

Life reading 2777-3 says:

> Take His word, the Holy Bible; it is man's attempt—through the direction of the spirit of truth, of universal consciousness—to indicate man's relationship to that Creative Force, God, and God's approach to man's consciousness of his relationship to God.
>
> Thus, take these portions particularly—not that there is one portion greater than the other, but these are the conclusions of the lawgiver—as indicated in the 30th chapter of Deuteronomy, as indicated in the King James' version (as called). These are the conclusions of the matter with that individual entity, Moses, after a hundred and twenty years of seeking his relationships to God. Then take the 14th, 15th, 16th and 17th of John; here we find the conclusions of Him who is the way, the truth, the light.

Study of the Scriptures

A lawyer once told me that he had studied the Bible in college as literature. He said that he had read a good bit of it and that it was just average as literature. He went on to say that we know so much more today than they did in those days, that he really couldn't see much need for using it as a guide today. Perhaps he had forgotten what a powerful influence the Mosaic Law had on the English common law upon which much of our legal system is based. This fact is pointed out to Mrs. [3350] in her reading, which recommended that she study the Bible:

> First, analyze and study the characters indicated—Moses as the lawgiver, Joshua as the leader. These are the basic principles of all material law. And these applied in the mind and body of Jesus became the way. Do thou likewise. 3350-1

My conversation with this person was before the recent collapse of most of the secular systems of Eastern Europe. The faith of the people of those countries had not disappeared as the atheistic governments had expected. I have heard in recent years that Russian educators are now making an effort to teach Christian morals in public schools in Russia. According to reading 900-232, that might not be such a bad idea:

> ...what ere trouble there may arise in the life of the entity, in social, marital, home, business, or what not, that the dependence of the Book, the lessons, the truths, the exposition of the manifestation of the Holy Spirit in the earth's forces, is ever the Guide to everyone.

The readings don't just tell people to study the Bible so they will be religious. They speak of developing a relationship to God that will result in personal transformation:

> Do study scripture. Do analyze it. Begin with definite portions, as: Exodus 19:5. Then study thoroughly the whole of Exodus 20, then Deuteronomy 30. Then make the pattern of thy life the 23rd Psalm, and then the first ten verses of the first chapter of John. And then the 14th, 15th, 16th, 17th of John. And then the 13th of I Corinthians. These should not merely be learned, but used as patterns; not as a show, but as something to be used in the experience with others to become a little more patient, a little more sincere, with self, a little kinder to those less fortunate, a little more of brotherly love to those who are high-minded, who think and act as if they were the patterns of the world. 2969-2

> Read the Book, if you would get educated. If you would be refined, live it! If you would be beautiful, practice it in thy daily life! 3647-1

Many who wrote the Bible, though human like us, had an encounter with God through a dream, a vision, an inner voice, or some form of prophecy. We can have the same kinds of encounters. As reading 1173-8 says, "For in the study of these [the scriptures] ye will find that ye draw unto that force from which the writers of same gained their strength, their patience." If you followed the instructions on a map and found a hidden treasure, would you then complain about what you perceived to be imperfections in the map? Perfection in the Bible is not so much in the details as it is in the fact that it reveals, to those who will give it a try, One who can transform their lives.

Israel

In addition to the Bible, I also enjoy reading the Quran, the Tao Te Ching, the Vedas, the Zand Avestas, and other great spiritual writings of the world, and I find many parallels in them to the Judeo-Christian traditions. When we question where the Bible fits in with other ancient scriptures, the spiritual identity of the people known as Israel becomes a central issue. The Cayce readings often address this issue. They confirm that the Israelites were called by God, not for their own glory but to be an example to the whole world of what God's love could do for any people who would love and obey Him. Reading 587-6 puts this into perspective:

> Not merely in the thought of that termed in the present as the people of Israel, but rather that as understood by those peoples of the day—the greater meaning of the word Israel—those called of God for a service before the fellow man.

The readings do not put down other religions when they suggest that the people of Israel had a worldwide mission. Reading 2772-1 says:

> For those who seek are indeed Israel, and Israel indeed is *all* who seek; meaning not those as of the children of Abraham alone, but of every nation, every tribe, every tongue—Israel of the Lord! That is the full meaning of Israel. [See Galatians 3:29 and 6:16]

Reading 262-28 gives even more information about the meaning of Israel:

> Israel is the chosen of the Lord, and that His promise, His care, His love, has not departed from those that seek to know His way, that seek to see His face, that would draw nigh unto Him. *This* is the meaning, this should be the understanding to all. Those that seek are Israel. Those that seek not, have ye not heard, "Think not to call thyselves the promise in Abraham. Know ye not that the

Lord is able to raise up children of Abraham from the very stones?" So Abraham means call; so Israel means those who seek. How obtained the supplanter the name Israel? For he wrestled with the angel, and he was face to face with the seeking to know His way. So it is with us that are called and seek His face; we are the Israel. Know, then, the scepter, the promise, the love, the glory of the Lord has not departed from them that seek His face! [See Genesis 49:10, Hebrews 1:8 and Revelation 19:15]

Cayce worked closely with several Jewish people. The readings stated that it was important to have them as a part of the Work and that the "children of promise" should have the first opportunity to benefit from the Work. Nevertheless, the readings kept a perspective on the broader meaning of Israel. Even personal readings for Cayce's Jewish friends often encouraged them to seek God, making obvious references to the Messiah. Reading 137-118, given for a Jewish associate, says:

... that name—that becomes on every tongue that of the *crucified* one in the manner that self is crucified to the fleshly desires, that the spirit of man be not proud—but rather preferring the spirit of the Holy One before self, and considering the neighbor as thine self.

A New Meaning to the Words of Old
I have found myself going back to the readings many times to look for a deeper meaning to some particular passage of Scripture that I might be studying. Sometimes I find something like the following reading while looking for something else:

... first there must be within the information that may be obtained that which corresponds, or which awakens a chord *within* each individual, and that rings true to the individual's own plan, own spiritual desire; for the *spirit* is alive, the *flesh* is weak. The carnal desire must sooner or later, as in nature, *burn* itself out; so, as has been given, "all things are tried so as by fire." *this* to *some*, will give a new meaning to *many* of the words of old. 254-55

This reading has helped me to develop patience, especially with myself. In the Gospels of Matthew and Mark, the Master said, "The spirit is willing, but the flesh is weak." In the light of the readings, I see this to mean that if we stay awake and focus on the things of the spirit, the old, selfish patterns will burn themselves out in time. Paul dealt with this inner struggle in chapters seven and eight of Romans when he said, "It is death to limit oneself to what is unspiritual; life and peace can only come with concern for the spiritual." (Romans 8:6 JB)

Sometimes those who asked for readings had questions about some particular passage in the Bible. Study Group reading 262-111 is an example of one that adds dimension to one of the Beatitudes:

(Q) Please explain "Happy are the poor in spirit, for they shall see God." Who are the poor in spirit?

(A) They that have not allowed and do not allow themselves to be directed by other influences than that of Godly-Force itself. They that are not acquainted with the familiar spirits but with the Divine. They that are meek yet proud in their meekness and their humbleness. These are they that are poor in spirit.

Reading 853-9 gives an interesting meaning to Mark 8:36 when it says. "For as He gave again, what profit it a man though he gain the whole world and has lost sight of being a soul?" This reminds me of when I was going somewhere away from home as a teenager and my mother said, "Don't forget who you are." The readings often remind us that we are sons and daughters of the Most High and that we should act like it.

The gospel lesson in which the Master said, "...unless you change and become like little children you will never enter the kingdom of heaven" (Matthew 18:3 JB) is explained in reading 3395-3, which adds: "Unless you become as open-minded, unless you can get mad and fight and then forgive and forget. For it is the nature of man to fight, while it is the nature of God to forgive."

Behavior of Bible Characters

In one of the first "Search for God" study groups in which my wife and I participated, one person said that she could not accept the Bible because Abraham had lied to the Pharaoh and because

139

other biblical characters did things that were not moral. This may
have been a normal reaction to the way the Scriptures had been
applied in her experience, but was it worth the price of rejecting
the best book ever written? I did not argue the point at the time,
but later, found readings that spoke directly to the question.

> For as indicated in the law of the Book, the life of the
> man Abraham was not beautiful, yet that faith which
> motivated same is beautiful, and the memory of and the
> children of faith we find beautiful. 4035-1

> Remember what was said of him who was the greatest of
> men born of woman [John the Baptist], that he was the
> least in the kingdom of heaven, for he forgot to be humble
> and meek. 5089-2

> Using the experience of David the king as an example,
> what was it in his experience that caused him to be called a
> man after God's own heart? That he did not falter, that he
> did not do this or that or be guilty of every immoral
> experience in the category of man's relationship? Rather
> was it that he was sorry, and not guilty of the same offence
> twice!
> Well that ye pattern thy study of thyself after such a life!
> 5753-2

The readings recognize the weaknesses even of those who
wrote what we call the New Testament:

> (Q) Please explain I Cor. 15:51. Is the reference here to
> body? "Behold, I show you a mystery. We shall not all
> sleep, but we shall all be changed."
> (A) Referring to the body; though the individual here
> speaking (Paul) *looked* for this to happen in his own day,
> see? For what is the stumblingblock to us today? If we do
> a good deed we want God to repay us tomorrow! So did
> Paul! Did he not groan continually that the mark, that scar
> in him, was not removed? Did he not bring those things as
> said by Peter concerning same? That, "He speaketh many
> things hard to be understood, that many wrest with to their
> own destruction." To what did he refer? That their idea (of

many who spoke) of time and space was limited; for they had even less conception of same than the weakest among you here! 262-87

Sure, we can find examples of less than perfect behavior in many Bible characters, just as we can find the same in ourselves and those around us today. I believe, however, that some of the criticism that I hear is aimed at rejecting or eroding biblical standards that are perceived as being too difficult for mortals to live up to. The spirit of the law as taught by the Master often seems even more difficult to live by than the old letter of the law, but finding fault with others does not excuse us from making an honest effort to live up to God's standards. Wouldn't it be better to follow Cayce's advice and magnify the virtues and minimize the faults of every other soul? While we have many examples of what not to do, we also have an example in the Bible of One who is righteous in God's sight:

So manifesting same [the teachings of Jesus] in the lives and minds of those whom the self may meet day by day, learning that lesson as He so well manifested, that it was not in the separation as John, not in the running away as Elijah, not as in sitting in high places as Isaiah, not as in that form of Jeremiah—mourning; not in that lording as Moses—but *all things unto all men!* reaching them in their own place of experience; and not with long-facedness! 1472-3

For even in Elijah or John we find the faltering, the doubting. We find no faltering, no doubting, no putting aside of the purpose in the Master Jesus. 3054-4

Challenge for the Future

Have we trusted in God's promises by trying to live up to what He has asked of us in His Holy Word, or do we give up because it seems too much to ask? Reading 5758-1 says that all that is required of us is an honest try:

And it will be to each individual as was indicated to the children of Israel. They entered into the Promised Land not because of their righteousness but because of the love of the Father for those who tried, who *tried* to live the righteousness.

There are many more Biblical treasures awaiting any serious student of the readings. It is difficult to understand how anyone who loves the Bible would not recognize Edgar Cayce as a kindred soul. In spite of complaints about the difficulty of understanding both the Bible and the Cayce readings, the hardest thing may be making a commitment to devote the time it takes to study either of them. Studied together, I believe that they complement each other and both become easier to understand.

Reading 262-60, given to the group that spent more than eleven years producing the *Search for God* study books, even suggests that producing sacred writings is an ongoing process:

> ...as He gave, in righteousness may ye know those things that have been preserved from the foundations of the worlds in thine own experience. For, these are told there in the manners of those that recorded same in their own environ. What wilt *thou* write today that will be as the words of life to thy brothers in the ages to come?

I have found the material in these *Search for God* books to be a very powerful, biblically centered, practical guide for spiritual growth. I can heartily recommend them to anyone. I would also echo Edgar Cayce's admonition to study the "Book of Books" along with whatever else you choose.

11

The Master in All Ages and His Mission: Jesus Who Became the Christ

Then he said to them, "You foolish men! So slow to believe the full message of the prophets! Was it not ordained that the Christ should suffer and so enter into his glory?" Then, starting with Moses and going through all the prophets, he explained to them the passages throughout the scriptures that were about himself. Luke 24:25-27 JB

Picture of Jesus

At a Bible study program at our church, the minister pointed out the different styles of the writers of the four gospels and how they each portrayed Jesus in their own way. Our own image of Him is not just a picture of how He looked physically, but it involves why He came into the earth, what He taught, how He lived His life, and what He means to us today. No two artists or writers will see a person in exactly the same way, and the pictures they paint of that person will differ. Yet, each picture may convey some unique perspective that will add to our understanding of the person being portrayed.

One of the most important things that I can share with anyone about the Edgar Cayce readings is the picture they paint of the Master, Jesus. While essentially agreeing with the Bible, the Cayce readings add some powerful new dimensions to the significance of the Christ in the history of the world. They go well beyond many Christian scholars in seeing Him as a world-class figure. This can be seen in reading 5758-1, which says:

And as there is the analyzing of the Christ-Life, Christ-Consciousness, one realizes and finds that the Christ-Child was born into the earth as man; one born in due season, in due time, in man's spiritual evolution, that man might have a pattern of the personality and the individuality of God Himself.

143

A Catholic woman, who was an art student at the time, sought information about painting a picture of the Master. Her reading (338-4) said that He should not only be depicted as a man of sorrows, but should also be shown in his expression of power and might:

> Depict Him as that in the giving of the Supper.
>
> For there we find not only the shadow of Gethsemane, not only the sunlight of Calvary, but also the beauty of the glorious resurrection morn. For as He gave, "This my body, broken, *for you*—This my blood, shed that ye might have life and have it more abundantly."
>
> All of these that came then as the physical suffering, as the man, were pushed aside. And in His Face there comes that as He gave, "I drink it anew with thee in my Father's kingdom." *that* depict!

The readings were quite specific in giving details about the life, and even the appearance, of Jesus. Several artists have painted pictures of the Master based, at least in part, on the following word picture of the Last Supper, which was given spontaneously at the end of a physical reading:

> The Lord's Supper—here with the Master—see what they had for supper—boiled fish, rice, with leeks, wine, and loaf. One of the pitchers in which it was served was broken—the handle was broken, as was the lip to same.
>
> The whole robe of the Master was not white, but pearl gray—all combined into one—the gift of Nicodemus to the Lord.
>
> The better looking of the twelve, of course, was Judas, while the younger was John—oval face, dark hair, smooth face—only one with the short hair. Peter, the rough and ready—always that of very short beard, rough, and not altogether clean; while Andrew's is just the opposite—very sparse, but inclined to be long more on the side and under the chin—long on the upper lip—his robe was always near gray or black, while his clouts or breeches were striped; while those of Philip and Bartholomew were red and brown.

The Master's hair is 'most red, inclined to be curly in portions, yet not feminine or weak—*strong*, with heavy piercing eyes that are blue or steel-gray.

His weight would be at least a hundred and seventy pounds. Long tapering fingers, nails well kept. Long nail, though, on the left little finger.

Merry—even in the hour of trial. Joke—even in the moment of betrayal.

The sack is empty. Judas departs.

The last is given of the wine and loaf, with which He gives the emblems that should be so dear to every follower of Him. Lays aside His robe, which is all of one piece—girds the towel about His waist, which is dressed with linen that is blue and white. Rolls back the folds, kneels first before John, James, then to Peter—who refuses.

Then the dissertation as to "He that would be the greatest would be servant of all."

The basin is taken as without handle, and is made of wood. The water is from the gherkins [gourds], that are in the wide-mouth Shibboleths [streams? Judges 12:6], that stand in the house of John's father, Zebedee.

And now comes "It is finished."

They sing the ninety-first Psalm—"He that dwelleth in the secret place of the Most High shall abide under the shadow of the Almighty. I will say of the Lord, He is my refuge and my fortress: my God; in Him will I trust."

He is the musician as well, for He uses the harp.

They leave for the garden. 5749-1

The fascinating thing about this reading is the way that Cayce actually seemed to be looking at this scene as if he had a video camera that allowed him to look in on any time or place in history. Could he have been recalling a picture that he had seen or a book he had read? Or had he tuned in to the memory of some individual who had actually been there? Whatever the source, there are some unusual things about this scene.

I initially thought the comment about the long fingernail was strange. Later, I read in a children's book on the customs of Palestine at the time of Jesus that it was customary for those who played the harp to keep a long nail on the left little finger for the purpose of tuning the harp. I seriously doubt that Cayce consciously ever knew about this custom.

Many people insist that Jesus could not have had red hair and blue eyes. The Bible (I Samuel 16:12 and 17:42) says that David was "ruddy," meaning that he had red hair. Was Jesus not supposed to have been descended from David? I have also heard that the Israelites believed that there was something special about people with red hair. Even so, I would not be too quick to argue about the color of the Master's hair or eyes. I have no problem with artists who depict Jesus in a variety of ways to appeal to many people. The physical appearance of Jesus the Christ is much less important than the life that He lived. Nevertheless, most of us would want to see Jesus in the flesh if we had the chance. This is evidenced by continued interest in the Shroud of Turin. Some of us are also especially interested in knowing more about what He believed and how He really lived. Reading 341-44 gives a few more clues:

> For He was man *of* men and one with them, in their joys, in their sorrows—yet never uncomely, never unkempt, never tiring, never sorrowing; yet rejoicing with those who did rejoice, weeping with those who wept; giving to the needy, enjoying the good things of life with those who had abundance; and making equal *all* before the law of God...

Will the Real Jesus Please Stand Up?

Having been impressed with the above readings, I looked for more in the Cayce readings about the life of Jesus. I also read about the Dead Sea Scrolls and other archaeological studies. Then I became aware of what some scholars and theologians call the search for the "historical Jesus." At first I was puzzled as to why these scholars show little interest in the historical details found in the Edgar Cayce readings. As I learned more about their approach to the Bible, however, I realized that even if they could accept Cayce's method of giving readings, they would probably label most of the Cayce information as mythology and discount it along with much of the New Testament.

My first encounter with this kind of theology was in the late 1960s, when my wife and I taught a Catholic Sunday school class on the air force base where we were stationed. In a special class for Sunday school teachers, a young priest told us that the virgin birth of Christ was a myth or a "midrash." A midrash is a Jewish story in which each word may have an important meaning, but which need not be literally or historically true. It was assumed that the Gospel writers had been Jewish, and that the story of the virgin birth symbolized the importance of Jesus. Later, according to this theory, when the antipathy between Jews and Christians developed, the Christians began to interpret the story literally.

I talked to an older priest who was aware, and somewhat disturbed, that this theory was being taught in some of the seminaries. Had I not been familiar with the Cayce readings about the virgin birth, I might have been less saddened by such rationalizations, and possibly more sympathetic. Reading 5749-15, however, shows that Cayce knew that the immaculate conception created difficulties for some people:

> Neither is there much indicated in sacred or profane history as to the preparation of the mother for that channel through which immaculate conception might take place. And this, the immaculate conception, is a stumblingstone to many worldly-wise.

Later, I learned that many of the doubts about the biblical picture of Jesus were spearheaded partly by the German theologian, Rudolph Bultmann (1881-1976). While not denying, as some have, that Jesus lived and was crucified, Bultmann promoted a method of Gospel analysis called "form criticism." The Gospels were divided into short sections, which were analyzed according to their form. After Bultmann and his followers removed everything that they considered to be mythology, they concluded that the New Testament revealed very little about the historical Jesus. In their efforts to emphasize Jesus' humanity and play down his divinity, these theologians viewed Jesus' references to himself as the Son of Man *(bar adam)* to be one of the few authentic passages in the New Testament. Ironically, this may only add weight to Cayce's assertion that Jesus was an incarnation of the same soul that was Adam.

Cayce had no credentials that would cause scholars to even consider his readings, much less take them to be an authoritative source. The picture of Jesus found in Cayce's readings might make more sense, both historically and spiritually, however, than some modern and traditional interpretations of Scriptures. When the Spiritual Life Group of the Park Place Methodist Church asked Cayce for a reading, they were told:

> As with Him, He found no fault in others. This should be the first premise, then, of each individual; less and less condemning of others and more and more of self manifesting that love shown by the Father through the Son in the material world; that man, through this pattern, through this picture of God, may become a living example, may walk closer in that way of less condemning. 5758-1

Jesus/Christ

Those who would magnify the differences between the Cayce Work and traditional Christianity sometimes suggest that the readings emphasize the universal Christ rather than the man Jesus. The readings do often speak of having the mind in us that was in Christ Jesus (Philippians 2:5), and they sometimes call this state of mind the Christ Consciousness. The readings also emphasize, as did Jesus (John 4:24), that God is Spirit, but distinctions between Jesus and the Christ are probably as much from liberal Christian theology as from Cayce.

Having convinced themselves that they could not find Jesus in history, some theologians attempted to separate the historical Jesus from what they called "the Christ of Faith." Their dividing line between the two is what they called the "Easter Event." Perhaps it is to their credit that, believing they could not find the real Jesus, they still recognized the pattern of love and forgiveness as the Christ. In any case, this may have been the theological context in which the following question was asked of Edgar Cayce:

> (Q) What is the meaning and significance of the words Jesus and Christ as should be understood and applied by these entities in the present?
> (A) Just as indicated. Jesus is the man—the activity, the mind, the relationships that He bore to others. Yea, He was mindful of friends, He was sociable, He was loving, He was kind, He was gentle. He grew faint, He grew weak— and yet gained that strength that He has promised, in becoming the Christ, by fulfilling and overcoming the world! Ye are made strong—in body, in mind, in soul and

purpose—by that power in Christ. The *power*, then, is in the Christ. The *pattern* is in Jesus. 2533-7

In other words, he is saying that the power is in putting the spiritual welfare of others before our own self interest, and the example of doing this is to be found in Jesus. Rather than widening the distinction between the words Jesus and Christ, Cayce showed how they are complementary. The readings do, however, recognize the danger of worshiping one's own concept of Jesus as a man, without recognizing in His life the pattern of the universal Christ Spirit.

Jesus Who Became the Christ

The readings say that the awareness of the power of the Christ Spirit in our lives is something that we must grow toward through our experiences in the earth. Could that have been true of Jesus also? Compared to denying the virgin birth, it seems much less heretical to think that Jesus "increased in wisdom, in stature, and in favour with God and men" (Luke 2:52 JB); or that, "Although he was Son, he learnt to obey through suffering; but having been made perfect, he became for all who obey him the source of eternal salvation and was acclaimed by God with the title of high priest *of the order of Melchizedek*." (Hebrews 5:8-10 JB)

Throughout the readings over the years, Cayce frequently used the phrase "Jesus who became the Christ." Like several other key phrases or ideas, Cayce used this phrase in many different ways and contexts. Here are a few excerpts from the readings that have been meaningful to me in trying to grasp the full meaning, to the world and to me personally, of the mission of the man we call the Christ:

> ... as set in the example of Jesus of Nazareth, who became the Christ, the Son of God, as each soul as a son of God; but He was the first; the light, the way, the truth; the high priest of the soul of men, the brother in mind and body; that we as individuals might know the Father-God. 5252-1

> For it is true that light, that knowledge, the understanding of that Jesus who became the Christ, is indeed thy elder brother and yet Creator, Maker of the

universe; and thus are ye a part of same and a directing influence. 5124-1

But keep humble, keep patient, keep in the manner in which the pattern has been given. For it is even as that one manifested in the flesh, even Jesus who became the Christ, who offered Himself that ye through belief, through faith, through the pattern of His life, might find thy way, might find thy true relationship to the Creator, God. 3660-1

For freedom alone can come in the knowledge of the only true living God, and as was manifest in Jesus who became the Christ and the Way. Thus keep that as the ideal throughout. 3052-3

He, that Christ-Consciousness, is that first spoken of in the beginning when God said, "Let there be light, and there was light." And that is the light manifested in the Christ. First it became physically conscious in Adam. And as in Adam we all die, so in the last Adam—Jesus, becoming the Christ—we are all made alive. Not unto that as of one, then. For we each meet our own selves, even as He; though this did not become possible, practical in a world experience, until He, Jesus, became the Christ and made the way. 2879-1 [I believe that this reading could shed some light many theological arguments.]

And then the 14th, 15th, 16th and 17th of John, as to how the man of Galilee, Jesus, that became the Christ, instigated the life that may be lived within, in the application to others; and upon Whom each soul must rely for guidance in making the choice of those promptings that arise in the heart and mind. 2851-1

...the entity may remind others of the needs to live that life which was wholly, truly exemplified in the life of the man Jesus, who became the Christ through the things which He suffered, and through demonstrating in the earth the abilities to overcome *death,* the law of death. 1877-2

Look not for those disincarnate influences; for rather know that the promise, "As ye abide in me and love me and keep my commandments," is to *thee;* from the Maker, the Giver of all good and perfect gifts—even Jesus who became the Christ by being able to not condemn, but gave Himself a ransom for *thee* and thy friends; for thy world in which ye labor! 1010-12

Former Appearances of the Christ

For, karmic forces are: What is meted must be met. If they are met in Him that is the Maker, the Creator of all that exists in manifestation, as He has promised, then not in *blind* faith is it met—but by the deeds and the thoughts and the acts of the body, that through Him the conditions may be met day by day. Thus has He bought every soul that would trust in Him. For, since the foundations of the world He has paved the ways, here and there entering into the experience of man's existence that He may know every temptation that might beset man in all of his ways. 442-3

Before we go into the question of former appearances of the Master, I must reiterate a few points in order to put the Cayce readings into perspective. First, Cayce was a lifelong, active church member, even when some other church members shunned him. He himself struggled with some of what was given through the readings and only accepted those things that he could integrate with his faith. The readings never denied the divinity or the humanity of Jesus the Christ. The readings never denied the virgin birth of Christ, as many theologians do. The readings affirm that Jesus actually died on the cross and was resurrected. The readings call Jesus the Savior of the world and do not view Him as just another prophet or teacher, as many people around the world often do. The readings never condemn those who believe otherwise and never create any sectarian barriers among believers. In comparison to many other things happening in churches today, I would suggest that Cayce's comments about former appearances of the Christ are not so sensational.

Nevertheless, the suggestion that the soul who was known as Jesus of Nazareth had also appeared at other times in history certainly did cause me to question the readings. I was well aware that the preexistence of the Christ was an established Christian doctrine. The readings said, however, that Jesus had formerly appeared as Adam, Enoch, Melchizedek, Joseph, Joshua, Asaph, and Jeshua, among others. I talked to various people, asked questions, and tried to find out what others believed and why.

For some, even a few Christians, the whole idea of the soul having any kind of existence other than as a function of the body was out of the question. For them, my question was irrelevant. Others could accept the idea that we humans might have lived before, but not Christ. Yet another group could accept that Jesus might have appeared as Melchizedek, or as the fourth man in the furnace with Shadrach, Meshach, and Abednego, but they believed that preexistence applied only to Christ and that the rest of us could not have had former lives.

During this time, I heard three different evangelical ministers refer to what they called a Christophany, meaning a former appearance of the Christ. So I searched through my Bible and various commentaries for clues. To my surprise, I found some interesting correlations. The following is a chronological list of the names listed above, with a few of the comments I found, including some from the readings. Some of the references, abbreviated as "Si," are from a section of the apocryphal book of Ecclesiasticus (not Ecclesiastes) called the "Eulogy of the Ancestors," which scholars say is from the second century BC:

- *Adam:*

Shem and Seth were honoured among men, but above every living creature is Adam. (Si 49:16 JB)

The first man, Adam, as scripture says, became a living soul; but the last Adam has become a life-giving spirit. (I Corinthians 15:45 JB)

Cayce says that there is a pattern of Adam and a pattern of the Christ within each of us. We are all here because of our own personal error or fall. We can awaken the Christ pattern within by following the living pattern, Jesus. Study group reading 262-100 says:

For ye having partaken of *sin,* not *in* Adam but *as* Adam must as the new Adam learn that God is merciful, is love, is justice, is patience, is long-suffering, is brotherly love; for these are the law, not *of* the law but *the* law. And the law is love and the law is God.

- *Enoch:*

Enoch walked with God. Then he vanished because God took him. (Genesis 5:24 JB) [A footnote to this verse includes, "Enoch has a prominent place in subsequent Jewish tradition: he is held up as a model of piety, Si 44:16; 49:14, and certain apocryphal books (one of which is cited in Jude 14-15) bear his name."]

Enoch pleased the Lord and was taken up, an example for the conversion of all generations. (Si 44:16 JB)

No one else has ever been created on earth to equal Enoch, for he was taken up from earth. (Si 49:14 JB)

- *Melchizedek:*

A footnote to Genesis 14:18 (JB) says:

Melchizedek makes a brief and mysterious appearance in the narrative; he is king of that Jerusalem where Yahweh will deign to dwell, and a priest of the Most High even before the levitical priesthood was established; moreover, he receives tithes from the Father of the chosen people. Ps 110:4 represents him as a figure of the Messiah who is both king and priest; the application to Christ's priesthood is worked out in Hebrews 7. Patristic tradition has developed and enriched this allegorical interpretation: In the bread and wine offered to Abraham, it sees an image of the Eucharist and even a foreshadowing of the Eucharistic sacrifice—an interpretation that has been received into the cannon of the Mass. Several of the Fathers even held the opinion that Melchizedek was a manifestation of the Son of God in person.

This becomes even more clearly evident when there appears a second Melchizedek, who is a priest not by virtue of a law about physical descent, but by the power of an indestructible life. (Hebrews 7:15-16 JB)

Again there may be drawn to self a parallel from the realm of spiritual enlightenment of that entity known as Melchizedek, a prince of peace, one seeking ever to be able to bless those in their judgments who have sought to become channels for a helpful influence without any seeking for material gain, or mental or material glory; but magnifying the virtues, minimizing the faults in the experiences of all with whom the entity comes in contact day by day. 2072-4

Reading 262-55 says, "Melchizedek wrote Job!"

- *Joseph:*

And no one else ever born has been like Joseph, the leader of his brothers, the prop of his people; his bones were honoured. (Si 49:15 JB)

A footnote in the Jerusalem Bible to Genesis 37:1 says:

Betrayed by his brothers, Joseph is rescued by God who makes the betrayal itself serve the divine purpose... Here, as later with the Exodus, we have a preliminary sketch of the Redemption.

Because of this and his forgiveness toward his brothers, Joseph is often called "a type of the Christ" in Sunday school literature and other commentaries.

- *Joshua:*

Mighty in war was Joshua son of Nun, successor to Moses in the prophetic office, who well deserved his name, and was a great saviour of the Chosen People... (Si 46:1 JB) [The footnote to the above verse says, "Joshua means 'Yahweh-saves.' Hebr. has 'who was fashioned to be in his time a great salvation for his chosen ones.'"]

Who had ever shown such determination as his? He himself waged the wars of the Lord. Was not the sun held back by his hand, and one day drawn out into two? (Si 46:3-4 JB)

A footnote to chapter 3 of Joshua (JB), in which God parts the waters of the Jordan for Joshua much as He had done for Moses at the Sea of Reeds, says:

Thus, with Joshua the events of the Exodus receive their first fulfillment; the Passion and resurrection of Christ repeat and fulfill those events at the spiritual level, cf. I Cor. 10:1. The Fathers therefore regard Joshua as prefiguring his namesake, Jesus.

They were all baptised into Moses in this cloud and in this sea; all ate the same spiritual food and all drank the same spiritual drink, since they all drank from the spiritual rock that followed them as they went, and that rock was Christ. I Cor. 10:2-4 (JB)

This rock probably alludes to the rock (identified with Yahweh himself by Jewish writers) from which Moses made water flow. It is interesting that Joshua was also present at that time. A footnote to I Cor. 10:4 (JB) also says, "Paul credits the pre-existent Christ with the attributes of Yahweh."

- *Asaph:*

There are only a couple of readings that seem to include Asaph as one of the former appearances of Jesus. However, Psalms 50 and 73 through 83, which are attributed to Asaph, reflect a writer who is impressed with the awesome power of God and worships Him above all others. It might be interesting to compare the style of these Psalms to the Book of Job.

- *Jeshua (also known as Joshua the high priest):*

How shall we extol Zerubbabel? He was like a signet ring on the right hand, so too was Jeshua son of Jozadak; they who in their days built the Temple, and raised to the

Lord a holy people, destined to everlasting glory. (Si 49:11-12 JB)

The third and sixth chapters of Zechariah include most of the biblical references to Jeshua. Cayce reading 5023-2 adds, "...Jeshua, the scribe, translated the rest of the books written up to that time."

These are the lives of the Master, as suggested in the readings, that relate to persons mentioned in the Old Testament. They are often mentioned in the readings as essential elements in our picture of the Christ:

Apply thyself in such a way and manner as to know what ye will do with this man, Jesus of Nazareth—Jeshua of Jerusalem, Joshua in Shiloh, Joseph in the court of Pharoah, Melchizedek, as he blessed Abraham, Enoch as he warned the people, Adam as he listened to Eve. 3054-4

Cayce said that the Master has also appeared in other places and times since the beginning of time:

Then, He has come in all ages when it has been necessary for the understanding to be centered in a *new* application of the same thought, "God *is* Spirit and seeks such to worship him in spirit and in truth!" 5749-5

There are other diverse beliefs about who Jesus might have been in former lives. Like the various church groups, they can't all be right. I do not know where Cayce got his information for these readings. I only know that they make Jesus and His ministry seem more real to me, and they provide a workable alternative to both materialistic and reactionary beliefs that are so popular today. I also know that the love of Jesus can be a real force in our lives, whether or not we know the exact truth about history.

The Way

The folk religion in China known as Taoism traces it's roots, at least partially, to a relatively short dissertation known as the *Tao Te Ching*. The *Tao Te Ching* appears to be quite spiritual in nature and has many similarities to Christianity such as extolling generosity, goodness, humility and moderation. The One Tao is referred to as the "Way of Heaven," the "Creative Nature," or the "gate to all spirituality." I do not know if there is an actual connection between the Chinese word *Tao* and the word used in John 14:6 (JB), where Jesus says, "I am the Way..." (He did not say, "I wrote the Way," or "I teach the Way," but "I am the Way") However, I suspect that a Taoist might have understood Jesus to say, "I am the Tao."

Here are a few readings in which we can see Cayce's interpretation of Christ as the Way:

But by one man sin came into God's creation. By one man death came. By that same man death was overcome.

Thus He is the way, the truth and the light; and through no other way may the individual entity attain to its greatest ability in the mental or the material world, save by having that spiritual ideal as set in Him. 2784-1

The *way*, then, is that manifested in the Creative Force through Jesus, the Christ, the Son: for He is the way, the truth, the light in which the body, the mind, the soul may find that security, that understanding, that comprehending of the oneness *of* the spiritual with the material that is manifested in an individual entity. 2600-2

For He is the way and the truth and the light, and they that climb up some other way are thieves and robbers of their own selves, and they alone will eventually suffer for such. 3213-2

As to how to meet each problem:
Take it to Jesus. He *is* thy answer. He is Life, Light and Immortality. He is Truth, and is thy elder brother. 1326-1

The Pattern/Example
(Q) Should the Christ-Consciousness be described as the awareness within each soul, imprinted in pattern on the mind and waiting to be awakened by the will, of the soul's oneness with God?
(A) Correct. That's the idea exactly! 5749-14

During a Sunday school class, I once said that Jesus is the example or pattern for our lives. Another person in the class challenged that idea, saying that He died for our sins and that we did not have to do anything but accept it. She knew of, and had expressed concern about, my ideas on reincarnation. To her, the idea of Jesus as the pattern seemed to condone an "Eastern" concept of karma and works for salvation. I tried to share my perception that Jesus was seen as an example even in traditional Christianity, but the class was over before the idea could be developed further. I was pleasantly surprised during the church service that followed, however, when we sang a hymn that referred to Jesus as our example and our pattern.

After Jesus washed the disciples' feet, he said, "I have given you an example so that you may copy what I have done to you." (John 13:15 JB) Peter also wrote, "This, in fact, is what you were called to do, because Christ suffered for you and left an example for you to follow the way he took." (I Peter 2:21 JB)

Perhaps Jesus' greatest example of obedience to God was when He prayed, "...your will be done!" (Matt. 26:42 JB) The readings often admonish us to pray with that same attitude. Only because He actively focused on serving others did He have the courage to completely overcome self and the flesh. I believe that this is the great pattern. Only when we are willing to suffer in the service of others will we heal our own souls.

If Jesus is our pattern, then we must follow His example if we would lead a Christian life. There is a popular acronym today that can be seen on T-shirts, pendants, and coffee mugs: WWJD. It means "What Would Jesus Do?" Edgar Cayce may have heard this saying from his mother when he was a boy. It came through in reading 954-5, which says, "Then when doubts and fears arise, when discouragements and disappointments come—yea, when joy of body or mind or soul is thine—ask thyself the question: 'What would Jesus do?'"

Thus it became necessary that God in His goodness give an ensample, a pattern, by which man might conduct his life, his ideals, his hopes, his fears, all of his idiosyncrasies; a pattern laid out for man. Those who accept same may live in peace and harmony with themselves and with others. Those who reject same continue to find discordant notes between their own associates, and with every activity of life there is continued to be trouble. 5211-1

For the Master, Jesus, even the Christ, is the pattern for every man in the earth, whether he be Gentile or Jew, Parthenian or Greek. For all have the pattern, whether they call on that name or not; but there is no other name given under heaven whereby men may be saved from themselves. 3528-1

Most individuals find, as self does at times, "If I can do this it will be pleasing to God." Who made thee a judge of God's pleasing? Who made anyone? The pattern! Cut to the pattern. Don't draw too close the hem or don't leave it too loose, for the bagging shows just as much as the overstitching. 3357-2

Love Manifested
We ourselves have known and put our faith in God's love towards ourselves. God is love and anyone who lives in love lives in God, and God lives in him. 1 John 4:16 (JB)

Love is universal and is understood by all people. If people do not recognize the essence of love in Jesus, it is because Christians still have room for improvement when it comes to demonstrating God's love for the world. Cayce frequently equated the law of love with giving. This means not only good intentions or a warm fuzzy feeling, but also giving of ourselves to others:

...without that love as He manifested among men, nothing can, nothing did, nothing will come into consciousness of matter. Not that we may deny evil and banish it, but supplanting and rooting out evil in the experience, replacing same with the love that is in the consciousness of the body Jesus, the Christ, we may do all things in His name... 436-2

Love then, *divine*; as was manifested in Jesus of Nazareth, must be the rule—yea, the measuring stick—the

159

rod, by which ye shall judge thy motives, thy impulses, thy associations. For without Him there is not anything made that is made—to endure. 1497-1

The Servant

Know it is in the little things, not by thunderous applause, not by the ringing of bells, not the blowing of whistles, that the Son of Man comes—humble, gently, kind, meek, lowly—for "He that is the greatest among you serveth all." 3161-1

Forgiveness

If you asked everyone you met to define the essence of Christianity in one word, I believe that second only to love would be forgiveness:

For the Lord loveth those who put their trust *wholly* in Him.

This, then, is that attitude of mind that puts away hates, malice, anxiety, jealousy. And it creates in their stead, in that Mind is the Builder, the fruits of the spirit—love, patience, mercy, longsuffering, kindness, gentleness. And these—against such there is no law. They break down barriers, they bring peace and harmony, they bring the outlook upon life of not finding fault because someone "forgot," someone's judgment was bad, someone was selfish today. These ye can overlook, for so did He.

In His own experience with those that He had chosen out of the world, if He had held disappointment in their leaving Him to the mercies of an indignant high priest, a determined lawyer and an unjust steward, what would have been *thy* hope, thy promise today? 357-13

For He stands in thy stead, before that *willingness* of thy inner self, thy soul, to do good unto others; that willingness, that seeking is righteousness, if ye will but understand, if ye will but *see*—and *forget* the *law* that killeth but remember the spirit of forgiveness that makes alive! 1436-3

The Cross

In reading 5277-1, Cayce was asked if the greater sufferings of Jesus were in the tests to which He was subjected before He began His ministry. The answer was, "No. The real test was in the garden when in the realization that He had met every test and yet must know the pangs of death." Reading 281-5 gave:

> *All* must pass under the rod as of that *cleansing* necessary for the inflowing of the Christ Consciousness, even as *He* passed under the rod, partook of the cup—and *gives* same to others.

There are those who would question why we cannot just forget about the cross and focus on love, but the cross is the path to love. There are numerous readings that explain why the cross was a necessary way for God to demonstrate His love for us. Here are a few of those readings:

> How if He is Life, could He die? Why did He die? These were the burdens. *Why* should He die?
>
> Yet as He gave, "For this purpose came I into the world." Just as He gave, "If ye would have life, give life."
>
> ...If ye would know Jesus, the Christ, then be like Him; who died for a Cause, without shame, without fault yet dying; and through that able to make what this Season [Easter] represents—*resurrection!* 1158-9

> For thy body is indeed the temple of the living God. There He has promised to meet thee. There He has promised to make Himself known to thee, His will, His purpose with thee.
>
> That may *not* be supplied by another. If that were true, that it might be supplied by another, why the need of the Son to suffer the death on the Cross, to offer Himself as a sacrifice? He offered it not alone for thyself, for the world, for the souls of men, but for His *own* being!
>
> For, ye—too—are *his* son; and ye, too, are brethren one with another. 877-29

...do not attempt to shed or to surpass or go around the Cross. *This* is that upon which each and every soul *must* look and know it is to be borne in self *with* Him. 5749-14

Why is the Cross the emblem of shame yet necessary, for the Crown that is to be in the experience of those that bear same? For we have reached that place in the experience where *we*, as individuals, will walk no more with this thought or else say as Peter, "Thou alone hast the words of eternal life, to whom shall we go?" 262-35

Resurrection
For ye in the present have the knowledge that He lived, that He not only lived but that He *lives*—and is mindful of those that seek to honor the Father! 1497-2

My impression is that some Bible scholars and ministers who question the virgin birth of the Christ still believe in the Resurrection. However, many mainline theologians now consider the Resurrection to be a myth as well, even though they may be less willing to say this from the pulpit.

Those who sought readings from Edgar Cayce sometimes wanted to know how they might discern the validity of sources from which they received guidance through meditation or other intuitive processes. Whether such a person or source would acknowledge the resurrection was usually one of the criteria given. Reading 422-1 says, "Test ye the spirits, for there are divers activities; but have no part with those that know not the Lord, the *risen* Lord—and Him crucified and risen!"

It is comforting to know that the readings support the spirituality of Christian beliefs, but many nonbelievers will not be convinced just because of the readings. Cayce often told people that the best way to witness to others was in the life that they lived:

And as the little leaven leaveneth the whole lump, so do thy gentlenesses, thy kindnesses, thy longsufferings, thy patience, bring into this world that for which He gave His life, His hope—into thy hands and to thy friends' hands, and into those that have named His Name, the *power* to bring glories of a risen Lord. 1158-5

Personal Relationship

Reading 5083-2 says that "every soul must take Jesus with him if he would succeed in any undertaking." When we are dealing with habits that we would like to correct, we especially need to have Him with us. I believe that we subconsciously hope that God will not notice when we are doing something that we know is not good for us or for those around us. Jesus was tempted in all things, however, and He knows how to forgive us and encourage us to change. Even though He forgives, we tend to lose our desire to do wrong when we feel that He is present at all times.

Press *on* to the mark of the higher calling as set in *him, and* in *thee*—if ye walk, if ye talk often with Him. Invite Him by name, by purpose, by desire, to be thy companion in all that ye do, all that ye say. He rejecteth not those who willingly, honestly, sincerely, invite Him to be with them. As He never rejected an invitation by any as He walked in the earth as an individual, neither does He reject the invitation of a soul that *seeks*—in sincerity—His companionship. 622-6

But let the theme of the mental body ever be *Jesus*, the Savior, the merciful companion to those who seek to know God's way with men. For He *is* that friend that would ever guide, direct and *accompany* thee, in trials, temptations, in thy joys as well as sorrows.

So, take Him with thee as thy companion in thy studies, in thy preparations, in thy thoughts of others, in thy *joys*. For would ye as a friend to man hear only sorrow as each and every word of those that sought thee! The heart of God in the Christ seeks the *joy*; as He did in giving His Son that we might know Him the better. 1173-10

(Q) Should I hope and seek for personal experiences or contacts with Jesus as a personality now?

(A) As has been indicated, this may be—but this ye live. Not as a desire for self-exaltation; that is, self-proof, self-evidence; but it is evidenced *in* thee when ye *are* (in thy living, in thy thinking, in thy acting) One with Him.

Then, and thus—how hath the angel given? "As ye have seen Him go, so will ye see Him come." Were those just as words? No.

Thou hast seen Him oft in the acts of others... 1158-9

If we have our eyes open, we too have seen Him in the acts of kindness, forgiveness, and selfless giving that we see around us every day.

Atonement

Did thy Lord bleed when the nails were driven in His hands and feet? Did He give up the ghost? Did He die?

Yes. For as He gave, without His death—yea, without His resurrection—there is no hope in man's estate. 1152-5

A friend who belongs to a Spiritualist organization once asked me if I believed in vicarious atonement, the belief that Jesus had died in our place, for our sins. I told him that I did believe that Jesus had brought the opportunity of salvation to us through His crucifixion and resurrection, but that I did not necessarily agree exactly with all other Christians on that subject. To many individuals or groups whose beliefs are different from those of the more orthodox churches, the concept of salvation can be seen almost as the line of demarcation that separates them from the orthodox. However, the variations among beliefs, even among mainline Christian churches, makes that line somewhat obscure.

Rather than trying to find one definitive statement from the readings about salvation, I have discussed the subject in various chapters, hoping to provide food for thought and to share many perspectives that Cayce offered for people of various backgrounds and persuasions. Here are a few more suggestions:

Then in that as the Christ He came into the earth, fulfilling then that which makes Him that channel, that we making ourselves a channel through Him may—with the boldness of the Son—approach the Throne of mercy and grace and pardon, and know that all that has been done is washed away in that *he* has suffered that *we* have meted to our brother in the change that is wrought in our lives, through the manner we act toward him. 442-3

Then there came in the entity's experience the full meaning of the priesthood in Israel, and how that the lowly Nazarene was that fulfilling of that priesthood in His offering of Himself as the lamb that was not to roll back but to take away the sins of the people. Not as an escape but as an atonement in which each soul does find, would find, the lamb standing *ever* as that offering in its relationships as an individual to its fellow man. 1000-14

For His yoke is easy, if His grace and mercy is thine— and this ye obtain only by showing others the way to same! 1402-1

For by faith are ye saved, and that *not* of yourself—for it is the gift of thy Maker. 1681-1

From what must we be saved? The readings say that we must be saved from ourselves. Reading 3528-1 told a person, "And as ye find in thyself, it is only thyself from which ye are to be saved— hardheadedness and your pessimism!"

Other Biblical Names Used in the Readings

In Him *only* is the way, the water of life, the bright and morning star, the rose of Sharon; the *glorious*, the mighty, the *holy* One! 1089-3

For He is the rock of salvation; the bright, the morning star; the rose of Sharon; the *wonderful* counsellor. In Him *is* thy Destiny. 262-75

...Lord of Lords and the King of Kings and the Prince of Princes and the Son of man; yea the Son of God! 1497-2

...that man of God, that lover of men, that Savior of a sin-sick world. 811-2

He is the Alpha and Omega, the bright and morning star; He is the water of life and they that take thereof shall not thirst, neither shall they weary—When they weary of the Christ—too bad! 792-1

165

...the high priest of the soul of men, the brother in mind and body... 5252-1

Jesus, the Christ is the light of the world. As ye reflect His tenets, His truths in thy relationships to thy fellow man, ye shine out as a star in the crown of thy Master, thy Lord, thy Brother. 5149-1

12

Children of the Living God:
The Early Church

The Cayce readings contain some interesting stories about the early church. Most of this information was given in bits and pieces for individuals who were told that they had lived in or around Palestine in the first century. One of those persons was Edgar Cayce himself, who was told that he had had a former life in which he was active in the early church in Laodicea. Consistent with a statement from the readings implying that Cayce was more likely to give information about the times and places in which he himself had had an incarnation, there were dozens of readings that touched upon this time period.

These readings seldom differ significantly from the Gospels, but they do add a lot of details that make the scriptures more real and understandable. I suspect that Cayce's love for the Bible and the language and the flavor of the readings were all greatly influenced by his first-century experience. One example of this is Cayce's frequent references to God as the Creative Force. This is very similar in meaning to the *Word* or the *Logos*, as used in the first chapter of John. The Hellenistic Jewish writer, Philo of Alexandria, also refers to the Logos as God's "creative power."

Another example of possible first-century influence upon the readings is Cayce's frequent references to Jesus as *the Master*. A retired minister with editorial experience was kind enough to review some of my earlier chapters. He was concerned that it might not be clear to some readers that Cayce was speaking of Jesus when he spoke of the Master. Another person objected because his image of a master was an adept in the esoteric sciences or some kind of potentate in a secret society. I understand these concerns and have made some attempt to clarify this issue. I believe, however, that Cayce's use of the name Master is more a reflection of his early church experience and his frequent reading of the Bible than of any other use of the word. In the New Testament, I found numerous occurrences of the word master, many of which were used by the apostles when speaking to Jesus. (See Matthew 23:8, Luke 8:24 and 45, 9:33 and 49, and 2 Timothy 2:21.)

Birth of the Church

I once heard a discussion on a religious talk show about the birth of the church. There was a question as to whether the church began at Pentecost or in the upper room. Of course, this is only an academic question, but the readings did give some interesting ideas about the beginnings of the church.

The readings say that a group called "the school of prophets," from earlier times, had been reestablished by Ezra and others after the Jews returned from exile. The following readings give some details about this group, known to us as the Essenes:

> In those days when there had been more and more of the leaders of the peoples in Carmel—the original place where the school of prophets was established during Elijah's time, Samuel—these were called then Essenes; and those that were students of what ye would call astrology, numerology, phrenology, and those phases of that study of the return of individuals—or incarnation...
>
> These having been persecuted by those of the [Jewish] leaders, this first caused that as ye have an interpretation of as the Sadducees, or "There is no resurrection," or there is no incarnation, which is what it meant in those periods. 5749-8

> Much might be given as to how or why and when there were the purposes that brought about the materialization of Jesus in the flesh.
>
> In giving then the history: There were those of the faith of the fathers to whom the promises were given that these would be fulfilled as from the beginning of man's record.
>
> Hence there was the continued preparation and dedication of those who might be the channels through which this chosen vessel might enter—through choice—into materiality.
>
> Thus in Carmel—where there were the priests of this faith—there were the maidens chosen that were dedicated to this purpose, this office, this service.

Among them was Mary, the beloved, the chosen one; and she, as had been foretold, was chosen as the channel. Thus she was separated and kept in the closer associations with and in the care or charge of this office.

That was the beginning, that was the foundation of what ye term the Church. 5749-7

More than seventy-five other readings also have some mention of the Essenes. Even though the historian, Josephus, does mention the Essenes several times, it is significant that these readings were given before the more recently discovered Dead Sea Scrolls sparked greater public interest in this sect. Reading 254-109 says that the meaning of the term *Essene* was "expectancy," and that the central purpose of the group was to prepare people who would be "fit channels for the birth of the Messiah." According to this reading, both Mary and Joseph had been dedicated to the Essene mission by their parents, but they were free to accept this training or not. This reading also says, "This was the beginning of the period where women were considered as equals with the men in their activities..." Rather than implying, however, that the Essene organization itself was expected to become the church or even that Essenes were to be sent out into the world to proclaim the Messiah, Cayce says that most of them expected the Messiah to establish the new order by His own pronouncements.

Sects/Heretics/Gnostics

There were divisions enough among the Jews when the Church began. In addition to the Pharisees, Sadducees, and Essenes, there were Zealots, Nazarenes, Therepeutae, and others, all with their subsects having various shades of beliefs, sometimes overlapping and sometimes intertwined with each other. The following readings offer a few bits of information about some of these groups:

(Q) Were the Essenes called at various times and places Nazarites, School of the Prophets, Hasidees, Therapeutae, Nazarenes, and were they a branch of the Great White Brotherhood, starting in Egypt and taking as members Gentiles and Jews alike?

(A) In general, yes. Specifically, not altogether. They were known at times as some of these; or the Nazerites were a branch or a *thought* of same, see? Just as in the present one would say that any denomination by name is a branch of the Christian-Protestant faith, see? So were those of the various groups, though their purpose was of the first foundations of the prophets as established, or as understood from the school of prophets, by Elijah; and propagated and studied through the things begun by Samuel. The movement was *not* an Egyptian one, though *adopted* by those in another period—or an earlier period— and made a part of the whole movement.

They took Jews and Gentiles alike as members—yes. 254-109

But remember the Essenes had the divisions, just as you will find that most churches have their groups and divisions, these [wife and husband for whom this reading was given] were in opposite groups of the Essenes. One held to—that it can happen—the other that God makes it happen. Which comes first, the hen or the egg? 2072-15

Besides the various Jewish groups in the Holy Land, other teachings from various parts of the known world had their influence on first-century Israel. The New Testament account of Pentecost precludes a simplistic understanding of the beliefs of the occupants of Jerusalem. The second chapter of Acts refers to the presence in Jerusalem of "Parthians, Medes and Elamites; people from Mesopotamia, Judaea and Cappadocia, Pontus and Asia, Phrygia and Pamphylia, Egypt and the parts of Libya round Cyrene; as well as visitors from Rome—Jews and proselytes alike—Cretans and Arabs..." (Acts 2:9-11 JB)

From the writings of Philo, we can see several differing facets of the Greek or Hellenistic influences. Some scholars believe that the lack of belief in spiritual matters on the part of the wealthy Sadducees was due to their worldly Hellenistic education. It is thought that these Sadducees were swayed by followers of the Greek philosopher, Epicurus, who taught that the soul dies with the body. The beliefs and practices of the Jews had also been influenced by Zoroastrianism, to which they had been exposed during the time of the Exile. The teachings of Mithraism,

Brahmanism, and even Buddhism, as well as indigenous pagan beliefs, were also not unknown to this part of the world. Especially after the decision was made to disseminate the Gospel to the Gentiles as well as to the Jews, it was inevitable that all of these beliefs would have to be dealt with.

Even though the readings credit the Essenes with making the way straight for the Messiah to enter the earth, Jesus did not confine his ministry to these sects. He also had a great love for the orthodox temple and the Jewish nation as a whole. In fact, according to Cayce, Jesus was the author of Judaism from the beginning. Reading 2067-11 could be taken to imply that even most Essenes, including John the Baptist, probably did not fully understand Jesus' emphasis on the spirit of the law: "For, John was more the Essene than Jesus. For Jesus held rather to the spirit of the law, and John to the letter of same."

Some church writers have tended to lump most all of the sects that were not orthodox into one group that they call "Gnostics." On the other hand, some of the church fathers use the term "gnosis" (the root word for Gnostic) in a positive way while, at the same time, writing against some of the sects that are now called Gnostic. Some writers seem to imply that gnosis meant knowing God personally rather than just knowing about Him. Others suggest the opposite, that Gnostics believed they were saved by their secret knowledge rather than by how they lived.

I believe that the core of the secret knowledge, or gnosis, that some sects taught was that souls are eternal and that we are all children of God. I would have to agree with them that this awareness is an essential part of our spiritual growth. I would also agree with St. James, who says that even our faith has to be applied in our relationships to others to be worth very much.

From Josephus and from the questions asked in the Gospels, we can see that many first-century Jews (probably mostly Essenes and Pharisees) believed in reincarnation. This had little to do with the bizarre myths and beliefs of some of the fringe sects. Most of the Essenes probably would never have made a distinction between Yahweh of the Old Testament and the Father to which Jesus refers in the New Testament. Yet this was one of the more troubling beliefs held by some of the other sects that were resisted by the orthodox groups.

Many other metaphysical questions that were discussed in the culture of the day were factors in the growth of the early church.

171

For example, it seems to have been widely accepted that anything that was created would also have an end and that only that which was eternal from the beginning could be immortal. But others thought it blasphemy to think that human souls could be immortal. To further complicate matters, Philo, as well as some of the early Christian sects, seemed to argue that the matter that makes up the physical world is eternal. Some sects even thought matter to be equal to God. These and other beliefs helped set the stage for the myriad of arguments about the nature of Jesus, God, and man that tended to splinter the growing Church.

Reading 1541-11 explained to a person who wanted to overcome an abhorrence of the Catholic religion: "This arises from those periods of the controversy which arose between the followers of Cephas and the Paulites; that made for those changes wrought in the foundation of that first or early group." The method given for correcting this feeling was: "Overcome same in giving expression in those manners in which the young will weigh well in their own lives the teachings of the Master, without condemning any—as He, yet requiring that all be sowers in the life journey."

Children of the Living God

One summer—I think it was in the early 1980s—my wife and I visited the A.R.E. headquarters in Virginia Beach. While we were looking around, a member of the staff invited us to attend a study group that met in someone's home near the A.R.E. This was a very interesting meeting to me because Gladys Davis Turner, Edgar Cayce's secretary who had recorded most of the readings, was there. The lesson from the Search for God book included a phrase from a reading that said, "Ye are Gods." Gladys's brother, a Methodist from Selma, Alabama, took exception to this phrase. A lively discussion ensued, but the subject was changed before I could get a word in edgewise. My thought later was that the gentleman might have questioned Psalms 82:6 and John 10:34 rather than Cayce, who had only quoted these Scriptures.

The original reading, which was quoted in this lesson on "Desire," was study group reading 262-64: ·

Apply that ye know, for in the application comes understanding. For, as the Master gave, "Ye are gods," if ye will use His force of desire and will in His kingdom, but *not* thine own.

A few years ago, a New Age writer popularized the saying, "I am God." I am not sure how much I might differ with this statement in the context in which it was meant to be taken. It might, however, lend itself to being taken the wrong way by some people. As mentioned in the chapter on creation, Cayce said that we are to become one with God, but still an individual and not the whole. Reading 4083-1 gives this perspective:

> So, as in the self, whether the individual entity or soul entertains its relationship to the Creative Forces or not, the relationship is still existent or possible. For indeed in Him, the Father-God, ye move and have thy being. Act like it! Don't act like ye think ye are a God! Ye may become such, but when ye do ye think not of thyself. For what is the pattern? He thought it not robbery to make Himself equal with God, but He acted like it in the earth. He made Himself of no estate that you, through His grace, through His mercy, through His sacrifice might have an advocate with that First Cause, God...

In spite of the dangers of thinking ourselves above the law, I still believe that the fact that we are souls, created in the image of God, with the hope of eternal life, needs to be reiterated. Reading 699-1 says, "So are ye gods in the making, saith He that walked among men as the greater teacher of all experiences and ages." This belief that we are a part of God is shared even by many evangelical and charismatic Christians today. This concept, however, can be a bit difficult to share in some of today's liberal theological environments just as it was for Jesus when he said, "Is it not written in your Law: I said, you are gods? So the Law uses the word gods of those to whom the word of God was addressed, and scripture cannot be rejected." (John 10:34-35 JB)

Reading 5749-6 helps to define where the Cayce information stands on this question:

> How, why, was there the need for there to be a resurrection? Why came He into the earth to die the death, even on the Cross? Has it been, then, the fulfillment of man's estate? Else why did He put on flesh and come into the earth in the form of man, but to be one with the Father; to show to man *his* (man's) divinity, man's relationship to

the Maker; to show man that indeed the Father meant it when He said, "If ye call I will hear. Even though ye be far away, even though ye be covered with sin, if ye be washed in the blood of the lamb ye may come back."

The first chapter of the Gospel of John says, "But to all who did accept him he gave power to become children of God..." (John 1:12 JB). It is clear that when the New Testament speaks of our power to become children of God it does not only mean that we are created in God's image, but also that we should choose to act in a godly manner. One of the most frequently quoted Scriptures in the Edgar Cayce readings is this excerpt from Romans:

Everyone moved by the Spirit is a son of God. The spirit you received is not the spirit of slaves bringing fear into your lives again; it is the spirit of sons, and it makes us cry out, "Abba, Father!" The Spirit himself and our spirit bear united witness that we are children of God. And if we are children we are heirs as well: heirs of God and coheirs with Christ, sharing his sufferings so as to share his glory. Romans 8:14-17 (JB)

Both the readings and the Scriptures speak of our relationship to God as being a growth process, conditional on our acceptance of the Christ and on our being responsive to the Holy Spirit. Reading 1709-3 makes this point again:

For, thou art in thyself divine! The mere fact or knowledge of thy existence in a material world, prompted by the activities or the movement of the Spirit itself, indicates thy own divinity; but to be attained! And this may never be done by holding grudges or disputations with any.

If both St. Paul and Edgar Cayce emphasized that one's body is the temple of God—if Divinity actually resides within each individual—then how can it be wrong to look within ourselves to that still small voice for answers and guidance? This is not selfishness or rebellion, but obedience to the same Holy Spirit that dwells within all souls who will allow themselves to be channels of God's blessings to others.

If it is true that Jesus came to remind us of the eternal nature of our souls, then it took less than a century for some early church writers to begin to question that truth. Several ministers, perhaps with thinking similar to that of some of the church fathers, have told me that it seems a bit presumptuous, perhaps even blasphemous, to believe that we are a part, or a facet, of God. Would we not treat others better, however, if we thought that they were God's children? If we believed that Divinity lives within every human being, would it not be harder to demonize those who believe differently from ourselves?

Gnostic vs. Orthodox: Faith Watered Down
A lot can change in a hundred years, especially in times of turmoil such as existed in first-century Israel. I believe that some of the church fathers who denied the eternal nature of the soul were simply mistaken about the beliefs of Jesus and the Jews of His day. Other than the New Testament, Josephus is still probably one of our best sources of knowledge about the beliefs of the Jews of the first century. He said:

> The bodies of all men are indeed mortal, and are created out of corruptible matter; but the soul is ever immortal, and is a portion of the Divinity that inhabits our bodies. [Here Josephus speaks strongly against suicide, then adds:] Do you not know that those who depart out of this life, according to the law of nature, and pay that debt which was received from God, when he that lent it us is pleased to require it back, enjoy eternal fame? That their houses and their posterity are sure, that their souls are pure and obedient, and obtain a most holy place in heaven, from whence, in the revolution of ages, they are again sent into pure bodies; (*The Wars of the Jews* 3.8.5)

As mentioned earlier, it is quite clear from Josephus that most Jews of his time believed not only in the divinity and the immortality of the soul, but also in a kind of metempsychosis, or reincarnation, in an age to come. Then how is it that this belief began to be questioned long before Origen or the church councils?
Having found no single authoritative source, I have read some of the works of early Christian writers such as Clement of Rome, Tertullian, Irenaeus of Lyons, Origen, and others. Many of these

writers expressed a strong reaction against those Hellenists who taught transmigration. Not being uneducated, however, these and other early church writers were probably influenced, as the Jewish writer Philo must have been, by some of the other popular forms of Greek thinking. Like many scholars today, they would have been familiar not only with the Greek classics, but also with some of the more worldly philosophers. Perhaps some Jewish members of the early churches were also influenced by Sadducee beliefs.

Groups of believers were, in any case, clearly polarized between the orthodox and the more esoteric thinkers. This is not to suggest that there were not many different schools of thought on both sides of the fence. St. Irenaeus of Lyons, for example, argued that our souls do not exist prior to our physical birth but that they will continue to exist after the body dies. In *Adversus Haeresus* (between C.E. 180 and 199) Irenaeus says, "...souls not only continue to exist, not by passing from body to body, but that they preserve the same form as the body had to which they were adapted, and that they remember the deeds which they did..." The notion that the soul could have existed prior to the body seems, however, to challenge his belief that "God alone, who is lord of all, is without beginning and without end..." He also argued strongly against transmigration. Most of Irenaeus's writings were directed against what he believed were false teachings of the various sects. It was during this time that the term "orthodox" (or "straight thinking") came into use.

I do not question the sincerity of these early orthodox Christian writers. Some sects may have been legitimate expressions of Christianity. Other sects did articulate erroneous, even idolatrous, beliefs about which people needed to be warned. There were other individuals who claimed to be the messiah. These people often claimed to work miracles and even attempted to mimic the works of Jesus. Sometimes, their followers tried to influence the Christian movement. The followers of Simon Magus may be an example of this phenomenon. Some of the more mystical sects are said to have believed that any new initiate had to distinguish himself or herself by writing some prophetic work. Today, many of their writings are seen as fiction or, at best, allegory.

Theological or philosophical questions may not have been the primary concern of many early Christians whose faith was largely experiential. Their Gospel taught that there was no other name by which spiritual healing could be found, and they had seen changed lives when people accepted the power of the Christ. Still, the more educated leaders knew that Jesus claimed to be one with God, and this brought up some theological questions that they felt compelled to answer. The dilemma for some of these church fathers seemed to be a fear that if all human beings were really children of God, who shared in His Divinity, then how could they insist on the necessity of believing in Jesus the Christ? On the other hand, how could Jesus be an example for us if He was not a soul made of the same substance as the rest of us?

Those who attempted to answer such questions often assumed that they spoke with some claim to authority. Few would question that there should be reverence for the apostles, respect for gifts of the Holy Spirit, and admiration for those who take the time to study things of the Spirit. However, the readings emphasize that God speaks directly to all and that Jesus is our advocate with the Father. Bishops, synods, liberals, conservatives, doctrines, and dogmas may all have their place, but the final church authority is Jesus who became the Christ. Speaking of the power struggles that took place in his day, Paul wrote: "So there is nothing to boast about in anything human: Paul, Apollos, Cephas, the world, life and death, the present and the future, are all your servants; but you belong to Christ and Christ belongs to God." (I Corinthians 3:22-23 JB)

Whether metaphysical or ecclesiastical, these questions about the eternal nature of the human soul profoundly affected the long-term beliefs and pronouncements of the early churches. Much of the resulting confusion is still woven into the fabric of modern Christianity, and has even affected the beliefs of Judaism and Islam.

Church Councils

The readings suggest that those early Christian sects known as Gnostics (some of whom may have also believed in reincarnation) thought that their knowledge gave them a shortcut to salvation. This may have pushed some of the church leaders in the direction of rejecting such knowledge altogether, but, in spite of all the sectarian differences, the early church continued to grow. The church in Rome and in other places took seriously the words of Jesus when He said that the way we treat others is the way we treat Him. While these early Christians may have been confused about some theological issues, they were not afraid to take up their cross and build their church on the massive charitable works that they did for the poor.

It is understandable that many Christians still felt the need for a greater degree of unity. Some church leaders, such as Clement of Rome, warned against partisanship. Eventually councils were held in the hopes that some of the divisive issues could be settled. These councils probably did serve to extend the church's influence in the world, but the balance between centralization of authority and the catholic or inclusive nature of the church was never easy to achieve.

While many of the pronouncements were organizational in nature, the church councils did address some theological questions. Their answers, however, were not always sufficient to create peace in the church. For example, the conclusion that the preexistent Christ was both God and man was not far off base, but, the question of the nature of mankind may not have been handled so well. In any case, many differing factions continued to exist among those who called themselves Christians.

Conclusions

Subsequent centuries are full of stories of sects, schisms, and isms. From the first century on, there have been numerous cycles of charismatics, puritans, and worldly philosophers, as well as those who have been called Gnostics. A good example of a Gnostic-like movement in the Middle Ages is the group known as Cathars. They combined a kind of belief in reincarnation with Persian myths. These groups generally opposed the ostentatious and worldly lifestyles of the orthodox church clergy of the day (possibly a reappearance of some of the ideas of the earlier Greek Cynics). Some of them renounced the material world as evil and even condemned conception as causing light (souls) to be trapped in darkness (physical bodies). In spite of their common anti-orthodox theology, different Cathar churches also argued vehemently with each other. Vestiges of some Cathar practices can still be found in orthodox traditions, but their rejection of the God of the Old Testament, the orthodox church's perception that they indulged in abhorrent sexual practices to avoid conception, and their rejection of Papal authority eventually resulted in many of them being brutally exterminated by the Inquisition.

In more recent times, the advent of the printing press precipitated many changes in the ways that human institutions operate. The church was no exception to this evolution in human affairs. Just as the Spirit of Truth had been available from the beginning to all that would listen, the written Word now became more universally accessible to all. The resulting changes were not always peaceful within the Christian Church.

If we could rewind the videotape of history and review the last two thousand years, what might we do differently? Could we avoid the divisions between orthodox and esoteric factions? Would we emphasize Christ as the common ground where extremes can meet? Could we avoid the religious over-zealousness that the Cayce readings warn against?

> Well if such had then learned the lesson given of old by Gamaliel, "If it be of God it will carry on, if it be of man it will of itself fail, and if of God we would only be fighting God." The influences and powers then in the earth indicate purposes, purposes! O what crimes have been committed in the name of religion!...
>
> From that sojourn the entity will find itself at times becoming overzealous of something that may deal with religion, and yet it is selfish in its nature. 3344-1

In addition to enriching our historical perspective on the Christian movement, the Cayce readings can renew our awareness of our potential for becoming children of God. While the readings call for tolerance and patience and abhor the selfish things that have been done in the name of religion, they never fail to champion the cross of Christ as the answer to the world's problems. Reading 2946-3 says:

> For, as given, ever must the cross of Jesus, who became the Christ, go before the entity, leading the way, as it were—to bring to mankind that alone which may bring peace in the hearts and souls of men.

13

From Denominationalism to Inspired Democracy: Unity in the Body of Christ

> Consider, for the moment, that the Master was the creator, the maker of all that was; and yet in establishing the church did He ask any? Rather He gave His blood, His body as the memorial. As this crystallized in the mind and the desire of those with the means materially, from the same arose spires, cathedrals, church buildings and schools.
>
> Do thou likewise. 1561-18

I was from a Catholic background. My wife had attended the Methodist church. After we were married and as we changed locations, we often chose a church home because of the congregation more than because of the denomination. The readings have been useful to me in various ways in my work in each of the churches that we have attended. When other church members have been aware of my interest in the readings, it has not caused any serious problems for me, but I am concerned that a few people have felt that this Work is not compatible with Christian beliefs. I would consider some of the comments in the readings to be strong constructive criticism of the churches, but I see no way that they could be construed as "against" the church, any more than Jesus was "against" the orthodox faith of His time.

As you can see from the following readings that contain advice to the A.R.E., Cayce was very careful to insist that the Work his readings inspired should not be in opposition to existing churches:

> To be sure, those phases of the activity of the Association, in the material plane, must take concrete evidence... of its being grounded in mental and spiritual truth. But not that it is to build up any organization that is to be as a cism [schism] or a cult or ism, or to build up money or wealth or fame, or position, or an office that is to function in opposition with *any* already organized group.

How did the Master work? In the church, in the synagogue, in the field, in the lakes, upon the sands and the mountains, in the temple! And did He defy those? Did He set up anything different? Did He condemn the law even of the Roman, or the Jews, or the Essenes, or the Sadducees, or any of the cults or isms of the day? All, He gave, are *one*—under the law! And grudges, cisms, isms, cults, must become as naught; that thy Guide, thy Way, thy Master, yea even Christ—as manifested in Jesus of Nazareth—may be made known to thy fellow man! 254-92

And if they are healed, helped, aided, in body, in mind, in purpose, all of those that time gives, be satisfied. For it is either the Lord's work or it is nothing at all. He will provide.

Let each and every soul, then, do their part. It is not the lauding of the Association or its purpose. For, the Association is such that it may never become a tenet or as that to supplant any organized work. As an ecclesiastical group may individuals work, but it must supply to the needs of every character of individual, whether they be of this or that faith. For the faith must be in the good, in the God, that is presented in same. 254-114

[Given to those who were preparing the A.R.E. study group program]...do not become a cism, an ism, laying down laws as to the morals or as to any set rules. For these as have been set have *one*—the Christ! Let those, those manners be, then, so that—whether these be the Parthenians, the Jews, the Catholics, the Protestants, the atheists or the agnostics—all will be seekers for truth, and seeking to know the *individual* relationship to Father-God and the relationships to the fellow man. These should be the burdens and these then find only those activities that correlate denominations, correlate the cisms, correlate the thoughts for a greater service for the fellow man... 262-100

I would guess that at least half of those who become interested in the Cayce readings also have some kind of church affiliation. It is inevitable that some of these individuals will try to apply the spiritual laws learned through this Work as they go about their work in their church.

Even with their human frailties, our churches have been the guardians of our spiritual, ethical, and moral values. In a reading for a person who was writing a book about sex education, Cayce said that little could be accomplished unless it could be presented in a way that would be used by the churches. The same advice may apply to the spiritual ideals given in the readings. I believe that we can learn to present these truths in a way that will help to bring about a spiritual renewal that has no denominational boundaries.

Church Politics

The readings say that much of what we call religion is really, to some extent, political. Originally, the term "Catholic" (universal), as used in the church, was very inclusive of many different traditions. Later, it was seen by some as being used to solidify power and to dictate modes of worship. Even after the Gutenberg press had made Bibles more available to the masses and the Protestant Reformation had occurred, church politics still had a great influence on spiritual beliefs. Luther emphasized Paul's writings about salvation through faith to disarm the authority of the Roman Catholic Church much as Paul had used the same principles to counter the legalism and exclusiveness of the Jewish establishment of his time.

It was an important step toward freedom of worship for such people to assert that they could not be told what to do by those who had assumed authority. Yet, those who followed the dissenters often set up new power structures of their own. In addition to the power struggles for leadership of various social and religious organizations, sociologists recognize that national, regional, economic, class, and racial agendas have often influenced the development of the various denominations. These new organizations often justified their authority with reactionary spiritual beliefs, some of which have been not only divisive, but possibly also quite detrimental to the whole Christian movement in the long run.

In the early days of the American experiment, there was a proliferation of various church expressions, most of them imported, to some extent, from Europe. There was nothing inherently wrong with having different organizations to meet the needs of various people, but there was far too much bickering, bigotry, and condemnation among these groups to suit some people. Perhaps the Body of Christ was not working as harmoniously as Paul had envisioned in I Corinthians 12:12-30.

With the intent of bringing about greater unity among the Protestant churches, Thomas Campbell, the Scottish reformer, along with Barton Stone and others, fostered the Restoration Movement, which sought to heal the centuries of divisions and to reestablish the unity of the New Testament church. Campbell suggested the motto: "Where the scriptures speak, we speak; and where the scriptures are silent, we are silent." He believed that if all Christians agreed on the essential biblical truths, then there would be room for diversity of expression. At least a part of this movement became known as the Christian Church (Disciples of Christ).

Although the readings reflect no particular bias for or against any particular group, Edgar Cayce was raised in the Christian Church (Disciples of Christ) and, to some extent, was a product of the Restoration Movement. This might help explain his belief in the unity of the Church. We might even see a glimmer of Campbell's desire for simplicity in the following reading:

> Also the entity may find, as it did then, that not only are political and religious views the basis of many of the disputes in the lives of individuals, but that the entity may hold to *all*—or that the purpose, yea the intent of religion is that *peace* may be to body and mind of those who embrace same.
>
> Then the fewer definitions there be of that to which an individual is to subscribe, the greater may be the peace and the harmony in the experience of every soul.
>
> *Hold* to those things. For, as then, they are as lights to the many that find troubled minds in the confusion of the varied groups or sects of peoples.
>
> ...the simpler the life the greater it may be. 1467-3

Church Membership

Knowing of the many misguided or outright selfish things that have been done in the name of religion, I can understand why some sincere spiritual seekers have removed themselves from the confines of traditional "churchianity." The Cayce readings warn against the dangers of blind adherence to manmade doctrines, the narrowing mentality of denominationalism, and the spiritual atrophy that results from too much dependence upon ritual. When I read from 262-17, "If *form* becomes that that is the guiding element, then the hope or the faith is lost in form!" I knew that the Spirit was speaking to me. I also felt a resonance with reading 1767-2 which says:

> Yet for the entity, the basis of that taught by Him *is* that the way, the truth, the light may be free for all; and that the choice in the present, as then, must be within the individual rather than that as may be given as authoritative by any group or individual who would act in the capacity of a director.

After studying these ideals, I could never again be bound by sectarian or provincial modes of worship. With A.R.E. study groups that are so interesting and fulfilling, it is easy to question why one should belong to a church at all. There are secular ways to get married, counseled, and buried.

Not all church experiences are negative, however. Even after being freed from doctrines and dogmas, there is a natural attraction to associate with others who love God. Even though there may be no such thing as a perfect church, most of us find people who care when we are in need and people who need our love and concern. If, by default, we are excommunicated from the churches, we will miss the fellowship, worship, and charitable works that take place there. If we have a Christian perspective such as that found in the Cayce readings, we may also miss opportunities to share this spiritual heritage with those faithful people who have made a commitment to work within the churches.

Life reading 2780-3 was given for a ten-year-old boy who was somewhat indifferent or cynical about spiritual matters and perhaps not too happy about going to church:

> Because the entity is averse to being dictated to, or of being in the form of policy, is no reason that there is not truth in the tenets of the church, or the laws and regulations thereof. Because others have made a sham of same is no reason for thee to make a sham.

For as ye will analyze and study in thy life, that place or that community without the house of worship is not sought after—by even the most wicked of men. 2780-3

Another person was told, "Keep not thyself away from that thou *knowest* to be good. Attend the Lord's house more often." (934-7) The question of which church to attend touches on some much more complex issues:

Thus we find that through the formative years the directions as should be indicated for the entity should be close in touch with the teachings of the church—not as that of a dogmatic influence, but for its beauty, its truth, its basic forces, that should be the principle in each and *every* life.

...and especially the voice training should be a part of the entity's experience. And then choose for itself, as to the directions in which these may be taken, *after* its seventeenth or eighteenth year...

(Q) In what church should the entity be taught?
(A) There's only one church! 1990-3

(Q) Should I affiliate with any particular church organization?
(A) A particular church organization is well. For it centers the mind. But don't get the idea that you have the whole cheese. 3350-1

Someone once told me of a person who told a preacher that he didn't attend church because it was too full of hypocrites. The preacher replied, "That's no excuse. We always have room for one more." Thank God, we are free to go or not go to church in this country. We are also free to change churches if we find some other affiliation to be more constructive. Reading 3342-1 told a thirty-one-year-old woman who asked what church she should join, "...choose that—not as a convenience for thee but where ye may serve the better, whatever its name—let it be thy life proclaiming Jesus, the Christ."

The True Church

After a family member had joined a particular church about which I knew very little, I was in the A.R.E. library in Virginia Beach, looking for information on that group. A lady who worked in the library was helping me find what I was looking for. Talking mostly to myself, I said, "I wonder why there are so many different churches?" The librarian suggested that perhaps this was a natural part of the growth process of the church. Just as our physical body starts from a single cell and divides into different types of cells for different purposes, so it is natural for new churches to form. However, because of our desire to have our leaders speak with absolute authority, many of these groups have claimed to be the only "True Church." Some leaders of cults, sects, or even mainline churches, feel that they, their guides, or their sacred documents, have the most direct line of communication with God and, therefore, they are the only dispensers of truth.

As a young adult, I talked with many of my friends as they struggled with making a commitment to follow some particular faith. In today's world, it is becoming less common for people to share a religious background with spouse or friends. Interfaith marriages sometimes seem to be the rule rather than the exception. I once knew a person who was one of ten children. This person told me that each of the ten had married someone of a different faith. The resulting conflicts had destroyed what had been a very close and loving family. This kind of divisiveness is working in opposition to the higher purpose of any church. Yet, those within many of the sects (or denominations) seem to be unaware of the poor souls who may be hurt or confused by their claims to be the only correct church.

Cayce's ability to make some sense out of this confusing array of religious expressions is one of the things that impressed me the most about the readings. His advice to various individuals was more discerning and astute than any other source that I had ever experienced. Quite refreshingly, Cayce never made any claims of authority for himself.

A young Lutheran missionary, who was courting a Catholic girl, asked Cayce if the Roman Catholic Church was "the true Church founded by Jesus Christ through the Apostles?" He also asked if it would benefit him to "change to the Catholic religion." The answer was:

This would depend upon who was asking for such. As we would give here, the *church* as founded by Jesus Christ was, is, the Catholic Church; but *not* the *Roman* Catholic Church! This has rather been added, as have most of those—in their activities—that call or classify themselves as churches. For, the true church is within you, as the Master, as the Christ gave Himself: "I to *you* am the bridegroom—I to *you* am the church. The kingdom is within *you!*" Hence that which has been coordinated into the bodies in any activity is a representation *of* that which has gathered together for coordinating activity in whatever field; but are most man made. 452-7

After the above statement, Cayce went on to tell this person that there should be no problem with changing his membership to the Roman Catholic Church if it was consistent with his conscience and his existing relationships. Just in case you are wondering, the young man did not make this change, but later became an accountant and married a Baptist girl.

Methods of Salvation

Most religious people understand the idea that our sins or mistakes have spiritually separated us from God. The process of being reconciled to God is usually called "salvation." While many liberal and New Age thinkers may tend to reject the concept of salvation altogether, many others still see some correlation between their faith and their salvation. The question of how salvation is effected has been a divisive issue among various religious groups.

During one of our study group meetings several years ago, we discussed the question of whether salvation comes to a person through faith or by works. My wife had been very interested in this discussion, and that night she had a dream about it. In the dream, she had asked someone how a person could be saved. The answer she was given was, "Salvation is by faith and works, and it comes to those who love the Lord." I don't know where this answer came from, but it seemed to resonate with my understanding of the Bible. I later found this in reading 262-75: "While ye wander, search thine own heart and *know* as of old that faith is counted as righteousness to those that love the Lord."

James, the brother of Jesus, wrote his epistle partly to correct those who had misunderstood and misapplied Paul's teachings about salvation. Taken in context, Paul obviously knew that we are saved (from our own selfishness that separates us from God) by nurturing our relationship with God and being "faithful," rather than just by believing in God. In Romans 2:6-7 (JB) Paul says, *"He will repay each one as his works deserve.* For those who sought renown and honour and immortality by always doing good there will be eternal life." In other words, salvation is dependent on our trying, with God's help, to live up to our purpose for having been created—to be companions to God. Even so, some Protestant reformers also tended to stress faith as the only requirement for salvation, and even suggested that perhaps the letter of James should be removed from the New Testament.

The best that we can do today is to see the best in every organization and hope that they will all continue to reform and grow toward the truth. I wonder what John the beloved would write today if he had a revelation about modern churches?

I have worshiped in traditions that emphasize a sacramental system and have a well-defined liturgy. Most people in these organizations are well aware that their rituals are only symbolic of inner changes that must be made, but it may be possible for a person to feel justified by having performed the outward signs without really being in a right relationship with God.

I have also worshiped with groups who, referring to the teachings of the Apostle Paul, insist that works do not count and that salvation comes by faith alone. Many of these people will admit that faith that does not produce good results is not the real thing. Yet, there may be those who feel comfortable in their salvation, while ignoring the part that individual and social responsibility play in spiritual growth.

Still other groups emphasize obedience to the Scriptures or salvation by being baptized into the church. Such groups may provide a social structure that helps members conform to standards that they might otherwise be unable to live up to. These groups can be very good for some individuals, as long as the group is not expected to do the work of the Holy Spirit.

There are also those who look for the manifestation of some spiritual gift as evidence of their salvation. The Gifts of the Spirit, as spoken of in Acts and elsewhere in the Bible, are wonderful manifestations of the Holy Spirit and can be useful for building up the church. The Bible cautions us never to try to suppress or speak against such gifts, but we are also cautioned not to be lulled by these gifts into losing our humility and our relationship to Christ in the process.

During reading 281-34, Cayce was asked to explain the symbol of the second beast in Revelation 13:

> As has been given by Him, the power as attained by the study that has been shown in the first portions is to be applied, or may be applied unworthily—as is shown by the beast with two ways, two horns. Then here, how hath it been given? One Lord, one faith, one God, one baptism, one way! Yet in the experiences as ye watch about you there are constantly shown the influences by the very forces of the beast with the double-mindedness, as showing wonders in the earth yet they must come even as He hath given, "though ye may have done this or that, though ye may have healed the sick, though ye may have cast out demons in my name, I know ye not; for ye have followed rather as the beast of self-aggrandizement, self-indulgence, self-glorification," even as the beast shown here.

The above approaches to religion are effectively used to varying degrees in many churches, but methods or forms of worship cannot take the place of a personal relationship with God. While always encouraging us to be a part of the community of faith, the readings frequently challenge us to keep our focus on the Christ:

> For indeed as has been said, this or that teacher or exhorter may water, may even plant the seed, but only in *Him* that *is* the truth and the way and the life may such seed, or such hopes, such understanding, such peace and such security of every nature that is sought be found. 1809-1

> Hence we will find that experience gradually making for the advancement by the close adherence to those principles as He set; not as dogmatic influences of an orthodox activity—these He did not teach! For the whole gospel as He gave is, "Thou shalt love the Lord, thy God, with all thy

heart, thy mind, thy body; and thy neighbor as thyself."
1401-1

Denominationalism or Sectarianism

The readings often referred to the lack of tolerance for those who believe differently from us as "denominationalism." This tendency to divide people into various factions might also be called "partisanship" or "sectarianism." At the risk of seeming redundant, I would like to explore what the readings say about this subject in a little more depth.

If our religious affiliations are motivated by faith in the One God, then we might wonder why there is contention among various groups. People seem to have a great need to belong to something that gives them an identity. This is not just a religious phenomenon. Traditionally, tribes, states, nations, schools, families, and other organizations have also given people a sense of identity. Within these groups, we learn cooperation and teamwork, but there is also the danger of false pride. We need to discern whether our institutions really help us to grow spiritually or whether they become self-justifying and self-perpetuating for their own worldly purposes. Nothing really satisfies the soul except knowing that we are growing in our relationship to God. The following reading warns against idolizing even our church:

Man is hedged about by beliefs, by cults, by schisms, by isms—yes. And those things have been created by man that he hath given power in themselves to rule his days. Yet this is only because man has given them such power. For the spirit of truth and wisdom is mighty, and a bulwark of faith and hope to those that trust in Him. But they that give others, other things, power over themselves become subject unto them. Thus hath He declared, as was given of Him who is the way, the truth and the light, the first, yea the whole of the commandment of the Lord is encompassed in this: "Thou shalt have no other god before me, neither in heaven nor in earth, nor in things seen or unseen, but thou shalt love the Lord thy God with all thine heart, thine soul and thine body, and thy neighbor as thyself." 2454-4

In its simplest definition, the word *cult* applies to any religious practice. We use the word in a different way, however, to denote those sects that seem to be too controlling of their members, and we also tend to think of cults as being small fringe groups. Being a large mainline denomination, however, does not automatically exclude a church from being manipulative of its members or of becoming self-serving. The readings warned of these dangers:

> Press and impress each more and more...that the trust must be in *Him*, not *in* the group! The group is only lending their power, their ability, to make more aware the needs of each individual so seeking of that power! ...Let thine purpose be in expressing, in manifesting, His power. All praises give unto Him! Not in what I did, we did, or the other! The praise, the power, is in Him. 281-9

I have known many people who have been turned off by what they felt to be oppressive practices in their church, while the same church environment may have seemed comfortable to others. If our church does not provide opportunities for service and spiritual growth, then we should consider Galatians 5:1 (JB); "When Christ freed us, he meant us to remain free. Stand firm, therefore, and do not submit again to the yoke of slavery."

Cayce also frequently dealt with the problems created when differences occur among groups. As usual, he told them to look for areas of agreement. He even said that stressing differences would bring spiritual death to the organization that does so:

> Minimize rather than magnify disagreements in every organized group for the teaching of the holy word. For know that these in their true spiritual meaning are unchangeable. For God is one Lord, and the Christ is the same, yesterday, today and forever.
>
> There may be different channels of approach, yes. For not all peoples walked in the field when the wheat was ripe. Neither did all stand at the tomb when Lazarus was called forth. Neither were they all present when He walked on the water, nor when He fed the five thousand, nor when He hung on the Cross. Yet each experience answered, and does answer to something within each individual soul-entity. For each soul is a corpuscle in the body of God. And when differences arise in a body, where corpuscles are at variance to a common purpose for all, sin enters, and

death by sin, to whatever may be that group, that organization, that is stressing differences rather than the coordinating channels through which all may come to the knowledge of God. 3395-2

We find the same contentions arising in that· called in the present denominationalism, and each one crying, "Lo, here is Christ—Lo, this is the manner of approach—Lo, unless ye do this or that ye have no part in Him." "He that loves me will keep my commandments." What are the commandments? "Thou shalt have no other *God* before me." and "Love thy neighbor as thyself." In this is builded the whole *law* and gospel of every age that has said, "There is *one* God!" 364-9

...there is needed in the earth those who will constantly remind the young of their obligations to God and to man, and to remember that the greater service to the Father-God is the manner in which one treats the fellow man, for this is the manner in which one treats one's Maker.
This in itself should convince anyone of the senselessness of denominationalism, and how hard for the entity to give it up! Yet the growth has gradually come. For God is not a respecter of persons, it is true. Neither does He care in the way that individuals do for a name, or as to what people will say. Truth is truth and it convicteth the soul. The soul alone is eternal. 3179-1

(Q) In what way can I best serve as a member of the Association? [A.R.E.]
(A) ...It is Association by name only, the work is within thine own heart and mind to the glory of Christ, the King. 5277-1

Cayce spoke firmly against denominationalism, but that does not mean that he believed that there should be only one large organization or that each of the churches did not have a purpose:

As He has given, it will ever be found that Truth— whether in this or that schism or ism or cult—is of the One source. Are there not trees of oak, of ash, of pine? There are the needs of these for meeting this or that experience. Hast thou chosen any one of these to be the *all* in thine own usages in thine own life?

Then, all will fill their place. Find not fault with *any*, but rather show forth as to just how good a pine, or ash, or oak, or *vine*, thou art! 254-87

For there must be every type, else where would the opportunity come for those who seek to manifest God in the earth? It is indeed not strange there are even in the protestant churches, Methodist, Christian, Baptist, Congregational or the what, but it is to meet the needs. What is God? All things to all men that all might know Him. Not that one is better than the other. 2072-15

A few readings mention specific denominations. Several excerpts are included here, not to draw attention to these groups, but to demonstrate Cayce's open-mindedness:

[For a 58-year-old Protestant woman who asked what she should do about her favorite niece who married a Catholic] Art thou a good Catholic thyself? If thou art not, have ye not missed the way?

That is not as of finding fault because of some material manifested way. Is He not God and Lord of the Catholic as well as of the Protestant and of the Jew? Did He not make them all? Does He not love one the same as another? Know ye not that He is not a respecter of persons? Art thou?

Then, *who* is at fault? 2783-1

[For a person who had been a Quaker in a previous life] You will find greater strength, then, in those tenets of the brethren than in any other organized group. But remember, all that have the truth, that recognize the coming of God in the flesh, have a place and will contribute to the greater development of all. So, look upon same not as a closed organization. For, He is all things to all men, that there may be the true answer in "The Lord is one." 3053-3

(Q) Am I the chosen channel for the enlargement of Methodism in more vital, Christian relationships, as given through the call of the W.E.C.?

(A) A channel. Few would choose to be *the* channel. For, *the* channel must be *Him*. But as a representative of Him in such a service, *well* chosen. Well to magnify, not any cult or denomination—for Christ is Lord of all. Through that organization, well—but magnify the Christ, *not* the method. 2574-1

In several health-related readings, Cayce told a person to find a nurse who was trained in Christian Science or Unity. He told them that this would help them to depend upon the healing forces from within. When a college student asked if Unity was the best spiritual endeavor for her, however, the reading said:

Unity is a field of endeavor. The *truth*—as in Him—is the way! The church is in thyself. For, thy body is the temple of the living God. *there* He hath promised to meet thee. Hence not in an organization, not in a name, not in a title; for there is only one Name given under heaven whereby man may be saved, and He hath promised, "If ye love me and keep my commandments, I will come and abide with thee."

Make that not merely a saying, that may be passed by, but—as ye are practical—*live* it! As ye are living, *do* it! As ye are kind, live it in *every* way. *that* is the Christ way; and bespeaks unity of purpose with all that would do good. 2403-1

Cayce seemed to be saying that the way to avoid denominationalism is not by self-justification, but by living our faith without condemning anyone:

...if thou art worthy, Christ-like in the material, ye are Christ-like in the broader sense in the mental—and how much greater in the spiritual! The same as in those who are very devout without—as a Catholic, as a Protestant—as of such and such creed or faith; how much smaller have they grown within! 281-32

Walk with it—not talk it, but *live it—be it;* and ye will find while that which is so orthodox or denominational will not be so apparent, the love as He speaks of, the new commandment "Love ye one another" will persuade, will direct, will aid, will keep thee. 2205-2

Arguments will seldom change the aspects or the views of any. And truth itself needs no champion, for it is of itself champion of champions—and needs no defense; only for self to live according to that which *is* the truth! 1669-1

Church Unity

St. Paul wrote against the partisan spirit that affected the early church. Near the end of the first century, Clement of Rome was still warning Christians against partisanship. We are still dealing with divisiveness today, but if one authoritarian church organization is not the solution to the confusion of competing isms, then how do we move toward unity? In other words, what centripetal force can we apply to counter the centrifugal forces that pull us apart?

When the only unifying force is a claim to orthodoxy accompanied by narrow dogmas, then other groups tend to spin off and claim their own authority. On the other hand, when inclusiveness is taken to mean "anything goes," the promise of eternal life is often sacrificed to accommodate the worldly minded.

According to the readings, spiritual unity can come only from being one in purpose, not necessarily one in actions or modes of worship. In sports, in work, and even in the military, we often learn teamwork. We cannot prevail against the opponent if we are fighting and competing among ourselves. Having a common ideal helps us to rise above sectarianism. When I am asked what church I belong to, I often tell people that I belong to all organizations that are dedicated to following the Master. It is a little like having a "Master Card" that is acceptable anywhere.

We can even achieve a degree of unity with those of other religions when we are in agreement about our ideals. A Jewish businessman was told:

The entity gained much in the experience [a prior life], and in the present from same the entity finds that whether the associations are with those within or without the own faith—if they are true to *their* purposes—they are one! In this has tolerance come... 619-5

Baptism and Communion were two practices, both mentioned in the Bible, that held the early church together. At times, however, they have both been interpreted in ways that have contributed to the divisions among believers. Cayce's own church may have believed in adult baptism by immersion, but reading 2072-15 seems to demonstrate a degree of tolerance for other expressions when it says, "Just as an individual, seeking God, finds in self. He must have lots of water to wash his sins away and the other may do it with a drop, but the water and the blood must be there."

Many of these issues that have divided churches in past centuries have been almost forgotten, only to resurface from time to time. They will continue to plague us until we learn to put them to rest by focusing on our common ideals. Here is another reading that was given for the A.R.E:

(Q)   ...How is the best way to cooperate with other organizations who are in sympathy with or who have an understanding of this work?

(A) As has so oft been given. Let those that are sincere, that are honest with themselves, seek not the differences in the organizations but where they may cooperate. And as they do, you will find—as with these that are gathered here, they are of many faiths, many creeds, yet they find one common purpose—*good* to thy fellow man! So, as those that have found in this vision, in this interpretation, or in that promotion or in that experience of this or that nature, seek rather the common interest where there *is* cooperation, rather than the differences. And then if any group, if any organization, if any association has not this, it has not the full soul. 254-95

Reading 1152-11 speaks about the need for unity among all seekers:

...and its [1152's] abilities as a speaker, its abilities as a writer should be directed in those conditions and affairs that will more and more *unite* seekers in every phase of life, in every position, in every portion of the country, to that standard set by Him. Not as in a church, not as in an ism or cult, but in that every soul does the best he can where he is—and all with one ideal: "I am my brother's keeper— Christ the Lord is my brother!"

We should constantly be on guard against condoning any barriers within the Body of Christ. The readings do warn, however, that we must also be careful not to be a part of anything that is based on unbelief. Reading 333-6 says, "Join not with unbelievers, yet let thy yeas be yea and thy nays be nay. Be not unequally yoked together with those that make for stumbling in any direction." I believe that some of the issues that have been so divisive in churches in recent years are really red herrings that distract from the fact that much of modern theology has ignored the great human need for knowledge about the continuity of life. Believing that all souls are children of the Living God does not cause us to take advantage of our fellow man. It makes no sense, for example, that some see economic and social justice as being at odds with belief in eternal life. The following statement may have been a reaction to the spiritual pessimism that has permeated many of the issues that have divided churches:

That these (the theological and the spiritual) have grown and are growing farther and farther apart in the affairs of man as a whole, as is viewed by the entity, is a fault—a failure of man to grasp the *one* thought, the *one* ideal, that would be held in such a way as to know that these must be *one*, in that "I *am* my brother's keeper!" 1473-1

If churches are to be effective, then those who believe in God's justice, eternal life, and the power of Jesus the Christ must continue to reform them, not through any reactionary process and not by some kind of prophetic finger pointing, but by the silent power of unselfishness.

Lean upon the arm of the *Divine* within thee, giving not place to thoughts of vengeance or discouragements. Give not vent to those things that create prejudice. And, most of all, be *unselfish!* 254-87

Jesus Is the Church

Cayce's answer to questions on church authority is that Jesus himself is the Church. In Him, we make up the Body of Christ. Church organizations are merely physical manifestations of that Body. Perhaps these readings will speak to you as they did to me:

[Speaking of the Work of the A.R.E.] Not a new doctrine—not even a new thought; but rather showing that there *is* something that each individual can do *about* the fact that Jesus the Christ is the way! Wherever the individual is, or no matter in what position in life he may be. 254-108

For here ye may find the answer again to many of those questions sought concerning the Spirit, the Church, the Holy Force that manifests by the attuning of the individual; though it may be for a moment. He asked, "Whom say men that I am?" Then Peter answered, "Thou art the Christ, the son of the living God!" Then, "Upon this I will build my church, and the gates of hell shall not prevail against it." He said to Peter, "Flesh and blood—*flesh* and blood—hath not revealed this unto thee, but my Father which is in heaven." Heaven? Where? Within the hearts, the minds; the place where Truth is made manifest! 262-87

The better is the church within self, not by name or place. For the church is the living Christ. Make association first with that, and whether it is in this, that or the other name, Christ ye serve and not a church! 2823-3

Then *who* is the bridegroom, and who is the bride? Thyself—thy Lord!
Trust not any other than Him. For as He gave it was not that ye should come unto Peter nor to Paul, but "unto *me!* If ye will abide in *me*, I will come and abide with thee!" 1597-1

And if He chooses a director or guide to walk with thee day by day, well; but why walk with a disciple when ye may walk with the Master! 2441-2

There were times when Edgar Cayce was rejected by some of the people in his own church because of his Work with the readings. Much to his credit, he remained loyal to the church throughout his life. But I am glad that he continued to seek the truth directly from the source of all truth and light.

Inspired Democracy

Ours is not the only country today in which people are free to attend the church of their choice or to stay at home. We may act out of habit, but to the degree that church attendance is voluntary, there is an element of democracy in all churches. We vote with our feet by going where we choose to go. My wife and I once stopped attending a church where many members had been very warm and friendly to us, but where we did not want our children to hear the negativity that was preached toward other denominations. I have sat through several sermons in my life when, in retrospect, I should have simply walked out.

As people have become more educated, churches, like governments and other organizations, have become more democratic and participative. Although democracy does not ensure correctness, it gives each person the opportunity to be a channel of God's spirit. Jesus said that where two or three are gathered in His name, He will be there. We can all read our Bibles. We are children of the new covenant, and God's law is written in our hearts. We are a nation of priests. (See Exodus 19:6, Isaiah 61:6, 1 Peter 2:9, Revelation 1:6.) We have a responsibility, as well as a right, to have an input into the organizations within which we function, but we should also be willing to be accountable for the outcome of our decisions. The Bible warns us that there will be those groups that give people whatever they want to hear. If our churches focus only on membership or sidestep the cross to make the Gospel more palatable to the material-minded, then the democratic process will not work.

I like to think of the church of the future as an "inspired democracy," wherein each individual speaks, not out of self-interest, but out of concern for all, while expecting God to direct him or her through the still, small voice within. When we listen to God for guidance, the answer may not always come in a loud voice or in an utterance from a prophet. We will have to develop the gift of discernment and, as we work within any organization, we will

199

most likely also have to develop the gift of tolerance. For many people, the difficult part of applying the democratic process is accepting the fact that every other person has just as much potential for listening to the Holy Spirit as we do. Some of the Jews at the time of Jesus did not accept the writings of the Prophets that we know from the Old Testament. They considered the Mosaic Law to be the last and final revelation. Some Christians believe that the New Testament is God's final revelation to humankind. But, we worship a living God and we have a living Church. Some churches revere the great leaders of their various movements, but we are all called to be builders of the Church. The churches should not be saying to people, "We have all the answers and we need your help to spread our message." They should be saying, "We need your help in listening to God so that we can have a better vision of how to build God's kingdom in the earth."

Someone once suggested that, if all of the mainline denominations would separate into liberals and conservatives, then they could combine all of each faction into a single group and there would be only two large groups where everyone would be happy. Life, however, is not always that simple. Without some cohesive force, factions would develop in any group and, eventually, result in more divisions.

In a life reading, a nineteen-year-year-old college girl who was considering a teaching career was told that she would find herself in many situations where there would be those with opposing views. The reading went on to say:

> Remember, only in Christ, Jesus, do extremes meet. And in thy activity through each experience, ask self oft, "What would Jesus have me do?" For He faileth not those who seek. 1981-1

This is pretty good advice for getting along with others in any situation. I believe that this kind of inspired democracy within the churches will eventually make it easier to apply spiritual lessons, such as those found in the Cayce readings, in any organization.

No Patent on Spirituality

Jesus said that those He sent out to preach deserved their wages. Those who labor professionally within the churches should be able to earn a living doing so. But churches and other spiritual organizations do not have to create systems that attempt to make people artificially dependent upon them.

"The silver and the gold is mine," saith the Lord. Begin—as was given to the prophet of old—"What hast thou in hand?" and this same rod, cast before Pharaoh, brought the plagues to the nation. The same spread over the sea divided same. The same brought consternation when smiting the rock, and said, "Shall I (not shall God) give this stubborn and stiff-necked people?" 254-31

It might be better if every church and congregation would strive to be *a* true church rather than *The* True Church. Jesus said, "Then let all who are thirsty come: all who want it may have the water of life, and have it free." (Revelation 22:17 JB) Jesus was not concerned that a man who was preaching the Gospel was not one of His disciples (Mark 9:38). Likewise, when church leaders see spirituality practiced in the business place or elsewhere, they need not automatically feel that their turf has been challenged. According to the readings, this may be a good thing:

These are not principles that are for the church alone, nor for the lodge, nor social organizations; but more and more the principles to be applied in the experience of the business man, the social man, in the everyday life. Thus may better the glory of the Lord shine through thine experience. 416-7

Witness to the Readings
If the Work of the A.R.E. is seen by some as an "alternative" spiritual expression, this speaks more to the failure of established institutions to answer spiritual needs than it does to any purpose in the readings to set up anything new or to detract in any way from the work of the Master that is being done through other organizations. Reading 254-115 says, "Do not ever attempt to convince, to impress, even to 'expose' the work to those who do not of themselves seek same." On the other hand, the readings say that we should not miss any opportunity to share the Gospel with those who are ready to hear it:

In the Lord's house are many mansions. In thy mind and heart are many possibilities, many opportunities. Lose not a single one to make known the love that the Master has for the children of men. 5758-1

If ye would find and know mercy before Him, be merciful and kind to those in whatever faith or whatever group ye may find them.

Oft ye will find, if ye so live, that others may say, "What has caused you to do this or that?" Not as a crank, not as one bereft of this or that. Live even as He, in thine social life, in thine home life, in thine business life, in thine own expressions everywhere, in such a way and manner as to bespeak that which thou would have thy God, thy Christ, to do or to be to thee. 254-87

(Q) How can this group best meet the conditions that have arisen in relation to the Church?

(A) Do the lessons not make the individuals that are members of individual churches *better* Christians, better or nearer Christ-like; thus filling their lives with such love that dogmatic principles (as in some churches) must be taboo? But present them to those that are weak, *living* them before those that *stumble*—but do not cram them down anyone's throat! Neither argue with them! Did thy Master ever argue, even when there were the greater railings or abuses? He presented that which each *has* found, did find, convicted them. What said He respecting that? "I do not condemn thee, for thou art condemned already in thine own self." So, in the approach to those influences, the truths and lessons as presented—and *lived* by individuals—should fill the needs, even in the greater or higher places in any individual organization; and may fill some with awe—and they may speak evil. So did the High Priest condemn thine Lord! So did those of the Sanhedrin wreak their own purposes upon Him. Yea, art thou willing to live that which has proved and does prove in thine experience that which makes thee closer with thy God? If these lessons are not founded in such, have nothing to do with them. 262-61

I know that this Work has changed my life for the better, and I am comfortable sharing it with other seekers because I know of the strong commitment in the readings to the Christian faith, but I am also aware that living these principles is not always easy.

"Feed My Sheep"

The readings also say that the church should be a place where souls are fed: "Then the partaking of those emblems—or of that body and that blood—supplies or becomes food for the soul." (262-89) Perhaps there are those in the churches who have experienced the power of Christ and are trying to keep the faith, who might be pleasantly surprised to know what a source of comfort the readings can be.

In the late 1960s, I attended an interdenominational weekend retreat that included many Roman Catholic participants. A priest, who was a part of the team sponsoring the program, said that he had been troubled by some of the changes that had occurred, both in theology and in moral values within the churches. He said that he had spent some time out in the woods alone, as he did from time to time, to pray and meditate about his concerns. Then he felt that he had received a clear answer: "Don't worry about what others do; just feed my sheep." He knew that all he had to do was to continue to teach the Gospel. This same message was often given in the readings:

And then as He gave to that Disciple, He requires of everyone, "feed my lambs, feed my sheep." For all have fallen short, yet recognizing in self that of thyself ye can do nothing, but only as the spirit of truth directeth, ye may accomplish much. 5758-1

For, as He gave, "If ye love me, feed my lambs. If ye love me, feed my sheep."

As the entity finds in its contact with individuals daily, many have forsaken—as ye would be tempted to do—daily communion with the Christ-Consciousness, the daily attuning of self. For, as everyone—and as this entity should comprehend, God in Christ is the same, ever. Not that any individual may by persuasion attain to having the Christ or the Father on his side, but rather there needs to be the attuning of self to the Christ-Consciousness, the oft and regular attuning of self in body, in mind, in spirit, to that oneness to which each soul may attain. 540-18

Then, as He gave to those ever, ye that have gained, that have tasted of the bread of life, "Feed my sheep, feed my lambs." 1150-1

14

Finding Common Ideals:
Other Religions

Fortunately, much of my formal education came after I had begun to study the Cayce readings. My study of religion was intellectually and historically informative and therefore helpful in understanding others. However, while carefully designed to avoid being partial, many of the books that I read on religion seemed like an affront to my faith, and I suspect that adherents of other religions must feel the same way. I was not bothered by the objectivity but by the subtle assumption that mankind had invented God. There also seemed to be an avoidance of any coherent awareness of the action of God's spirit in the affairs of mankind.

While most of the Cayce readings are clearly Christian in purpose, they avoid portraying other religions as being in opposition to Christianity. Even though he recognized that beliefs differ, Cayce often told people to look more for the parallels and the things on which all may agree. This information also recognizes that other paths sometimes teach service and humility, and the readings even call them "lights along the way" to becoming sons and daughters of God. Still, Cayce did put Jesus above other prophets and teachers, and I know that this may not be comfortable for everyone.

Within most religions, there is a wide range of beliefs. There are those who insist that they have the exclusive truth. They believe that membership in their organization or observance of their rules is the only path to salvation. Some of them even tend see all other religions as demonic. Toward the other end of the spectrum are those who say that faith in any prophet or teacher is the same. These people often assume that every soul will blissfully return to God sooner or later, no matter what they do. Rather than accepting either extreme or no faith at all, most of us would rather try to discern what really works for us to make our lives better.

Religion is a vital part of the fabric of most cultures, and it will not just disappear. As our world shrinks and people move around more, it is natural that there would be more friction among belief systems. Reading 3976-8, given in January 1932, addresses the problems of interfaith conflicts:

With the advent of the closeness of the worlds coming into being, so that the man upon the other side of the world is as much the neighbor as the man next door, more and more have been the turmoils that have arisen in the attempt of individual leaders or groups to induce, force or compel, one portion of the world to think as the other, or the other group to dwell together as brethren with one bond of sympathy, or one standard for all.

With the present conditions, then, that exist—these have all come to that place in the development of the human family where there must be a reckoning, a one point upon which all may agree, that out of all of this turmoil that has arisen from the social life, racial differences, the outlook upon the relationship of man to the Creative Forces or his God, and his relationships one with another, must come to some *common* basis upon which all *may* agree. You say at once, such a thing is impractical, impossible! What has caused the present conditions, not alone at home but abroad? It is that realization that was asked some thousands of years ago, "Where *is* thy brother? His blood *cries* to me from the ground!" and the other portion of the world has answered, *is* answering, "Am I my brother's keeper?" The world, *as* a world—that makes for the disruption, for the discontent—has lost its ideal. Man may not have the same *idea.* Man—*all* men—may have the same *ideal!*

As the Spirit of God once moved to bring peace and harmony out of chaos, so must the Spirit move over the earth and magnify itself in the hearts, minds and souls of men to bring peace, harmony and understanding, that they may dwell together in a way that will bring that peace, that harmony, that can only come with all having the one ideal; not the one idea, but "Thou shalt love the Lord thy God with all thine heart, thy neighbor as thyself!" This [is] the whole law, this [is] the whole answer to the world, to each and every soul.

In another world affairs reading, during even more difficult times (June 1942), Cayce was asked about how to deal with religious differences:

These are the swords He brought into man's material understanding. And more wars, more bloodshed have been shed over the racial and religious differences than over any other problem! These, too, must go the way of all others; and man must learn—if he will know the peace as promised by Him—that God loveth those who love Him, whether they be called of this or that sect or schism or ism or cult! The Lord is *one!* 3976-27

It is reasonable to assume that God's Holy Spirit, which Cayce sometimes called the Christ Consciousness, has been available to all people in the world from the beginning of time. The Holy Spirit is mentioned many times in the Old Testament. Jesus himself said that David prophesied by the Holy Spirit [see Mark 12:36]. The following reading, given for a Jewish person who was intimately involved in the Cayce work, speaks of a baptism of the Holy Spirit of several individuals who were not all Christian by name:

[Q] While reading, a sudden quivering came over me. I felt every pulsation of my heart, of the nerves, of the blood—I became conscious of a vibratory force moving everything within my body—even the chair upon which I was sitting seemed to be in motion. I was not asleep—
[A] (Again interrupting) This, as we see, is as to the entity that manifestation of the action of the Spirit Forces giving that vibration to the physical from within, and is as of the result of consecration of self, self's impulses, self's inner self, to that of the manifestation of force, as applies to this entity, and is the spiritual reaction, and the *physical effect* of same. An experience as some have been endowed with through the various ages of man's development, as may be seen in these illustrations:
Swedenborg, as he studied.
Socrates, as he meditated.
Paul, the Apostle, as he meditated upon the happenings of the hour, with the purpose meeting that spiritual force in

man that brought this self-conviction; the entity, then, being over-shadowed by the force as seen, see?

And as was by Buddha, in that position when meditation in the forest brought to the consciousness of the entity the At-Oneness of *all force* manifested through physical aspects, or physical, in a material world.

Then, this entity, [900], *sees, experiences,* through this, as a personal baptism of that "My spirit beareth witness with Thy Spirit, whether ye be the Sons of God or not,"... 900-187

Even though he saw the good in other faiths, Cayce was still faced with the same problem with which many Christian missionaries have to deal: How do we present our beliefs about Jesus the Christ without offending others? I am painfully aware that some religious people present their understanding of Jesus in ways that are abrasive and difficult for others to accept. That is not helpful. We can only plant the seed and then leave the increase to God. The readings say that the best way to do that is to demonstrate some evidence of what our relationship to the Christ has produced in our lives. Cayce also had some unique personal opportunities to share his faith with those of other religions.

Judaism

In spite of their common roots, Judaism and Christianity have often been cast as rival forces on the stage of Western history. Cayce was well aware of these differences as he worked with his Jewish friends, several of whom were quite instrumental in helping him with his Work. He not only shared his faith with them, he also invited them to share the unusual picture of Jesus found in the readings with others in the world.

One of Cayce's Jewish associates, Morton Blumenthal, asked, "How may we regard the truth regarding Jesus in relation to the Jewish and Christian religions, and to all the other religions of the world?" He was told:

In that the man, Jesus, became the ensample of the flesh, manifest in the world, and the will one with the Father, he became the first to manifest same in the material world. Thus, from man's viewpoint, becoming the only, the

208

first, the begotten of the Father, and the ensample to the world, whether Jew, Gentile, or of any other religious forces. In this we find the true advocate with the Father, in that He, as man, manifest in the flesh the ability of the flesh to make fleshly desires one with the will of the spirit. For God is spirit, and they who worship Him must worship in spirit and in truth, just as Jesus manifested in the flesh, and able to partake of the divine, for making all laws susceptible to the mandates. For the will was one with the Father, and in this we find He takes on all law, and a law unto Himself. For with the compliance, of even an earthly or material law, such a person *is* the law. And in that Jesus lived as man, and died as man, and in that became the ensample to all who *would* approach the Throne of God.

As we see in all religions of the world, we find all approaching those conditions where man may become as the law in his connection with the divine, the supreme, the oneness, of the world's manifestation. In Jesus we find the answer. 900-17

A life reading was given in 1935 for thirty-nine-year-old Dr. [991], whose religious preference was listed as "Rabbi, Hebrew, Christian." Dr. [991] was going through some severe turmoil about career choices. He also felt that he was experiencing some pressure from the Jewish community because of his interest in Christianity. In response to his question about which profession he should pursue, he was told:

...as a teacher, as a lecturer, that would *coordinate* the teachings, the philosophies of the east and the west, the oriental and the occidental, the new truths and the old...

Correlate not the differences, but where all religions meet—*there is one God!* "Know, O Israel, the Lord thy God is *one!*"

Set that upon thy brow; keep it as a frontlet upon thy speech; make it such that thou may hand it on to thy brethren.

Who is thy brother? Who is thy sister? Who is thy mother? He that doeth the will of the Father, the same is thy mother, thy brother, thy sister. He that would not forsake all to join hands with those who have attempted to do such, or who have same as their purpose and desire, is not worthy of His house...

(Q) Should I remain in spiritual work as a Rabbi, or go into business?

(A) Remain in spiritual work; not as a Rabbi, rather as—yes, as a rabbi in its *truest* sense; that is—a teacher, a minister. *not* as bound by creeds! Not as bound by modes! Not as bound by any law! ...

(Q) Why do I have a leaning more towards Christianity than Judaism?

(A) Hast thou not tried both? [No. 991 had been told that he had had a prior incarnation in this country as a French Catholic.] Hast thou not found that the *essence,* the truth, the *real* truth is *one?* Mercy and justice; peace and harmony. For without Moses and his leader Joshua (that was bodily Jesus) there *is* no Christ. *Christ* is not a man! *Jesus* was the man; Christ the messenger; Christ in all ages, Jesus in one, Joshua in another, Melchizedek in another; *these* be those that led Judaism! These be they that came as that child of promise, as to the children of promise; and the promise is in thee, that ye lead as He has given thee, "Feed my sheep." 991-1

I believe that Jews, as well as members of other religions, do sometimes follow the Christ in the way that they live. Jews have played an intricate part in world history in the last two thousand years. The Jewish faith today is still a multifaceted force in our culture. It is understandable that some Jews, being a minority in this country, would see the Christian community as a threat to the survival of their religious traditions, just as Christians experience the same difficulties in some other countries. Still, there are many efforts between Christians and Jews to understand each other and to work together. The Cayce readings would encourage us to do more of that.

Islam

There is not a lot said in the readings about the Muslim faith. However, we can get a glimpse of Cayce's tolerance from reading 1220-1 for a person who was said to have been in the crusades:

And when illness befell them, and the entity came into the hands of those now known as the Mohammedans—or the peoples that were overrunning the land, in those surroundings did the entity gain an understanding that the Lord is *one,* and that the activities of mercy, peace, justice, longsuffering, brotherly love, kindness and grace are attributes of those fruits that are indeed of the spirit of the Master; and though they may be manifested in the lives and the experiences of those that are called unbelievers, yet they become them and fit them to become as sons of a *living* Father.

While the Jewish, Muslim, and Christian faiths all trace their roots back to Abraham and much of the Old Testament, there are some variations in beliefs and hundreds of years of history, that make cooperation a real challenge. Any challenge, however, is also an opportunity. Our common belief in one God should be an area where we can find some agreement. Some have suggested, however, that Muslims and Christians do not even worship the same God. Perhaps they do not know that *Allah,* the Muslim name for God, is an Arabic form of *Elah,* a name for God that occurs about ninety times in the Old Testament. The Christian concept of the Trinity is also difficult for others to understand. The readings offer some interesting perspectives the Trinity that might be helpful to many. Their emphasis on forgiveness and the universal language of love can also overcome many barriers.

Hinduism/Buddhism

It is quite true that there appears to be some similarity between Cayce's suggestions on meditation and reincarnation and the beliefs of some Eastern religions. Without condemning anything, however, he continued to hold up the Christ as the Way for everyone.

For an individual who was interested in various religions, especially "the banyan, the Buddhist or Theosophy," reading 3054-4 said:

These are well in their place but they lead to that which is indicated in the figure in the right upper corner [the Cross], in this life's seal. For this is the culmination of God's approach to man in his phase of unfoldment in the earth. Thus as He expressed Himself, it was not merely an individual entity, but His son, His chosen son, as with the great teachers of the earth. For even in Elijah or John we find the faltering, the doubting. We find no faltering, no doubting, no putting aside of the purpose in the Master Jesus.

The readings say that it is necessary for some people to study and understand all religions so that they can know what has influenced others in their beliefs. Cayce also seemed to be saying that something of the spirit of the Son can be found in adherents of all of the major world religions, and that there may be times when we can learn from them. Cayce might have compared world religious leaders such as Buddha or Muhammad to prophets such as Moses or Elijah, but the Master is held up time and again in the readings as the ultimate answer for all people. Reading 5265-1 says, "To be sure, all power is of a first cause, but that light which was the light of the world from the beginning is crystallized in the entity known as Jesus of Nazareth, who passeth by today for thee, and unless ye take hold upon Him, ye must falter."

When reading 262-34 says, "So, He, with the Cross, represents something in the experience of every entity in their activities through the earth, and has led in all of the experiences of thought in *any* of the presented forms of truth in the earth, and comes at last to the Cross," it leaves little room for the uninformed criticism that Cayce's Work might put any other religion above his Christian faith. Cayce even cautioned several people not to lean too far in other directions, but always suggested healing rather than contention. Reading 2909-1 says, "Those interests [spiritual fields] especially in the oriental will necessarily be tempered. But *become* rather a unifier; for the Lord thy God is one."

King of Kings

The readings maintained a view of Jesus as a unique world figure, while still seeing the best in all others. In reading 364-9, Cayce was asked what part Jesus had played, in any of His incarnations, in the development of "Buddhism... Mohammedanism, Confucianism, Shintoism, Brahmanism, Platonism, Judaism." The reading said: "... the entity [the Christ]... influenced either directly or indirectly all those forms of philosophy or religious thought that taught God was One." It went on to say that He was associated with those who had guided these various religions "in the meditation or spirit," and that much of what was given by "Jesus in His walk in Galilee and Judea" had been assimilated into those other traditions in subsequent years. The reading also said that, in most of these, there had been that same "impelling spirit," but that individual teachers or leaders, just as in Christianity, had often later distorted what had been given in order to meet their immediate needs in a material world. In this reading, there was no question that the Christ was seen as the summation of all spiritual revelations to mankind: "Not as *only* one, but *the* only one; for, as He gave, 'He that climbs up any other way is a thief and a robber.'" Again it was emphasized that the whole law—love of God and neighbor—has been the gospel of every age that has believed in One God. The following reading, although quite difficult in places, seems to shed even more light on this question:

(Q) ...Is the faith of man in Buddha or Mohammed equal in the effect on his soul to the faith in Jesus Christ?

(A) As He gave, he that receiveth a prophet in the *name* of a prophet *receives* the prophet's reward, or that *ability* that that individual spiritual force *may* manifest in the life of that individual. Hence, as each teacher, minister or seer, or prophet, receives that obeisance as is giving the life from that faith and hope as held by that as an individual, in the Christ is found that as the advocate *with* the Father and the spirit of the Father glorified in him that approaches through that manner, without that as is approached in the spiritual activity of any individual; for individuality is last lost, even as man in spirit overcomes death in the material; even as He overcame death in the material, and able to put on immortality in a material world, bringing to man not only of flesh that endowed *with* the ability to be one *with* the Father but magnifying the Father *in* the individual yet in the material plane. Hence, as we find, each in their respective spheres are but stepping-stones to that that may awaken in the individual the knowledge of the Son in their lives. 262-14

Sharing the Faith

For if you can't spend a thousand dollars to preach the word, you can give ten cents and preach more in what you say and do to people ye meet every day. Yet it is true the entity has experienced, and may yet experience, that unless the missionary is sent, unless the missionary goes to others, those others may heathenize even America. 5112-1

When we do reach out to those of other faiths, we should keep in mind the difficulties encountered by persons who try to integrate new beliefs into their culture. Christianity does not have to be bound by rituals or creeds. Jesus tells us what is required when He says "I give you a new commandment: love one another; just as I have loved you, you also must love one another. By this love you have for one another, everyone will know that you are my disciples." (John 13:34-35 JB) This not only challenges us to manifest God's love, but it also defines love using Jesus as the standard or the ideal to be striven toward. Just as He dedicated His life to meeting our spiritual needs, we must do likewise for others. If those of other religions are trying to express love as Muhammad or Buddha loved them, is this a problem? They are also trying to learn to love. Even if the standard appears different, depending on their understanding, they are probably still moving in the right direction. When religion, ours or some other, teaches us to see those who are different as an enemy to be hated or feared, then it is not doing its job. When we emphasize our common ideals of love, forgiveness, and giving, then the fear and suspicion will fade away.

A Jewish friend of Edgar Cayce's, who was seeking work with an organization whose mission was to rehabilitate those in war torn countries, was told:

And these will give thee the opportunity to give greater understanding of the relationships that are borne by all who seek the face of the Lord, whether he be Greek or Jew, French or the children of Ishmael.

For, *all* have fallen short. Yet His mercy endureth forever. 257-250

PART FOUR

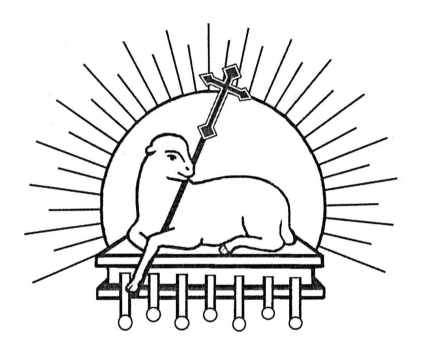

Christian Spirituality Applied

15

A Closer Walk:
Manifesting the Fruits of the Spirit

The door is open, the way is before thee. Let that as makes for a closer walk with Him guide thy every footstep in the choosing of the way before thee. 262-37

When I first learned about the Cayce readings, I often scanned books and other publications for direct quotes from the readings while paying little attention to what someone else might have said about them. If you feel the same urge, then you will enjoy this chapter. It is simply a collection of excerpts from readings.

Anger
Don't so oft act by the letting of your temper get away with you, so that you are really ashamed of yourself. And don't become so boastful of those activities. 3528-1

Remember, no man is *bigger* than that which makes him lose his temper. 254-55

For, remember, whoever they may be, whatever they may have done they are made in the image of thy God, or is it thy God? It depends upon what ye entertain. If it is saying hard things, ye are not entertaining the God of creation, ye are entertaining the God of destruction. Say something nice of everyone. 5103-1

Balance
But keep balanced—keep coordinated. Know that there are material laws, there are mental laws, there are spiritual laws. And just as it is necessary for the body to coordinate—mentally, physically and spiritually—so must the rules or the laws coordinate and cooperate. 1670-1

Be Good for Something

Know that it is not all just to live—not all just to be good, but good *for* something; that ye may fulfill that purpose for which ye have entered this experience. 2030-1

Economic Success

...do not be afraid of giving self in a service—if the *ideal* is correct. If it is for selfish motives, for aggrandizement, for obtaining a hold to be used in an underhand manner, *beware.* If it is that the glory of truth may be made manifest, *spend it all*— whether self, mind, body, or the worldly means—whether in labor or in the coin of the realm. 1957-1

Let the economic power, however, be *not* the first cause; let it rather be the *result* of careful, purposeful consideration of the use of abilities given to each entity... 1861-2

Only that ye give away, of self, of money, of time, of patience, of love, do ye possess! 1362-1

And if there is to be *soul* development, it must *not* be considered from the *monetary* basis! 1249-1

How much greater in the experience of each soul to at the end of any given day have the satisfaction of the best within self say to thee, "Well done!" than to have all the *glory* of man that you have tricked or have overstepped in some manner that may have been for material gain! 416-7

Expect Great Things

If an individual doesn't expect great things of God, he has a very poor God, hasn't he? 462-10

Friends

Be the real *friend—everyone,* as ye seek for the Christ to be *your* Friend. 4926-1

For He hath not willed that any soul should perish, but has with every temptation prepared a way, a manner of escape. And the more oft it comes through thy friends, thy associates. And as these have been and are oft representative of a savior, a means, a manner, a way, so must ye in thy association and thy activity make of thyself as one that would be a help, a savior, an aid, a *hope* for many. 1709-3

Thus the great admonition would be: Do the first things first. Learn this first —no soul or individual may have so many friends that he can ever afford to lose the least one. 3126-1

There is no friend that one could afford to lose. There is no friend one could afford to abuse! 1827-1

Fruits of the Spirit
Only those things that are just, those things that are beautiful, those things that are harmonious, that arise from brotherly kindness, brotherly love, patience, hope and graciousness, *live.* These are the fruits of those *unseen* forces that ye recognize as being the powers that rule this universe—yea, this heterogeneous mass of human emotions and human souls; that power which arises from *good*—not from hate nor malice nor greed nor covetousness. For these take hold upon the gates of hell and are the torments to man's soul! 1776-1

Give the Praise to God
As ye grow in appreciation of the love of thy fellow man, and the needs of such in thy daily experience, give the praise to the Father-God; that ye may be *used* more and more in a service for others. 262-121

Healing Love
He, thy King, thy Lord; yea thy Brother hath *shown* thee the way! "I am the way; I am the water of life." Drink ye *deep* of same, that the healing you each may administer to others may flow as His love through thee! For love healeth the wounded; it binds up the brokenhearted; it makes for understandings where differences have arisen. For *God is* love. 688-4

Heaven
There are children growing. Have you added anything constructive to any child's life? You'll not be in heaven if you're not leaning on the arm of someone you have helped. 3352-1

Humility
So in these applications, hold fast to that love that He gave, and ye will find peace and harmony, much strength and much power that is gained only in *humbling* of self and self's own emotions, self's own self! 688-4

Jesus Needs You
Know that He, thy Ideal, hath *need* of thee! 2449-1

Do It Today
Do not put off today that which will bring hope and help to the mind of another... Those things that make for the putting off become a joy never fulfilled. Use, then, the experiences from day to day as the basis, and these will *grow under thine very effort;* surprising even to self as to the joy that comes from same, and gradually taking shape to become a joy to self and blessings to others. 877-9

Keep the Faith
Keep that faith which has prompted the self to set thy ark to the port of the higher calling as found in Him. Let Him ever be thy pilot and thy commander. Listen oft to others, condemning none, but steer thine own purpose and way by the directions thou may obtain from Him alone. 420-6

Kindness
...the entity may speak to those who open the door of a morning ... in such a manner that the whole day is brighter because of a kindness expressed.

Would that men, then, *everywhere,* would learn such a lesson! 1472-12

Try in thine own experience, each; that ye speak not for *one whole day* unkindly of any; that ye say not a harsh word to any, about any; and see what a day would bring to you... 262-106

Let Others Do as They May
And whatever may be the choices of others, let self determine: "Others may do as they may, but as for me—I will serve a living God. I will manifest love, I will manifest patience, I will manifest longsuffering, I will manifest brotherly love." 1326-1

Line Upon Line
Not that some great exploit, some great manner of change should come within thine body, thine mind, but line upon line, precept upon precept, here a little, there a little. For it is, as He has given, not the knowledge alone but the practical application—in thine daily experience with thy fellow man—that counts. 922-1

Listen To God
Repeat three times every day, and then listen:
"Lord, what wouldst Thou have me do today?" Have this not as rote. Mean it! 3003-1

Make the World Better
And unless each soul ... makes the world better ... a little bit more hopeful, a little bit more patient, showing a little more of brotherly love, a little more of kindness, a little more of longsuffering—by the very words and deeds of the entity, the life is a failure; especially so far as growth is concerned. 3420-1

Mission
For, each soul enters with a mission. And even as Jesus, the great missionary, we all have a mission to perform. Are we working with Him, or just now and then." 3003-1

Patience
Beware lest ye as an individual soul, a son, a daughter of God, fail in thy mission in the earth today; that those ye know, those ye contact shall know the truth of God, not by thy word, bombastic words, but in longsuffering, in patience, in harmony, that ye create in thine own lives, for it must begin with thee. 3976-29

...few there be who comprehend that if they are patient first with their *own* selves they are then more capable of being ...patient with others. 1158-2

Do not grow anxious because those about thee deny thy faith. Only live it and be it; not in finding fault with others, not in condemning others. For as we forgive, we are forgiven; as we condemn others, we are ourselves condemned. Thus in patience condemn not, neither find fault; not condoning, not agreeing, but let thine own life so shine that others, seeing thy patience, knowing thy understanding, comprehending thy peace, may take hope. For such comes only from finding the presence of the Christ-Consciousness in self. 3459-1

Purpose
For the try—the *try*—is the righteousness in materiality. For God looks on the purpose and not as man counts righteousness. 880-2

Hold to that which is pure, in every form, in every phase and it will melt the obstacles away before thee as ye apply same ... keeping God and His purpose ever foremost... 1472-10

Salvation
...no one can destroy the soul but self! *No one* but *self!* 281-59

See the Best in Others
Hold rather to those things in which, in thy dealings with thy fellowman, ye may see only the pure, the *good!* For until ye are able to see within the life and activities of those ye have come to hate the most, *something* ye would worship in thy Creator, ye haven't begun to think straight. 1776-1

See Self in Other's Place
...ye cannot even *think* bad of another without it affecting thee in a manner of a destructive nature. Think *well* of others, and if ye cannot speak well of them don't speak! but don't think it either! Try to see self in the other's place. And this will bring the basic spiritual forces that must be the prompting influence in the experience of each soul, if it would grow in grace, in knowledge, in understanding... 2936-2

Selflessness
Become *selfless!* and there will grow that which makes the body, the mind, *strong*—and able to meet every obstacle in the physical conditions, in the social surroundings, in the family circles, with a smile; knowing that "If my life is one with Him the rest matters *not*," and *mean* it! and *do* it! and *be* it! 911-7

Service

For until ye are willing to *lose* thyself in service, ye may not indeed know that peace which He has promised to give—to all. 1599-1

Not "What does the world owe me?" but "What contribution can I, as an individual soul seeking God, seeking to know His face, make that may hasten the day of the Lord?" 3976-22

Smile

Brighten the corner where thou art from day to day. Let not a day go by without speaking to someone with the smile of the face and eye reminding them that somebody cares, and it is Jesus! 3357-1

Though ye may be reviled, revile not again. Though ye may be spoken of harshly, smile—*smile!* For it is upon the river of Life that smiles are made. Not grins! No Cheshire cat activities bring other than those that are of the earth, of such natures that create in the minds and the experiences those things that become repulsive. But the smile of understanding cheers on the hearts of those who are discouraged, who are disheartened.

It costs so little! It does thee so much good, and lifts the burdens of so many! 281-30

As ye look into the face of some child, see the smile of hope that ye have lost at times. Then bring to someone a smile again, where you have seen the tear start. The smile is as that look which the Master gave Peter, and he went out and wept—for he found himself. So may ye, as ye bring—by thy look, into the faces of others—that conviction of the love of the Christ as shown in Jesus the man. 3578-1

The Presence of God

"Be not afraid, it is I." Has this come to thee? Has it not oft been thy experience and ye, in thy doubt, in thy fear of being in His presence, have turned away? 5749-16

Yet in the day that ye accept Him as thy sacrifice and *live* thyself according to His precepts, *ye* become reconciled—through

Him—to the Father, and He—too—walketh and talketh with thee. 2879-1

That consciousness of His presence, then, must be the real criterion of thy choices that ye make day by day. 1151-12

The Try Counts
Study, then, to show thyself approved, *each day! Do what* thou *knowest* to do, to be aright! Then *leave it alone.* God giveth the increase! Thy worry, thy anxiety, only will produce disorder in thine *own* mind!

For the application in self, the *try,* the effort, the energy expended in the proper direction, is all that is required of *thee.* God giveth the increase. 601-11

The Way
For as has been intimated, each soul that has named the Name and who keeps in the Way may know, may hear, may see, may have a consciousness of that *entity;* yea, the consciousness of being at an at-onement with Jesus, the Christ. 1158-9

Trust in the Master
(Q) How can I shoulder responsibility with more grace and ease and poise, and assurance?

(A) Of thine self, thou may do little. Take the *Lord* in partnership with thee! But be honest with *Him* and with thyself, as you would have *Him* to be honest and sincere with thee! 815-3

Tolerance
For there the entity learned *tolerance,* which so few possess in *any* experience in the earth! Selflessness is the greater tolerance. For when self seeks exaltation, beware! 1298-1

Witness for Christ
Speak a word for thy ideal [Jesus]. Not as to force an issue but ever constructive. Sow the seed of truth, the seed of the spirit. God will give the increase. 3245-1

16

The Harmonious Triune:
Meditation—Listening to God

Attune yourself almost in the same manner as you tune the violin for harmony. For when the body-mind and the soul-mind is attuned to the infinite, there will be brought harmony to the mind... 1861-18

The practice of meditative or contemplative prayer was prevalent in the early church and persisted even into the Middle Ages. For various reasons, such methods of prayer seem to have been suppressed in recent centuries. However, there has been a renewed interest in meditation during the last thirty or forty years, even within the churches.

A few years ago, a minister from a nearby seminary was asked to conduct an evening Lenten service at our church. He led the congregation in a meditation that was very similar to that used in A.R.E. study groups that I had participated in as much as twenty-five years earlier. Wondering if there was any connection, I asked the minister and his wife if they had heard of Cayce's Work. They had heard of Cayce, but admitted that their knowledge of his Work was quite limited.

More recently, while using the *Search for God* books in an adult Sunday school class, I asked if anyone had had any experiences with meditation. Several persons had used very similar techniques in other churches or at special church programs. I have also heard conservative, liberal, and Pentecostal ministers preach or teach about the need for meditation.

When the study group readings were begun in 1931, members of that first group were already practicing meditation. The earliest reference to meditation that I found in the readings (4718-1) was given in 1921 for a person who had problems sleeping. During subsequent years, the readings offered many suggestions about purposes and techniques for meditation. As the *Search for God* books were being prepared, reading number 262-127 (April 23, 1941) said, "Though this [Cooperation] should be listed as the first lesson, put Meditation in the front. Let each know what it is about. And the form and manner of the meditations as presented here is among the first of the occidental ideas of an oriental theme according to that presented by the Master." Since that time, thousands of people have used those little books in *Search for God* study groups around the world. I have no doubt that Christians who have participated in these study groups have played a significant part in the recent renewal of the use of meditation in the churches.

What Is Meditation?

A common theme from the readings is that prayer is talking to God and meditation is listening to God, or "listening to the Divine within." (1861-19) The Glad Helpers Prayer Group often sought readings (the 281 series) from Cayce, asking for advice. Reading 281-41, given for an A.R.E. Congress meeting in 1939, was about meditation. This reading says that meditation is not just "daydreaming," but it is attuning "the mental body and the physical body to its spiritual source" while seeking to know our relationship to our Creator. It goes on to say that most of us have allowed our mental and physical faculties to atrophy through nonuse and even to be "glossed over" by "self-indulgences," and that we must learn how to meditate just as we have learned to walk or to talk. Here is an excerpt from a reading that speaks to the problems we encounter when we fail to meditate upon God's Word:

... have ye not wondered why in the sacred writings it is said that God no longer spoke to man in visions or dreams? It is because man fed not his soul, his mind, upon things spiritual; thus closing the avenue or channel through which God might speak with the children of men. 1904-2

The Harmonious Triune

The readings often speak of meditation as the process of bringing body, mind, and soul into harmony with each other, while focusing on the Triune God (Father, Son, and Holy Spirit) as the pattern. Cayce coined the term "harmonious triune" (252-108) to describe not only his own condition while giving a reading, but also the state of mind that we might hope to achieve through meditation.

The Body Is the Temple

In I Corinthians 6:19 (JB) Paul says, "Your body, you know, is the temple of the Holy Spirit..." Cayce quotes this passage hundreds of times in the readings, not only to echo the biblical admonition to keep one's body clean and free from immorality, but also to remind us that it is within our own body that God promises to meet with us when we pray and meditate. Reading 281-41 says, "That He gave of old is as new today as it was in the beginning of man's relationship or seeking to know the will of God, if ye will but call on Him *within* thine inner *self!* Know that thy body is the temple of the living God. *There* He has promised to meet thee!"

Preparation

The Cayce readings caution us not to allow formality to be our guide to the extent that faith is lost. They say that the important thing is the "humbleness" with which we approach the throne. Reading 281-13 does, however, give quite a dissertation on how to prepare for meditation. It advises us to consecrate ourselves and to cleanse our minds and bodies according to our own conscience. Then it suggests that one "Sit or lie in an easy position, without binding garments..." Other suggestions include breathing exercises, a head-and-neck exercise, chants, music, affirmations, or whatever is helpful for the individual. One person was told that, for her, a certain amount of ceremony was helpful and that burning sandalwood and cedar might be good. When asked about special diets or other practices, people were usually told just to keep a balance.

Like the Master's advice to "leave your offering there before the altar, go and be reconciled with your brother first" (Matthew 5:23 JB), Cayce said, "Approach not the inner man, or the inner self, with a grudge or an unkind thought held against *any* man! or do so to thine own undoing sooner or later!" 281-13

Protection

Cayce often warned of the dangers of using any tool, whether physical, mental, or spiritual, in the wrong way or for the wrong reasons. Meditation is no exception. "To be loosed without a governor, or a director, may easily become harmful," says 2475-1. It goes on to say that a person's director should not be any individual entity, but should be the "universal consciousness of the *Christ.*" Surrounding ourselves with the Spirit of the Christ is a constant theme of the readings. Here are a few examples:

(Q) Where can I get concrete guidance besides from the inner voice?
(A) Seek not other than that of His meeting thee within thine own temple. For beside Him there is none other...
Then listen—listen to that voice within. Prepare thyself, consecrate thyself, purify thy body, thy mind, in much the same manner as did those of old who were, or would be, the priests and priestesses to Jehovah. And then, open thy heart and thy mind to those promises; surrounding thyself with the consciousness of the Christ love. 2029-1

Surround thyself with that consciousness which comes in merely calling the name—Jesus, the Christ, the same yesterday, today and forever! 3357-2

Be sure it is Him we worship that we raise in our inner selves for the dissemination; for, as He gave, "Ye must eat of my *body;* ye must drink of *my* blood." Raising then in the inner self that image of the Christ, love of the God-Consciousness, is *making* the body so cleansed as to be barred against all powers that would in any manner hinder. 281-13

Be Still and Know—(Psalm 46:10)
Listening to the still, small voice within is a frequent suggestion in the readings. Whether it is because of the concerns of the world or because we don't want to hear what our conscience has to say, this is not always easy, but the following readings make a good case for making the effort:

(Q) Please advise the body as to how he may best gain control of himself and utilize his abilities to best advantage.
(A) Depend more upon the intuitive forces from within and not harken so much to that of outside influences—but learn to listen to that still small voice from within, remembering as the lesson as was given, not in the storm, the lightning, nor in any of the loud noises as are made to attract man, but rather in the still small voice from within

does the impelling influence come to life in an individual that gives for that which must be the basis of human endeavor; for without the ability to constantly hold before self the ideal as is attempted to be accomplished, man becomes as one adrift, pulled hither and yon by the various calls and cries of those who would give of this world's pleasure in fame, fortune, or what not. Let these [spiritual gifts] be the outcome of a life spent in listening to the divine from within, and not the purpose of the life. 239-1

...sources of [imaginative] impulse are aroused by the shutting out of thought pertaining to activities or attributes of the carnal forces of man. [Note that Cayce does not suggest that we try to make the mind a blank or to shut out all thought.]
...material sources are laid aside, or the whole of the body is *purified* so that the purity of thought as it rises has less to work against...
Meditation is *emptying* self of all that hinders the creative forces from rising along the natural channels of the physical man to be disseminated through those centers and sources that create the activities of the physical, the mental, the spiritual man; properly done must make one *stronger* mentally, physically... 281-13

When the soul, that image of the Creator is attuned to the divine, you are on the road to meeting thine own self, and all will be well with thee. 3174-1

Affirmations/Scriptures

While the Cayce readings never mentioned the word *mantra,* nor did they suggest using words or phrases in quite the same manner as they are used in some other methods of meditation, they did often suggest affirmations to be said aloud or held mentally.
Here is an affirmation that was asked for by an individual:

Father, as I surround myself with the consciousness of the Christ Spirit, wilt Thou be the guide. Send Thou, O God, that influence into my mind, my heart, my soul, my body, that will make and create the best in me, that I may

229

use the attributes of my mind, my soul, my body, for Thy glorification. 317-7

One person who was concerned about going to sleep during meditation was told:

This, as may be found, is the surer, safer, saner way of meditation. For, when the mind is absent from the body it is present with thy Lord, thy purposes, thy hopes. Let thy pronouncements ever be, then, as the beginning of thy meditation, of thy prayer, as may be put in thine own words—but after this manner:
Lord, Thou art the maker of heaven and earth. Thou hast shown Thy love in the gift of Thy Son. Make me, then, a channel of blessing through Him to others. 1152-13

Each of the lessons in the *Search for God* books begins with an affirmation that is usually used for a group meditation at the beginning of each study session. Some groups also end their meditation by saying the Lord's Prayer together. The first lesson, "Cooperation," uses the following affirmation:

Not my will but Thine, O Lord, be done in and through me. Let me ever be a channel of blessings, today, now, to those that I contact, in every way. Let my going in, mine coming out be in accord with that Thou would have me do, and as the call comes, "Here am I, send me, use me!" 262-3

Many of the affirmations given in the readings, like the one above, quote or paraphrase one or more Bible verses. Some people were also told to prepare by studying certain passages from the Scriptures. When a person asked for guidance in developing a healing and teaching ministry that a reading had suggested, the following was given:

Know it is within self, and it is found—the manner of approach—in the 30th of Deuteronomy, and in the 14th, 15th, 16th, and 17th of John. Not that other approaches may not be just as important, just as beautiful—but here the directions are crystallized into that of knowing thine own body is the temple. It is thy tabernacle. There He will meet with thee.

Seek not other entities. Not that many are not about; not that there is not the communion of saints, but there is also the communion of sinners! Ye seek not those!

Let that light be in thee which was also in the Christ Jesus, who went about *doing* good! bearing His cross, as ye must indeed bear thy cross, but bearing it in Him it brings peace, and most of all life everlasting, and hope and cheer!

Be not longfaced, but happy—*happy* in thy service to others. 2787-1

Gland Centers (Chakras)

Seven endocrine gland centers were mentioned in the material on meditation. These correspond in some degree to the nerve centers that yoga and related meditation techniques call *chakras*. From top to bottom, these glands are the pituitary, the pineal, the thyroid, the thymus, the adrenals, the leyden, and the gonads. It is interesting that the philosopher, Descartes, is said to have found his purpose of unifying all knowledge, while meditating. Descartes thought of the pineal gland as the point of contact between the body and the soul. The readings confirm this idea, although they include the other centers mentioned above in the process.

The Glad Helpers prayer group studied these gland centers and sought more information through readings. Each of the centers was related to a part of the Lord's Prayer and to passages in the book of Revelation. Although this study would be quite interesting for any serious student of Christian meditation, reading 281-29 makes it clear that such a study is not a prerequisite to meditation when it says:

To give an interpretation that the opening or activity through a certain center raises or means or applies this or that, then would become rote.

...It is not then as a formula, that there are to be certain activities and certain results... For, as has been given, man is free-willed. And only when this [the will] is entirely given, and actively given to the will of the Father may it be even as the life of the Christ.

231

Kundalini

The readings sometimes refer to a kind of energy or phenomenon, related to the spine and gland centers, which is called kundalini. The word means coiling like a serpent. My understanding is that kundalini, in the yoga traditions, is potential creative energy located at the base of the spine. It is symbolized as a coiled snake. Some think of kundalini as being related to consciousness, and it may also be thought of as moving through the various centers along the spine.

Many of the readings that mentioned kundalini were about physical health. Some were about the generative process in a fetus. At other times the reference was to a process that takes place during meditation. Kundalini was seen as a normal process that could release a person from self-indulgent physical desires and channel creative energy into service toward others. Still, the usual warnings were given:

> These [kundalini forces] arise from the creative center of the body itself, and as they go through the various centers direct same; else they may become greater disturbing than helpful. Surround self ever with that purpose, "Not my will, O God, but Thine be done, ever," and the entity will gain vision, perception and—most of all—judgment." 2823-3

> (Q) [Given for a Protestant music teacher] How may I bring into activity my pineal and pituitary glands, as well as the Kundalini and other chakras, that I may attain to higher mental and spiritual powers? ...
> (A) As indicated, first so *fill* the mind with the ideal that it may vibrate throughout the whole of the *mental* being!
> Then, close the desires of the fleshly self to conditions about same. *Meditate* upon *"Thy will with me."* Feel same. Fill *all* the centers of the body, from the lowest to the highest, with that ideal; opening the centers by surrounding self first with that consciousness, *"Not my will but Thine, O Lord, be done in and through me."* 1861-4

Pineal First: The Mark of the Lamb

The suggestions in the readings differ from some other forms of meditation that attempt to tune the centers of the body from bottom to top, forcing the energy to flow upward so that some power or spiritual gift might be manifested. Knowing that Cayce associates the pineal gland with the mind and that the mind is associated with the Son in the Trinity, the following reading seems to be suggesting that we start with the pineal center, which will then purify the other centers:

> If there has been set the mark (mark meaning here the image that is raised by the individual in its imaginative and impulse force) such that it takes the form of the ideal the individual is holding as its standard to be raised to ... *then* the individual (or the image) bears the mark of the Lamb, or the Christ, or the Holy One, or the Son, or any of the names we may have given to that which *enables* the individual to enter *through it* into the very presence of that which is the creative force from within itself—see?
>
> ...With the arousing then of this image, it rises along that which is known as the Appian Way, or the pineal center, to the base of the *brain*, that it may be disseminated to those centers that give activity to the whole of the mental and physical being. It rises then to the hidden eye in the center of the brain system, or is felt in the forefront of the head... 281-13

Purpose: Working Meditation

People were often told to be purposeful in meditation. It was suggested that one could find healing for self and others, find information, make decisions, and find a closer relationship to God through meditation. Here are some readings that emphasize these ideas:

> Seek experiences not as experiences alone but as purposefulness. For what be the profit to thyself, to thy neighbor, if experiences alone of such natures rack thy body—owing to its high vibration—without being able to make thee a kinder mother, a more loving wife, a better neighbor, a better individual in every manner? *These* be the fruits, that it makes thee kinder, gentler, stronger in body, in mind, in purpose to *be* a channel through which the love of *God*, through Jesus Christ, may be manifested in the world. Not as a vision, an experience alone. 281-27

The desire to seek the greater forces will gradually bring, draw, make, accomplish the desired end in the same manner as pennies accumulated finally reach to the desired amount... Apply all rules pertaining to life to that. 2725-1

Don't seek for unnatural or supernatural! It is the natural—it is nature—it is God's activity! His associations with man. His *desire* to make for man a way for an understanding! 5754-3

Take time first to be holy. Don't let a day go by without meditation and prayer for some definite purpose, and not for self, but that self may be the channel of help to someone else. For in helping others is the greater way to help self. 3624-1

When I think of meditation being directed toward helping others, I am reminded of many things that we have meditated about in our local study group. We have focused on helping members and friends with health problems, on helping our children with the many decisions that they make in life, on people being held hostage in other countries, on people who are suffering in wars and natural disasters around the world, on our leaders, and on many other concerns. The results may not be measurable by worldly standards, but our consensus is that these meditations have been most helpful.

Group Meditation
Someone in the Glad Helpers asked during reading 281-8 if all of the group members should hold the same prayer during meditation. They were told:

Each in their *own* way, but the purpose, the aim, *one,* the desire *one;* for, as just given, to *some* the song of the spheres is necessary for their comfort—to another the beauties in the sunset, in the water, or how, yet all are *acknowledging* the power of the Christ in the activative forces of *nature,* life, material, itself! *Know nothing but Christ, and Him crucified!*

In reading 281-13, it was suggested that thoughts in a group meditation could be conflicting and that it might be better for group meditations to be kept relatively short and to have a central thought, expressed by a sincere individual, along with a group effort to be cooperative. In response to a question from a person who was leading a morning devotional group, reading 3374-1 gave the following:

Open thy heart to God, surrounding self with the consciousness of the promises of the Christ—"If ye love me, ye will keep my commandments, and I and the Father will come and abide with thee." And as this is felt and spoken in body, in mind, visualize the coming of the Christ as He spoke in the day by the sea.

Problems

Even after trying to do everything right, people often feel that meditation is not working. This must have been true for the member of the prayer group who asked, "Why is it that at times my meditation seems unsatisfactory?" The answer came back:

For ye are *still* in the flesh. *Why* did He say, "Father, why hast thou forsaken me?" Even when the world was being overcome, the flesh continued to rebel; for, "When I *would* do good, *evil* is present with me—but, Though I take the wings and fly to the utmost parts of the heavens, Thou art there; though I make my bed in hell, Thou art there." So, when doubt and fear comes, close thine *senses* to the *material* things and *lose* thineself *in* Him. Not that ye shall not be joyous in the things that partake of the pleasures even of life; for so did He—but keep thine consciousness ever alert, ready and willing to be the channel that will make known His love, and *He* will speak with thee! 281-3

Another person who felt unsuccessful with meditation was told:

Do not *try*, or crave, or desire a sign; for *thou* art in *thyself* a sign of that thou dost worship within thine inner self ...do not be impatient. For what thou asketh in secret shall be proclaimed from the housetop. 705-2

One reading said that not attuning properly during meditation could cause a person to feel tired or dull. Ms. [1782] complained that when meditating on distant objects, she felt the sensation of "being unpleasantly suspended at a great height in the universe." She was told to find the tabernacle within self, "in the holy of holies; in the third eye—*not* above same!" (1782-1)

Probably the most frequently given advice, and the most relevant for most of us, was the admonition to use that which has been given before we seek for more. A thirty-six-year-old man who asked if he should seek more information through the readings was told, "Well, put some of it to use first, if you're going to seek further information! If you don't, you won't find any!" (1861-12) Cayce even said, "Knowledge without works is sin." (815-7) Reading 5502-4 also says:

> In the use of that in hand, in the direction as is purported, whether it be mental abilities, physical abilities, or the spiritual forces or the commercial side of experience, use that in hand and the increase comes with the use.

Why Reach Out to the Churches?

According to the Cayce readings, a commitment to follow the Christ is the first step to effective meditation. For many people such a commitment is often related to their affiliation with a church. This is why I feel that it is so important to present the Cayce material in a way that is useful to Christians where they are. There are several other Christian organizations or movements today that teach "centering prayer," or other contemplative forms of meditation. These are often quite parallel to the concepts discussed here, but I believe that the Cayce readings can add some unique dimensions to these ancient forms of wisdom. If this helps individuals walk closer with God, then the churches will grow along with their members.

17

Spiritual Growth:
Safe Ways to Use Dreams and Intuition

> As indicated, through the will power and its activities—
> as it has been—there is raised within self soul development.
> Do not think of it as being mysterious, or mystic, or
> something unnatural. It is unnatural for the soul *not* to
> develop before or towards its Maker. 457-3

Most of us have at least a streak of do-it-yourself in us. When
people read of the things that Edgar Cayce was able to do, they
often wonder if they could learn to do the same things. Even
better than that, Jesus said that we would be able to do the things
He did and even greater things (John 14:12). The A.R.E. and
other organizations have seminars and courses on developing our
natural spiritual abilities. Pentecostal churches devote more time
than most traditional groups to manifesting "gifts of the Spirit."
Self-help or self-improvement methods abound. One wonders how
the Bible characters from Abraham through the prophets
developed their ability to listen to God. Meditation, which is
discussed in the previous chapter, is a good start. However, the
readings also have much to say about other practices such as
prayer and fasting. To a person asking Cayce if he should pursue
psychic development, reading 3460-1 said: "Pursue rather
spiritual development; this is of the psychic nature, yes, but find
the spirit first—not spiritualism, but spirituality in thy own life."
When it comes to discerning the difference between what is
spiritual and what is based on selfishness or some kind of
materialistic psychology, reading 281-20 also suggests:

> Not so much self-development, but rather developing the
> Christ Consciousness in self, being selfless, that He may
> have *His* way with thee, that He—the Christ—may direct
> thy ways, that He will guide thee in the things thou doest,
> thou sayest. 281-20

GIVE GOD A CHANCE

The Cayce readings give hundreds of other suggestions about spiritual growth and attunement. Whether you wish to pursue spiritual growth through a *Search for God* study group, through a Sunday school class, or individually, the following Scriptural advice could suggest some safe ways to begin:

As we find, there are disturbances with this body. Much of these, however, are tied up with the emotional natures of the body. And here we find some of those conditions of which many bodies should be warned—the opening of centers in the body-spiritual without correctly directing same, which may oft lcad to wrecking of the body-physical and sometimes mental.

Know where you are going before you start out, in analyzing spiritual and mental and material things.

This is not belittling the seeking of knowledge, neither is it advising individuals—or this individual—to seek knowledge. But knowledge without the use of same still remains, as in the beginning, sin. And be sure your sins will find you out!

Here we have an emotional body well versed in the study of meditation, the study of transmission of thought, with the ability to control others.

Don't control others. Suppose thy God controlled thee without thy will? What would you become, or what would you have been?

But you were made in the image of thy Creator, to be a companion with Him—not over someone else, but a companion with thy brother and not over thy brother. Hence do not act that way, because ye have the greater ability or greater knowledge of control of others.

Then, as we would give for this body—for this is psychological as well as pathological—we would begin again to study—this time the Book.

Begin with Exodus 19:5.

Then read again and know thoroughly the 20th chapter of Exodus.

Study then thoroughly and apply personally the 30th of Deuteronomy, and apply it in the terms of the 23rd Psalm.

Thus ye will make thyself new. 3428-1

Prayer

The readings frequently recommend prayer and, especially, prayers for others who are in need of some kind of healing in their lives. Here are some excerpts from readings containing some typical advice about prayer:

Join with those that are helping, aiding others. The more oft in prayer for others, the closer ye draw to Him. For as He gave—as ye do it, as ye pray for them, as ye meet thy fellow man, so ye meet thy Lord. 2574-1

Be not overcome by failures in anyone's behalf, for good is accomplished in each individual prayer that may be sought by any, and in unison is the strength made more secure in Him. 281-9

For, the Father of light has never failed man that has cried in earnestness unto Him. It is when individuals have desired their own way that the *souls* have suffered in the sons of men. 552-2

He that would know the way must be oft in prayer, joyous prayer, *knowing* He giveth life to as many as seek in sincerity to be the channel of blessing to someone... 281-12

Another principle that I believe can be valuable in prayer is asking God to show us what we can do to heal our own diseases. So often we ask God just to fix everything for us, when it is we ourselves who have caused our own problems and may still have the power to do something to correct them. Taking the responsibility for correcting our own situation can help us to change the old patterns that started the problem in the first place. Asking God to help us help ourselves is not denying the fact that we still need His help. Cayce seemed to say that listening to the Holy Spirit will help us to recognize difficult situations earlier and deal with them constructively, rather than just praying ourselves out of trouble after we have made our usual mistakes. When a sixty-one-year-old woman asked how she could learn to discipline herself at her age to do what she needed to do, she was told:

Repeat three times every day, and then listen: "*Lord, what would Thou have me do today?*"

Have this not as rote. Mean it! For as He has spoken, as He has promised, "If ye call I will hear, and answer speedily." He meant it! Believe it! 3003-1

Sometimes people simply want to find answers to important questions in their lives. A question in reading 1861-12 asked if needed information could be obtained through meditation. The answer was, "On any subject! whether you are going digging for fishing worms or playing a concerto!" Here is a reading that gives a bit more details about how to go about getting answers from the Spirit:

...and here may be given as to how prayer may be answered and *know* you have the correct answer *when* you have the answer: The spirit speaks of itself. When such a question arises, *ask* of self yes or no—get the answer, yes or no—for it will come! This may be wholly mental, see? Whether yes or no—may be wholly mental. Then in thine prayer, in thine meditation, "*Is* my answer (whatever it may be) correct or incorrect?" Then the spirit answers. 5747-1

Fasting

Even though the readings are biblically oriented and usually in harmony with mainstream Christian beliefs and ideals, they often give some interesting emphasis or interpretation that enhances our understanding of spirituality. The emphasis on fasting in the following readings is an example:

For, fasting—as is ordinarily termed—is as the Master gave: Laying aside thine own concept of *how* or *what* should be done at this period, and let the Spirit guide. Get the truth of fasting! The body, the man's bodily functioning, to be sure, *overdone* brings *shame* to self, over indulgence in anything—but the true fasting is casting out of self that as "I would have done," [replacing with] "but as *Thou*, O Lord, seest fit—use me as the channel..." 295-6

For thy body is indeed the temple of the living God. Therein ye may meet Him in prayer, in meditation, in psalm singing, yea in the activities of fasting, in not only the foods but in opening the mind, the consciousness, consciously to that which may flow in from music, from prayer, those influences which may flow in from deep meditation, which may be gained in having regular periods for this shutting out from self of the voices or the sounds of nature and listening to the still small voice within. 3630-2

Conviction/Repentance

I once heard a sermon in which the preacher said that the first step toward healing one's relationship with God should be conviction by the Holy Spirit. We often tell ourselves that we want to know God's will for us, but we sometimes look to people for approval. We worship, pray, meditate, and read the Scriptures looking for answers, but are we ready to accept His conviction? Reading 3976-14 challenges us to do just that:

Blame not the other fellow. Seek first to know within self that which has prompted thee, and when thou hast set thine house in order, when thou hast made thine peace with thine own conscience (that would smite thee, if ye will look within your own heart), then may ye find the answers that will come to every soul that seeks. 3976-14

The next step after accepting conviction is to turn around, or repent. In a physical reading for a thirty-seven-year-old woman diagnosed as having a psychosomatic illness, Cayce told the woman that her attitude caused her to react negatively to things done by others around her. Then he added:

To bring about a nearer normal activity, "right about face", as it were, with the ideals. *Know* in self that *all* is well with those who love the Lord and His ways, and that His ways being past man's understanding do not attempt to do *His* portion of the work. 1192-3

Dreams/Visions

Dream analysis has become more acceptable to some psychologists as a result of the work of Carl Jung. Jung recognized that dreams often contain symbols that can have meaning to the person having the dream. Some symbols or events

241

seem to be common to people around the world, and such symbols are called archetypes.

Cayce also recognized that dreams were often symbolic, but he did not offer any shortcuts to dream interpretation. When he helped people interpret their dreams, he often recommended that they make note of their dreams and learn to interpret them for themselves. The following reading gave some advice that might be useful to anyone:

> While this [dream] may be explained, or unraveled—as it were—for the consciousness of the entity, the whole reaction must be *solely* within self, would the body be able to apply that gained through this experience, for remember, these are as illustrations only, and not means of an escape, but that one may have an understanding of how to apply in self that that self already has in hand, to the betterment of self in the spiritual sense *first*, and the *material* sense as an outgrowth of *doing* that known. Understand that! 4167-1

Considering dreams to be prophetic or inspirational is not without Biblical precedent. Joseph (Genesis 37 and 40-42) and Daniel (Daniel 1 and 2) are recorded in the Old Testament as having interpreted dreams. A few of the other Bible passages that deal with dreams coming directly from God, or from an angel of God, are found in Numbers 12:6, Judges 7:13, I Samuel 28:6, I Kings 3:5, and Matthew 1:20 and 2:13. Perhaps the most widely known passage dealing with dreams is Joel 2:28 (JB), which says, "I will pour out my spirit on all mankind. Your sons and daughters shall prophesy, your old men shall dream dreams, and your young men see visions." In Acts 2:16-21, Peter sees the Pentecost as the fulfillment of Joel's prophecy.

There are also several references in the Bible that warn about false dreamers and prophets (see Jeremiah 23:25 and 25:29 and Zechariah 10:2), but no blanket condemnation of finding guidance through dreams. Certainly cautious comparison with spiritual lessons already learned is necessary when trying to analyze dreams (see Deuteronomy 13:1-3). It is not hard to imagine the foolish ways that people could misinterpret dreams or the problems that could be caused by superstitious uses of dreams. Yet, when I hear someone denying all of the value of dreams, I wonder whether, if St. Paul were here today, he would repeat his admonition, "Never try to suppress the Spirit or treat the gift of prophecy with contempt..." (1 Thes. 5:19 JB). Or, perhaps, we should be reminded of Elihu's message to Job:

> He speaks by dreams, and visions that come in the night, when slumber comes on mankind, and men are all asleep in bed. Then it is he whispers in the ear of man, or may frighten him with fearful sights, to turn him away from evil-doing, and make an end of his pride... (Job 33:15-17 JB)

Here are a few more excerpts from readings that are typical of the advice given about dreams:

> In this age...there is not sufficient credence given dreams; for the best development of the human family is to give the greater increase in knowledge of the subconscious, soul or spirit world. 3744-5

> ...all visions and dreams are given for the benefit of the individual, would they but interpret them correctly... 294-15 (see also 4167-1)

> Dreams, visions, impressions, to the entity in the normal sleeping state are the presentations of the experiences necessary for the development, if the entity would apply them in the physical life. These may be taken as warnings, as advice, as conditions to be met, conditions to be viewed in a way and manner as lessons, as truth, as they are presented in the various ways and manners. 294-70

Dreams can often contain real inspiration if we can interpret them correctly. In the preface to his book titled *The Story of the Other Wise Man*, Henry Van Dyke said that he got the whole story in a dream. While he had to do a good deal of research for the details in the book, he had clearly seen the main character and knew his story from beginning to end. This is a very moving story that can still be found in many libraries.

Speaking in Tongues

There were only a few references to the phenomenon of speaking in tongues in the readings. Most of these refer to the early church and to the biblical accounts of the Pentecost. While the development of such gifts was not in any way discouraged, the emphasis was on learning to love:

> Ye saw phenomena in the household of Cornelius, in the servants, in thine own parents—which ye sought and yet never fully experienced. Ye learned later it was not necessary that ye speak with tongues, but with that tongue of love—which is the language of all who seek His face. 2205-3

Growth

Here are some readings that have been meaningful to me in my desire to understand spiritual laws that can be applied to bring about personal spiritual growth:

> In knowing Happiness ye find that it is the little things...the little kindnesses that bring it to the lives of others. So does it grow in thee. 262-109

> For, the body-physical becomes that which it assimilates from material nature. The body-mental becomes that it assimilates from both the physical-mental and the spiritual-mental. The soul is *all* of that the entity is, has been or may be. 2475-1

> For we grow in grace, in knowledge, in understanding of spiritual laws, as we apply gentleness, kindness, patience, longsuffering, to those we meet day by day. Not long-facedly, no; but in *joy* of the Lord! 1469-1

> Then, as the entity in this material plane has found, it is necessary physically to conform to certain moral and penal laws of society, of the state, of the nation, even to be termed a good citizen. Thus if there is to be preparation for the entity as the soul-entity, as a citizen of the heavenly kingdom, isn't it just as necessary that there be the conforming to the laws pertaining to that spiritual kingdom

of which the entity is a part? And there has been an ensample, a citizen of that kingdom, the Son Himself, has given the example to the entity as well as to others. Isn't it well, then, that the entity study to show self approved unto that kingdom, rightly putting the proper emphasis upon all phases of His admonitions, His judgments, His commandments, and thus become such an one as to be a good citizen of that individual kingdom? 3590-2

An experience, then, is not only a happening, but what is the reaction in your own mind? What does it do to you to make your life, your habits, your relationships to others of a more helpful nature, with a more hopeful attitude? 1567-2

Know that thou would worship, and self a part of same, seeing in others then that thou would worship in the Father; for the prayer was, "May they be one, even as Thou and I are one," for, as given, a *spiritual insight* brings the *seeing* of the best in each life. 262-12

18

Causes and Corrections for Dis-ease:
Spiritual and Physical Healing

The main focus of Edgar Cayce's gift was on helping people who were sick. Of more than 14,000 readings that Cayce gave during his lifetime, about sixty-three percent were physical readings. People who sought readings did not expect to be healed directly by the reading. The readings diagnosed their illnesses and gave advice for correcting them. In addition to the many physical remedies, mental or spiritual advice was also sometimes given.

There were also a few readings that dealt with the use of prayer, meditation, anointing with oil, the laying on of hands, and other spiritual disciplines in the process of healing. During Cayce's lifetime, there was a group that met for the purpose of applying the concepts of spiritual healing that were given in the readings. This group, called the Glad Helpers, received several readings that focused on their healing ministry.

I have participated in healing services at the A.R.E., in my own church, in homes and in evangelical, Catholic, and Pentecostal settings. The prayer, the laying on of hands, the Spirit, and the emotions involved in these different groups are certainly overlapping and, at times, almost indistinguishable. Methods change and evolve, but calling on God to heal in the name of the Master goes back to New Testament times. Cayce's concepts of meditation and other spiritual principles from the readings have helped me to better understand the process.

Illness Caused by Sin

One of the most important principles in the readings, and one with which many orthodox church people, from liberal to conservative, tend to disagree, is that illness is caused by sin. Reading 3174-1 sounds almost blunt when it says, "And all illness comes from sin. This everyone must take whether they like it or not; it comes from sin whether it be of body, of mind, or of soul, and these manifest in the earth."

There may be inappropriate ways of sharing this principle with a person who is suffering, but when the readings speak of sin, they are not being insensitive. They simply mean that we have misapplied some natural law—whether mental, physical, or spiritual—and gotten an undesirable result. In reading 659-1, Cayce was asked about the use of biotin in cancer research. After saying that biotin and some other substances would be found to be helpful, he added, "and yet there is really the greater necessity of man's comprehension of ills as related to erring from the path of righteousness—or that of sin, and its relationships to all such conditions that are in the experience of man."

Some of the problems people have in understanding this concept are caused by the negative connotations associated with the idea of sin. I would suggest that we might define sin as anything that causes suffering or separation from God. Without the concept of sin or error, we could have no free will, no personal responsibility, no basis for making decisions, and no hope of improving the world or ourselves.

It is not necessary to confuse sin with our feelings about blame, guilt, or punishment, nor is it necessary to react to our own or other peoples' mistakes with condemnation. The Bible says that we have all sinned. To some extent, we are all in a mess, and it is the amount of mercy and love that we show to others who have problems (even of their own doing) that we will receive back when we need it.

Events that may otherwise seem to be harsh or tragic might be seen in a different light in the context of reincarnation, karma, and grace. We may not consciously remember our actions by the time the law of cause and effect has run its course, especially if the error was in a prior lifetime. Reading 3395-2 says:

...all illness is sin; not necessarily of the moment, as man counts time, but as a part of the whole experience. For God has not purposed or willed that any soul should perish, but purgeth everyone by illness, by prosperity, by hardships, by those things needed, in order to meet self—but in Him, by faith and works, are ye made every whit whole.

Attitudes Affect Health

In high school biology, I learned about experiments with dogs whose digestion was disrupted when they were agitated. From these and other studies, psychologists began to learn about what they called psychosomatic illnesses. Cayce often spoke of the effects of attitudes and emotions on health and suggested further studies of such effects. Here are a few excerpts from some pertinent readings:

To be sure, attitudes oft influence the physical conditions of the body. No one can hate his neighbor and not have stomach or liver trouble. No one can be jealous and allow the anger of same and not have upset digestion or heart disorder. 4021-1

For anger can destroy the brain as well as any disease. For it is itself a disease of the mind. 3510-1

(Q) Is there likelihood of bad health in March?
(A) If you are looking for it you can have it in February! If you want to skip March, skip it—you'll have it in June! If you want to skip June, don't have it at all this year! 3564-1

Much of the condition is physical, and much of it is mental ... self-condemnation, and also condemning in others—which is the highest form of self-condemnation.
...In the mental and the associations, the mental outlook on life, the attitude of life that the world and the conditions and surroundings are at an advariance to self is *all wrong!* Rather do something for the *world,* than having the world do something for you! Act in a way and manner as that a *service* to *others* will be the highest service as may be rendered for self. That held in the mental forces of the body as a grudge can only create *poisons,* can only create distrust, disruption, disorder, discouragement through the whole activities of self. 719-1

All Healing Is From God

There is as much of God in the physical as in the spiritual or mental...

...Understand them as one, yet do not attempt, at all times, to heal with word when mechanical or other means are necessary to attune some disturbed portion with the mental and the spiritual forces of the body.

Remember, the spirit is ever willing; the flesh is weak. 69-5

All healing—body, mind, soul—must come from Him. All applications—as we have indicated, of a mechanical nature, of a medicinal or of a suggestive nature—are only to stimulate any portion of the body, mind or soul activities to coordinate and collaborate with the spiritual force of the body-soul itself. 1467-13

Not palliatives, but healing that is sincere—of whatever nature, whether spiritual, magnetic, mechanical, even drugs, electrical, heat, or whatever application—to be of real aid for the body—must bear the imprint or stamp of the universal or divine...

...Palliatives may be injected for a time; but half a truth is worse than a whole lie, for it deceiveth even the soul! 366-1

The Great Physician

Ms. [2269], a thirty-one-year-old registered nurse who was interested in psychic phenomenon, was told in her life reading, "But keep them [mystical interests], my child, spiritualized—in Him, who is the *great* Teacher, the *great* Physician, the *great* Healer!" (2269-1)

Spiritual healing might be defined as getting right with God. When Jesus healed the paralytic and others, he forgave their sins. He told one person, whom he had healed physically, to stop sinning or something worse might happen. Cayce told Mr. [3545] in a life reading:

For when man has learned that the physician must be the physician to the soul as well as to the body, he will have begun to find the meaning that the Great Physician gave to His ministry in the earth. As He indicated, which is it easier to say, "Son, thy sins be forgiven thee," or "Rise, take up thy bed and walk?" Learn the meaning of such. 3545-1

249

Healing From Within

Some people are confused by suggestions that we can find healing within ourselves. They think that the readings are telling us that we do not need God. Nothing could be further from the truth. The readings are simply echoing the 30th chapter of Deuteronomy—that God and His law can be found within:

> Know that all strength, all healing of every nature is the changing of the vibrations from within—the attuning of the divine within the living tissue of a body to Creative Energies. This alone is healing. Whether it is accomplished by the use of drugs, the knife or what not, it is the attuning of the atomic structure of the living cellular force to its spiritual heritage. 1967-1

Changing Old Patterns

Medical professionals often do not even attempt to tell patients how to change their habits and patterns of living because people so seldom follow through with these suggestions. Even with the Cayce readings, many people never tried to do what they were told to do for their illness. Here is a reading that speak to this kind of pessimism:

> Knowing these tendencies, these weaknesses, does not then indicate that there are those bugaboos continually before the entity. For, these are left behind when ye do that ye know to do, and leave undone those things ye must or else pay the price of neglect, over-indulgence, gratification for the moment that there may be the satisfying of an appetite or tendency as may exist in the body!
>
> Here we find the necessity for care, for exercise, for constant checking up on the bodily activities; not daily, necessarily—but we remember that the body-physical alters in its expression continually, and by the end of a cycle of seven years it has entirely replaced that which existed at the beginning of the period seven years ago. Replaced with what? The same old tendencies multiplied, the same old inclinations doubled—or eradicated? 2533-6

A Person Must Want Healing

The Glad Helpers group was often told that healing could only be accomplished if there was a sincere desire, on the part of the one seeking help, to be healed. The third reading for that group (281-3) said, *"God* cannot save a man that would *not* be saved!"

It was not enough just to want to be made physically whole. The readings said that a willingness to serve others and to be used by God for His purposes was needed for true healing:

> Then because of the fact that destructive forces arise in the physical forces, the impulse, the nature of the disturbance must be first eradicated with a purposefulness in the desire for self to be used in a constructive, helpful, hopeful way... 528-9

One person who, in a letter requesting a reading, sounded quite willing to be healed and desirous of knowing God's will, was nevertheless given this rather stern admonition:

> For the soul seeks its own—in Him, who is the light, the life, the Way.
>
> And when there are rebellions of body or mind against such, is there any wonder that the atoms of the body cause high blood pressure or cause itching, or cause running sores, or cause a rash, or cause indigestion? For, all of these are but the rebellion of truth and light, error and correction in a physical body.
>
> For thy body is indeed the Temple of the Living God. What have you dragged into this Temple? 3174-1

Group Effort

The Glad Helpers group once asked if group action was more effective than individual efforts, and if so why? The answer was:

> "Where two or three are gathered together in my name, I am in the midst of them." These words were spoken by Life, Light, Immortality, and are based on a law. For, in unison is strength. Why?
>
> Because as there is oneness of purpose, oneness of desire, it becomes motivative within the active forces or influences of a body. The multiplicity of ideas may make

confusion, but added cords of strength in one become of the nature as to increase the *ability* and influence in every expression of such a law. 281-24

Learning How to Heal

Those who questioned whether they could participate in the healing prayer when they were, themselves, in need of healing were told: "Healing others is healing self." (281-18)

Here are a few more readings that were given for those who wanted to learn how to heal others:

In the study, then, *open* self—but surrounding self with that presence of Him, that brings healing in its wings. As the thoughts in their currents run through the energies of one seeking, and one to whom such thoughts are directed, there is builded little by little that strength which— *enlivened* by Him—brings all healing, the awakening, the understanding that "All is well." 281-10

(Q) ...By what steps are developed the powers of spiritual healing?

(A) Through spiritual growth. By what powers doth a grain of corn maintain its ability to produce corn; that divine gift to the first corn? By not trying to be something else than a grain of corn! Thus may there come an understanding to any soul, to any that will say "Use me, O God, as Thou will." But not remaining idle! 705-2

(Q) ...Is spiritual healing a gift, or is it a talent we have developed from our past lives?

(A) Both. All force, all power, comes from the same source. To some is given the power of healing, to some the speaking of tongues, to some that of ministry, to some that of another—each as they have builded in their experience, and as they seek to be used as a channel of blessings through *that* they have builded for themselves does the blessing come to others. Being free, then let that not become a stumbling block to some. Rather let those efforts of self be in Him, that *all* blessings may come *to* those in their respective ways. He knoweth what we have need of before we have asked. In the asking, in the seeking, as individuals—and intensified in cooperative thought, cooperative intent, cooperative purpose—so do the activities come to each in *their* way. 262-3

Don't find fault, or try to be like someone else—or try to have someone else be like you. Be like Him—all of you!...
(Q) ...What do I yet need in giving my best service to the group?
(A) More understanding in self, of unselfish, unrequited, undisputed love, of the love *for* the *Master's* way, that ALL may be one in Him. 281-9

One must raise self to that consciousness of a physical perfection in spirit, to give the proper attitude or concept to another. *Doubt* never *accomplished* anything! 281-3

Meditation and Prayer
In giving advice to those who would send out healing to others, the readings often gave affirmations to be said by those who were meditating and by the person seeking healing.

Use for the meditation this, though in the own words:
Father, God! in Thy love, In Thy mercy, be Thou near unto me now; that I may choose to do and to be what Thou would have me be at this time. I ask it in the name of the Christ who promised to be near when we call.
Mean it, be it, live it! And ye will find a new life flowing into thy body. 3254-1

(Prayer recommended for parents of a fifteen-year-old girl, to be used while giving her a massage.)
We thank Thee for the opportunity, O Lord, that we may in some measure meet those things Thou has given for Thy children in this material world. Let the power of the Christ spirit, through those promises given, be made manifest in my life as I minister now—and in the life of this body, [552]—be done that, O God, as Thou seest is best at this time. 552-1

When there are karmic conditions in the experience of an individual, that as designates those that have the Christ-like spirit is not only in praying for them, holding meditation for them, but aiding, helping, in every manner that the works of God may be manifest in their lives, and *every* meditation or prayer: *Thy will, O God, be done in that body as Thou seest best. Would that this cup might pass from me, not my will but Thine be done!* 281-4

The Laying on of Hands

Several people were told in their readings that they had the innate ability to heal by the laying on of hands. Reading 2620-2 is a good example of this:

Thus the entity is given the ability as a healer, even through the laying on of hands, for those needing such as has been indicated...

Use thy abilities to heal, by the laying on of hands, by giving such suggestions that quiet the fears of those who are fearful and doubtful as to their relationships to the Creative Forces or God; thus bringing mental *and* material health and joy to others...

As has been given here, praying with others and letting the vibrations from self pass through or into their bodies. Not taking *on* the vibrations, but laying them all on Him. For He *is* the healer, He *is* life. He overcame death, hell and the grave. He overcame temptation. And in Him is peace, harmony, life. With this accrediting, begin; not by proclaiming—for remember, as He oft gave, "Tell no man." Just be thyself, and trust in Him—and these bring the spirit of truth in thy labor of love for Him.

Patience and Persistence

When we attempt to help others, we should not be too easily discouraged if we do not see results immediately. The healing group of Cayce's time had one particularly difficult case. Someone in the group asked how much longer it would take. In reading 281-5, they were told, "If it's a day or a year, what's the difference if it's accomplished! There is no time! If thou art weary in that thou art doing, then turn back!" Another individual for whom the group meditated subsequently died. Feeling discouraged, they asked why the healing did not occur. The reading told them that they had been of great help to the soul for whom they had prayed and that their efforts were still bearing fruit in the spirit.

Give God the Glory

Cayce always insisted that the credit for healing should be given to God. Is it possible to heal in the name of the Christ and still do it for selfish reasons? Reading 262-87 alludes to the words of the Master:

...He said, "Though in my name ye cast out demons, though ye heal the sick, I will say Depart from me, I never knew you." Why? For ye have your own glory when such is done that it may be seen and known and heard among men alone.

19

Signs in the Heavens:
Astrology—Science or Superstition?

Study also astrological subjects, not as termed by some, but rather in the light of that which may be gained through a study of His word. For, as it was given from the beginning, those planets, the stars, are given for signs, for seasons, for years, that man may indeed (in his contemplation of the universe) find his closer relationships. 5124-1

The Zodiac

Humankind's fascination with the heavenly bodies extends back before the time of recorded history. The above reading refers to Genesis 1:14. The book of Job, considered by some to be the oldest book of the Bible, says, "Can you fasten the harness of the Pleiades, or untie Orion's bands? Can you guide the morning star season by season and show the Bear and its cubs which way to go?" (Job 38:31-32 JB)

In 1884, Joseph A. Seiss wrote *The Gospel in the Stars,* explaining how the constellations of the zodiac were originally designed to depict God's plan of salvation. Other Christian writers have elaborated on this theme, some of them questioning whether modern astrologers have lost the original purpose.

It is only natural that we would observe the stars and try to find some meaning in their positions and movements. It is obvious that the sun and the moon have powerful effects on our lives, and it must have been logical for our distant ancestors to assume that the other heavenly bodies might also affect us in some way.

Biblical Warnings

Any serious student of the Cayce readings will eventually have to deal with references to astrology, numerology, gems and stones, and other related studies. These are areas that initially caused me to be concerned about the character of the readings. However, while I have not devoted a great deal of time to studying these subjects, I have come to appreciate the value of the treatment given to them in the readings. Most of the readings quoted here focus mainly on astrology, but the suggestions given generally apply to the other esoteric sciences as well.

I hope that including these aspects of the readings will be helpful to any reader who might otherwise develop a sincere interest in the Christian aspects of the readings, only to later find references to some supposedly occult practice that had not been mentioned. On the other hand, I would not want to encourage anyone to become engrossed in any practice without thoroughly testing it in the same way as they would test any other spiritual teaching. The readings themselves do a good job of balancing these two concerns.

As Christians, we are usually made aware of the biblical warnings against astrology and divination, and these warnings are still valid today. Life reading 993-3 told a forty-one-year-old-woman who wanted to develop her spiritual gifts, "They [astrological influences] are as *signs,* or *warnings,* and will be as stumbling blocks if allowed to rule *us, rather* than *we* them! and safety from, with, of, by, or *for* such, is in the *knowledge* of Him."

Most of the biblical references to astrology are found in the book of Daniel. The Scriptures tell us that Daniel himself had been appointed "head of the magicians, enchanters, Chaldaeans [some versions use *astrologers*] and wizards." (Daniel 5:11 JB) The difference between Daniel and the pagan wizards was his single-minded faith in God, not that he refused to use the knowledge of his time. The same is true of the other biblical prophets.

It is much easier to condemn or demonize everything that is questionable than it is to study each phenomenon objectively and to develop the gift of discernment. Scientific discoveries have often been opposed by the establishment of the day. It is the constructive application of such knowledge that facilitates its acceptance. While modern science has been used in many ways to aid humankind, there is still a temptation to let the use of medicines, machines, television, and other modern conveniences become habits that replace our dependence upon the Spirit within. If we study astrology objectively and find that some of it is effective, then we will have the same responsibility to use it constructively that we have with respect to other scientific knowledge. The fact that there are some who would use this knowledge selfishly may not be a valid reason to condemn it altogether. Being Christian should not make us so narrow-minded that we become "experts" on what can't be done.

We do not know just how much the ancients knew about the actual effects of the planets and stars upon our lives. Just as we look to environmental and hereditary factors to explain human behavior, however, they studied the planets and the cycles of the return of souls over thousands of years and believed that they had observed some cause-and-effect relationships. To throw out all of their knowledge, even though it may contain some superstition, may be foolish.

After having been exposed to the information about astrology in the readings, I have gradually been persuaded that Cayce's Christian ideals pervade even this aspect of the readings. Cautions such as those in 3356-1 were frequent. Referring to a previous life of the seeker, the reading said, "The entity then was a sand reader ... in the capacity of what might be called a soothsayer, or a crystal gazer, or a star addict." Later in the reading, the seeker was told, "And the other stars, the sun, the moon were all given to be the servants and not rulers of man. Don't forget it! ...these are to be used, yes—but not abused. They do not force men until men have given them the power to do so, as a habit of any other form..."

Proper Use of Knowledge

The readings contain much relevant information about the mechanics of astrology and how the influence of the planets could be studied in relationship to recorded history. They also bring up the fascinating subject of planetary sojourns between earthly experiences. I look forward to the day when we can study and apply such knowledge in the faith and confidence that there is nothing to fear when we have put out trust in God alone, as suggested in the following readings:

(Q) Is it proper for us to study the effects of the planets on our lives in order to better understand our tendencies and inclinations, as influenced by the planets?
(A) When studied aright, very, very, very much so. How aright then? In that influence as is seen in the influence of the knowledge already obtained by mortal man. Give more

of that into the lives, giving the understanding *that the will must be the ever guiding factor to lead man on, ever upward.*

(Q) In what way should astrology be used to help man live better in the present physical plane?

(A) In that which the position of the planets give the tendencies in a given life, without reference to the will. Then let man, the individual, understand how *will* may overcome, for we all must overcome, if we would, in any wise, enter in...

(Q) Who were the first people in the world to use astrology, and what time in history was it first used?

(A) Many, many thousands, thousands of years ago. The first record as is given is as that recorded in Job, who lived before Moses was. 3744-3

For as we have indicated, there are two, yea three phases or schools through which such information, such charts, such characters have been carried—the Egyptian, the Persian, the Indian.

The Persian is a combination and the *older* of all of these, and these are as logos (?), or as charts that have been set. That they have become as experiences in the activities of individuals, to be sure, is not disputed; but the world does not govern *man, man* governs the world! And the inclinations astrologically show whether man has or has not applied will!

Then the inclinations are good, but they may be stumblingstones if one submerges will to listen at inclinations! 826-8

Interplanetary Sojourns

In giving that which may be helpful... respecting the sojourns in the earth, it is well that the planetary or astrological aspects also be given. It should be understood, then, that the sojourning of the soul in that environ, rather than the position, makes for the greater influence in the experience of an entity or body in any given plane. This is not belittling that which has been the study of the ancients, but rather it is giving the *understanding* of same. And... it is not so much that an entity is influenced because the Moon is in Aquarius or the Sun in Capricorn or Venus or

Mercury in that or the other house, sign, or the Moon and Sun sign, in that one of the planets is in this or that position in the heavens; but rather because those positions in the heavens are from the *entity* having been in that sojourn as a soul! This is how the planets have the greater influence in the earth upon the entity, see? 630-2

Each planetary influence vibrates at a different rate of vibration. An entity entering that influence enters that vibration; not necessary that he change, but it is the grace of God that he may! 281-55

Not that ye maintain a physical earth-body in Mercury, Venus, Jupiter, Uranus or Saturn; but there is an awareness or a consciousness in those realms when absent from the body, and the response to the position those planets occupy in this solar system...

Thus ye oft find in thy experiences that places, peoples, things and conditions are a part of self as if ye were in the consciousness of same. 2823-1

Just as the entity's attending this or that university, this or that place of learning, would make for a parlance peculiar unto itself. Even though individuals may study the same line of thought, one attending Harvard, another Yale, another Oxford, another Stanford, another the University of Arizona, they each would carry with them the vibrations created by their very activity in those environs.

In the same way emotions arise from individual activity in a particular sojourn, and are called the *spirit* of the institution to which the entity may have carried itself in its activity.

So we find those astrological sojourns making these vibrations or impressions in the present entity... 633-2

As it [the soul] views itself into the worlds about itself, it recognizes not only that it is a part of this material manifestation of individual entities but a part of a universal consciousness of *worlds* apparently without end. Yet it realizes there is a chord in thought, in purpose, in that intangible something that makes it aware of its desires that may not be answered by the material things; and realizing that the greater influences or forces are the unseen powers that are within the ken of its own consciousness.

Then, as the astrological aspects are seen—these are but spheres of consciousness to which man in his desire to bring same into material manifestation has given names, to which he has accorded this or that influence; some to the weal, some to the woe.

It is not then because an entity was born at a certain season, or a certain phase of the moon, or a certain period of the sun's position to the earth, or any of the planets, or the position of this or that phase of the outer consciousness. But it is because of the entity's application of *self in respect to what* these planets or constellations bring by association of its activities. 1776-1

Free Will

Will is the greater factor, for it may overcome any or all of the others provided that will is made one with the pattern... no influence of heredity, environment or what not, surpasses the will... 5749-14

Study of History

As to those experiences paralleling the cycle of astrological activity now—beginning on the morrow—there will be the Sun, the Moon, Jupiter, Uranus and Venus all in the one sign.

When last this occurred, as indicated, the earth throughout was in turmoil, in strife...

The powers of light and darkness, as then, as sixteen hundred (1600) years before. As in those periods, so today—we find nation against nation...

Thus it will require—yea, demand—that there be an expression on the part of each as to that given thirty-two hundred (3200) years ago: "Declare ye today *whom* ye will serve! As for me and my house, we will serve the living God"...

But *fear not* ye that influence that may destroy the body. Rather give praise and glory to Him who may *save both* body *and* soul to everlasting joy. 3976-26

Signs Not to Be Worshiped

(Q) Must I continue the study of Astrology?

(A) There's no *must* in anyone's life, save "I must not fail to give that credit to God for everything I am or hope to be." 3356-1

As these are but lights, but signs in thine experience, they are as but a candle that one stumbles not in the dark. But worship *not* the light of the candle; rather that to which it may guide thee in thy service. So, whether from the vibrations of numbers, of metals, of stones, these are merely to become the necessary influences to make thee in attune, one with the Creative Forces; just as the pitch of a song of praise is not the song nor the message therein, but is a helpmeet for those that would find strength in the service of the Lord. So, use them to attune self. How, ye ask? As ye apply, ye are given the next step. 707-2

For unless thy numerology may lead in the same direction as the star of Astrology led the Wise to Bethlehem, ye stumble in thy way. For know it was true that the days were numbered, yea, His star had risen—and these were one; and they become again, as they ever were and ever will be, those things that show, that lead, the way. 1402-1

Planets are but steppingstones to the greater consciousness which He would have each soul attain... 2282-1

Rather...than the stars *ruling* the life, the life should rule the stars—for man was created a little bit higher than all the rest of the whole universe, and is capable of harnessing, directing, enforcing, the laws of the universe. 5-2

20

Mind Is the Builder:
The Psychology of the Soul

When asked about various kinds of treatment for physical problems that might have seemed to have a mental component, Edgar Cayce often recommended prayer, meditation, and reading of the Scriptures. For example one person asked, "Would hypnosis help the body conditions?" The reading said, "Not as we find indicated here. Spirituality is the most help. Deep meditation, prayer, will be the most helpful." (3450-1)

There were a few cases where hypnosis was suggested, and Cayce often pointed to physical causes for mental illness or depression, but the readings seldom suggested psychiatric types of treatment. They did, nevertheless, speak often about psychological principles and even suggested to a number of people that they should study psychology. When a twenty-eight-year-old man asked, "What book on psychology would benefit body?" he was told, "The psychology of life; preferably that given in John— the Gospel John. That *is* the psychology of life; for how does it begin? 'In the beginning was the Word, and the Word was with Him.'" (452-6)

Psychology deals with how people think and act, and why they think and act the way they do. Much has been learned about the mind in recent years, but we are still just groping in the dark as long as we choose to ignore our own spiritual nature. Cayce added a dimension to our study of the mind by pointing out that the mind partakes of both body and soul. That is to say that mind functions in both the physical and spiritual dimensions.

> And know that the mental *is* the builder, in character, in nature, in characteristics, in spirituality, in morality, and all influences that direct. For it, the mind, is both physical *and* spiritual. 759-13

Cayce also separates mental activity into the conscious, the subconscious, and the superconscious. This terminology may be a little different from that of secular psychology, but there is some exciting information in these readings for any student of the mind who has the patience to understand it. Many psychologists today have studied Cayce's Work, and it seems that some of them are becoming more aware of the spiritual side of the mind.

Mind Is the Builder

The phrase, "Mind is the builder," occurs in more than 160 readings. This implies that the choices that we make in our minds, with our wills, determine what we become mentally, physically, and spiritually. Again, the readings provide much food for thought on this concept. Rather than trying to summarize this idea, I have included a somewhat condensed excerpt from a Search for God reading on the lesson of destiny:

In the beginning God created the heavens and the earth. How? The *mind* of God *moved*, and matter, form, came into being.

Mind, then, in God, the Father, is the builder. How much more, then, would or should Mind be the builder in the experience of those that have put on Christ or God, in Him, in His coming into the earth? For as He has given, "Let that mind be in you which was in the Christ, who thought it not robbery to make Himself equal with God," but living in materiality in the earth, in matter, as a body; but with the Mind, with the thought, with the manifestations of a Creative Force all together...

That ye think, that ye put your Mind to work upon, to live upon, to feed upon, to live with, to abide with, to associate with in the mind, *that* your soul-body becomes! That is the law...

How does matter, how does the seed of the oak or of the grass or of the flower or of the tree or of the animal or of the man, find within itself that which impels, propagates the specie? the activative force that moves on in its realm of activity in whatsoever sphere it may find itself, giving expressions of that first thought of the Creative Forces? That is Destiny, which the easterners say was set in the first. But, as ye see, this is only half a truth. For if the Mind dwells upon the spiritual things, then it follows that it becomes what it has dwelt upon, what it has lived upon, what it has made itself a portion of. But if the Mind dwells upon self-indulgence, self-aggrandizement, self-exaltation, selfishness in any of its forms, in any of its variations, then it has set itself at variance to that First Cause...

Yet we find the law, the same law, applying throughout the universe. For what was that which enabled man, or a mind, to first comprehend? "Know, O ye people, the Lord thy God is *one!" One* from the beginning to the ending, to those that use, to those that become constructive in their thinking, that are ever constructive in their Minds, in their indwellings, in their resting upon, in their thoughts, in their meditations, and *act in the same manner,* to build towards that which does make, that creates in the experience of each and every soul that knowledge. How easily, then, must it have been said, that it hath not yet entered the mind of man as to the unspeakable glories of him who has washed his raiment in the blood of the Lamb, who has made himself one in thought, in deed, in body, one with that thought, that purpose, that mind, of God.

So as ye contemplate, as ye meditate, as ye look upon the Mind, know the Mind hath many windows. And as ye look out of thine inner self, know whereunto thou art looking, thou art seeking. What is thy ideal? What would you have your mind-body to become? 262-78

Ideals
He without an ideal is sorry indeed; he with an ideal and lacking courage to live it is sorrier still. 1402-1

The readings refer to an ideal as an image of perfection to be striven toward even though we may never expect to reach it in this life. The word *ideal* is very close in meaning to words such as *spirit, purpose,* and *standard,* which are also used frequently in the readings. Ideals are different from ideas that we may have about how to go about applying our ideals. The readings also differentiate between having high ideals and being too idealistic. Cayce said that our growth or success in this life is a function of what we set as our ideals and what we do about those ideals:

As has been given, it [knowing self and the ideals of self] is the most powerful influence in the experience of man— and that which is constructive and to the glory of the

265

Father is worth while, but that which is done without first knowing self—and that is only to see what will happen—you will find self in a maze! 440-14

First, as given, know thy ideal. The abilities are within. Of thyself ye may do little, but if ye bear witness of His spirit working in and through thee ye may accomplish that ye set thyself to do. 2784-1

Reading 642-2, speaking to a florist, makes the analogy that our mind is like a plant or flower, and the ideals that we choose are like the plant food that we give it. Like the plant, our mind will grow to be the best that God made it to be only if we feed it with the highest ideals:

As to negative influences or forces, *rather* should the body maintain from the mental attitude a *positive* state throughout. For Mind as the builder will work with that the bodily functions to are given to act upon. Just as may be seen in nature, or in the entity's or body's own business or surroundings. Any of the plant life will produce the best it can with what it is given to *act upon!* So with the mind of the body, as related to its habits, as related to its relations with things, as related to peoples and activities of various natures; it acts upon that in whatever environ or that expediency that is set or held before it (the mind) as the ideal, see? Hence these changes from the morbid to more of the joyous happiness create, brings about in the experience of some individual unable to do for itself, some happy experience each day, and you will find the greater optimistic outlook, the greater constructive influence in the experience.

Some of the greatest changes that I have seen in the lives of individuals as they participate in study groups using the Cayce material occurs when they consciously attempt to change their ideals away from the mode of self-gratification and more toward that of service to others. Several times the readings suggested that a person should make three columns on a page—mental, physical, and spiritual—and write down their ideals. Here is a typical example:

Not merely as what you may say, but write them [your ideals] down: Body, mind, soul. What is thy spiritual ideal? One God, or many gods? A full belief in faith and in trust, in oneness of all force as manifested in an individual or just nature or just chance, but write it down. As thy experiences cause thee to change, change them.

So in the mental, what is thy mental ideal? That ye should or can cultivate the mind in given directions or that which arises from one source without, or arises from a source within or a combination of same? If so, from whence does it come? From the material impressions or the spiritual insight? What spirit do ye entertain consciously? That of Creative Forces as of God manifested in Christ, or that of a physical evolution of self? But write it down, change it as ye find the growth comes to thee.

Then the ideal in the material: An opportunity to serve all, or opportunity to rule someone else? Remembering, he who would be the greater will be the servant of them all.

The ideal, then, of the material: Is it plenty of money, or position? Or the opportunity to use that thou hast in hand for the glory of the God, for the benefit of thy brother, for making the world where ye are a better place to live? For, if ye are a "taker" and never a "giver", what have ye accomplished?

But write it down. Change it from day to day, and ye should eventually find Jesus, the Christ as the head of body, mind and soul. 5253-1

The readings contain plenty of suggestions on where to start when we want to raise our ideals to the highest possible standard. Here are two more of those suggestions:

Find what is self's ideal. And as to how high that ideal is. Does it consist of or pertains to materiality, or spirituality? Does it bespeak of self-development or selfless development for the glory of the ideal? ... And do not be satisfied with a guide other than the Throne of Grace itself! ... And who better may be such a guide than the Creator *of* the universe? 440-8

There is one ideal—that which manifests in the earth in the Christ-Jesus. *That* should be every entity's ideal—physically, mentally, materially.

What was His application of His spiritual ideal, thy spiritual ideal?

He thought it not robbery to make himself equal with God. So He made Himself of no estate, that He might thereby save the more. 2533-7

Thoughts are Things

If we think of our life as a garden, then negative thoughts are weeds, and good thoughts are vegetables or flowers. We must constantly remove the weeds and cultivate and nourish the desirable plants. You can see the effects of this discipline in people's lives as well as in their gardens.

As thoughts take form, they are something like the physical things that we build in the material world. If we build a house of a certain character, then that is what we may have to live with for some time. If we dwell upon gratifying some desire, even if we don't intend to follow through with it, we will have much less resistance should the opportunity present itself.

The following readings are typical of Cayce's comments about thoughts:

For mind is the builder and that which we think upon may become crimes or miracles. For thoughts are things and as their currents run through the environs of an entity's experience these become barriers or stepping-stones, dependent upon the manner in which these are laid as it were. 906-3

Each thought, as things, has its seed, and if planted, or when sown in one or another ground, brings its own fruit... 288-29

Give then more thought, *for thoughts are deeds...* What one thinks continually, they become; what one cherishes in their heart and mind they make a part of the pulsation of their heart, through their own blood cells, and build in their own physical, that which its spirit and soul must feed upon, and that with which it will be possessed, when it passes into the realm for which the other experiences of what it has gained here in the physical plane, must be used. 3744-5

Personality/Individuality

Even though the definitions of personality and individuality used in the readings may differ somewhat from those of modern psychology, they have had a powerful effect on my thinking. Far from being just semantics, they allow an awareness of the spirit to shine through the mundane studies of the mind of man:

Make then, more and more thy personality shine with the individuality of thy ideal. 5083-2

Do not look on personalities. Look on the individuality of the individual, and know that comes from the spiritual and not from the personal self. This will make it much easier for decisions to be made in relationship with things, circumstances and individuals. 2582-3

Personality is that which the entity, consciously or unconsciously, spreads out before others to be seen of others. As to whether you will say Good Morning to Jim or John, and ignore Susan or not—these are parts of the personality, because of some difference or because of some desire to be used or needed by *that* others would have to give.

While individuality in that same circumstance would be: I wish to do this or that for Susan or Jim or John, because I would like for Jim or John or Susan to do this if conditions were reversed.

One is for the universal consciousness that is part of the soul-entity's activity. The other is the personal, or the desire for recognition, or the desire for the other individual to recognize your personal superiority. 3590-2

Few people, few individual souls really enjoy the companionship of themselves. Not merely because they love themselves the less or that they despise themselves the more. But... their individuality and their personality don't reflect the same shadow in the mirror of life. 3351-1

Right Thinking

In some kinds of group work today, one might hear talk of raising consciousness. Nowhere else have I seen or heard this concept spoken so well, however, as when reading 31-1 said, "...for when duty—love—reason are one, then such consciousness approaches near that of universal love that gave all that man might be one with that universal love."

Even after we have experienced spiritual truth, however, we can be overwhelmed by the materialistic thinking of a secularized world:

> Let not intellectual reasoning, as is sometimes called, dissuade thee from the trust in that birthright which is promised and given to each soul; that indeed thy body is the temple of the living God, and that there, in thy holy of holies, He will meet thee—and His promises do not fail. 2173-1

> The entity then was among those who were in the Ibex Rebellion, being among those of the household of the young King's brother; keeping the tenets of those who expressed in that activity: "If you don't take care of yourself, no one else will do it for you."
> This isn't true. If you live right yourself, everyone will take care of you. 3479-2

> As would be said in very slang manner, the entity is ever ready to "go to bat" for somebody that's been abused, and yet feels itself abused oft. The entity likes to think of itself as being a martyr. Remember He has been the martyr for thee. Ye are to glory in thy strength and in thy abilities, that His may be one day glorified in the earth. He that is the martyr without a purpose is ashamed of self and might well be. For the glory must be in the Cross. 3418-1

Shortcuts

I occasionally get ads from various self-help programs that offer instant bliss and self-fulfillment. There may be some truth in what they are promoting, and it may be a welcome change from everyday pessimism, but I am skeptical of anything that is too easy and instantaneous.

The readings say that truth is not just discovered or professed, but it must be lived. They frequently caution against trying to take shortcuts to knowledge, to wisdom, to righteousness, to peace, to patience, to harmony, to physical or mental success, to God, or to spirituality (See readings 830-2, 1058-5, 1167-1, 1414-1, 1901-1, 2117-1, 2771-1, 5392-1, and 5749-14.).

While the readings do not offer any shortcuts they do offer some real hope:

Do not consider that there is no escape. While there indeed are no shortcuts to spirituality, there are no ways of not meeting in self that self has done unto others except in the material concepts, but there has been and is set before each and every soul this:

There *is* an Advocate with the Father... 1167-1

Mind Control

Jesus often emphasized the spirit of the law rather than the letter of the law. This means that we must control our thoughts and intentions, as well as our actions. Under the spirit of the law, hatred is equated with murder and lust equals adultery. While we do need to acknowledge our feelings and forgive ourselves for negative feelings, we can no longer make excuses, even for our thoughts. Reading 2936-2 says, "Think *well* of others, and if ye cannot speak well of them don't speak! but don't think it either!"

Self-control

If it is true that God's law is perfect and that we build our destiny by our relationships to God and our fellow man, then all of the problems experienced in this earth have an answer in self-control. As we bring our will into harmony with God's will, we begin to experience the joy and peace that He created us to have. Reading 1231-1 says, "The Father, God, hath not willed that man should even *worry*, much less perish; but hath in His direction to His people pointed the way wherein strength, vitality and work come with the closer walking with Him."

When we first begin to realize that our choices have consequences, we begin to try to modify our behavior. Like St. Paul, however, we often find that we cannot easily change patterns that may be very deep-seated in our consciousness from many lives of self-centered attitudes. Cayce suggested that we must have an ideal or image of what we would like to become and then have the courage to grow in that direction.

Churches and other social institutions sometimes give some very constructive guidelines about how people should behave, but they don't always have answers as to how the individual might control self to change behavior patterns. The readings deal frequently with what we call urges and how they change through time in response to our ideals:

> Urges arise, then, not only from what one eats but from what one thinks; and from what one does about what one thinks and eats! as well as from what one digests mentally and spiritually! 2533-6

> Let those influences in the intuitive activities of the mental and emotional body be rather in the control, than allowing same to be continually submerged by the mental on account of material or physical forces that surround the body. For these in their expression may bring to the body that awakening within self that is constantly seeking expression. 718-1

> The information will not do it for you. Did the Lord prevent Abel from being slain? Did He prevent Cain from slaying? Did He not say, "It is in thine own self to do"? So it is with individuals who may be warned or directed. It is within yourself to do or not to do. 2828-5

Learning

Being a parent and a teacher probably predisposed my mind to catch the following reading. When a twelve-year-old boy asked how he could improve his school work and his memory he was told:

> That which ye would attain in the studies as to that which is a text, a thesis or a theory—mull same as it were in thy mind, in thy consciousness. Then lay it aside, and meditate rather upon its application in every way and manner. Do this especially just before ye would rest in physical consciousness, or from physical consciousness—or in sleep. And ye will find thy memory, thy ability to

analyze, thy ability to maintain and retain greater principles will be thy experience. 1581-2

Attitude

Many years ago, while working in a juvenile detention home, I had to make contact with a young man who had been separated from the group because of his violations of the rules. When I asked him what he thought was the cause of his problem, he said, "I have an attitude." This was the first time that I realized that some people think of an attitude only in the negative sense. The readings often speak about attitudes. Fortunately, they usually encourage us to have the positive type:

Some individuals like to have their own way, irrespective of what anyone thinks...

These will never accept other suggestions unless the mental self is changed.

Thus it became necessary that God in His goodness give an ensample, a pattern, by which man might conduct his life, his ideals, his hopes, his fears, all of his idiosyncrasies; a pattern laid out for man. Those who accept same may live in peace and harmony with themselves and with others. Those who reject same continue to find discordant notes between their own associates, and with every activity of life there is continued to be trouble. 5211-1

First, then, the mental attitude towards self, towards the world, towards others, must be changed. For, if ye recognize in self the truth, that which is and was manifested in the Christ-Consciousness, ye will change thy mental attitude—towards self, towards others, towards conditions about thee. *Then* ye may see change in the physical results or manifestations in self. Then ye, too, as He gave of old, will wash and be clean every whit! 3078-1

Resentment

One of the interesting things about the readings is the way they look at the effects on both the sender and receiver of resentment:

273

How does a cross word affect thee? How does anger, jealousy, hate, animosity, affect thee *as* a son of God? If thou art the father of same, oft ye cherish same. If thou art the recipient of same from others, thy brethren, how does it affect thee? Much as that confusion which is caused upon the earth by that which appears as a sun spot. 5757-1

...the manner in which ye treat others ye are treating thy Maker. Keep this much in mind, and resentment will not be so much a part of thy conclusions. 2982-1

Self-esteem vs. Guilt

Modern psychology has put a great deal of emphasis on self-esteem. I share the concern that many of our customs and institutions cause us to put excessive emphasis on comparing ourselves with others. I would also agree that low self-esteem can have a devastating effect on a person. However, I sometimes suspect that thinking too highly of ourselves may be an even greater problem in today's world. We might do well to read the story in Luke (18:9-14) about the Pharisee and the tax collector praying in the temple. Who was justified—the man who felt good about himself or the one who recognized his guilt and was sorry for it?

Think not more highly of thyself than ye ought... For ye have not begun to think straight until ye are able to see in the life of those whom ye utterly dislike, something ye would worship in thy Maker. For each soul-entity in the earth, with life, whether of this, or that shade or color, or whether this or that disfigurement of body or mind, is in the earth by the grace of God. 3575-2

The problem with our focus on self-esteem is that some people attempt to improve their self-esteem simply by the denial of guilt. Understanding this problem is further complicated by psychological semantics (psychobabble) which confuses guilt with feelings of self-condemnation, sorrow, or repentance. Guilt is not really an emotion. It is awareness of the fact that one has failed to live up to some standard. That standard might be manmade laws, God's laws as written in the Bible or in our heart, or our own conscience, which may or may not be attuned to God's laws. The following readings give some examples of that process of becoming aware that we have fallen short:

> These doubts, these fears that come in thine experience are but thine own conscience—or the mind of thy subconscious self—*smiting* thee. 784-1

> For how has it been given? They that would believe must believe that God *is!* And if they do not, don't ask them to look at their own souls—for they are *not* beautiful! 254-96

The process of acknowledging our guilt may be quite healthy, especially if it produces sorrow for our actions and repentance. We should not, however, ignore the problem of false guilt. That is guilt that is produced by false or ungodly standards or by a false assessment of our own responsibility for some action of others over which we really had no control. Of course, psychologists are quite right to help people to recognize false guilt and to avoid any negative consequences that they might experience as a result of it. It might be just as important to recognize false self-justification and make the appropriate corrections.

The real problem created from any kind of conviction of guilt begins when we indulge in self-condemnation. I found well over 100 readings that warned people not to condemn themselves. A thirty-five-year-old woman was told, "Now, while we find there are many abnormal conditions with this body, a great many of these are produced more by self-condemnation than from physical conditions produced by physical reactions." (4358-1)

Here is a reading that demonstrates that we can not fool our higher selves just by lowering standards to avoid "guilt feelings." In fact, it suggests that setting higher standards is the solution to the problem of self-condemnation:

> ...a tendency to at times condemn self for the little things that the body has allowed to interfere with purposes and aims. Not that the body-mental or physical should express self in such a manner as to be one that would act as lauding self, or seeking applause or praise even from associates, or to think of self more highly than he ought to think, yet do not condemn self; rather set a moral, mental

and spiritual standard or ideal and work toward that at all times. Will the entity look back upon the experiences, these will often be found to have been faults or causes of failures, in thinking that self could do or act in the capacity that is felt or seen that another one held in esteem does and get away with it! ... The standard or ideal, then, has not been set high enough. 5489-1

Condemnation

Condemnation of others is not very different from condemnation of ourselves. When we resent ourselves for errors that we have no hope of changing, we often direct that feeling toward others around us. Conversely, when we condemn others for their actions, we often find ourselves compelled to do the very same things.

...and *find not fault* with others. For as the Psalmist has said of old, that ye hate, that ye despise, becomes thine own self. For what ye sow must ye reap. 633-5

Make thy individuality so bright in Him—who is the truth and the light—that ye may *never* condemn thyself nor others, even as He. 2420-1

Know in self that in giving a helpful influence, the magnifying of virtues in others and the minimizing of faults is the beginning of wisdom in dealing with others. not that the evil influence is denied, but rather that force within self is stressed which when called upon is so powerful that those influences about self may never hinder. 2630-1 [See also I John 4:4]

For where would thou be, had God condemned thee and not shown mercy? "Mercy ever, then—not sacrifice—Mercy, Lord, for all." 3155-1

Mental Illness

Much research has been done on the ways that mental illness was treated in the readings. Books about this subject can be found through the A.R.E. I have included here only a few of the simpler and more universal spiritual preventive measures that the readings recommended to guard against mental illness:

(Q) Am I slightly mentally ill?
(A) No, save as to who would be the judge. Every individual is slightly mentally ill to someone else. 5210-1

(Q) Just what should be my attitude and action in regard to same [mental illness in father's family], in order to offset or avoid such influences in my own experience?
(A) Keep the eye single to a service for *spiritual* understanding, and a mental aberration or a mental disturbance may not touch thee! 1442-1

(Q) To what extent have childhood home influences incapacitated the entity for a normal, happy marriage?
(A) Just as much as the individual entity lets it have. For when ye were a child, ye thought as a child, but when ye became a man ye should have put away childish things and not blamed others for same. 4083-1

...and the chorus of self is rather, "Thy will be done in me." Hence there may never be, unless self allows self to become led far astray, any periods when oppression or depression may ever influence the real abilities of the entity in a material or spiritual activity. 282-7

Humor Heals the Mind
Doctors and other health care professionals have been emphasizing the healing power of humor in recent years. The Cayce readings certainly would agree with them. Here are a few examples:

Cultivate the ability to see the ridiculous, and to retain the ability to laugh. For, know—only in those that God hath favored is there the ability to laugh, even when clouds of doubt arise, or when every form of disturbance arises. For, remember, the Master smiled—and laughed, oft—even on the way to Gethsemane. 2984-1

Don't think a grouchy man can ever raise a headed cabbage or a tomato that will agree as well as those raised by a man who laughs and tells a good joke, though it may be smutty! 470-35

One that should cultivate more the humorous side of life; see some wit, some humor. Not that which is at the expense of another; that is, never laugh at anyone, but laugh *with* others often. 2327-1

Remember that a good laugh, an arousing even to what might in some be called hilariousness, is good for the body, physically, mentally, and gives the opportunity for greater mental and spiritual awakening. 2647-1

At least make three people each day laugh heartily, by something the body says! It'll not only help the body; it'll help others! 798-1

One whose sense of humor has and will oft save many an unpleasant situation. Keep that humor! 5262-1

Peace: Contentment vs. Satisfaction

How often do we find people searching for peace of mind? The readings suggest that knowing the difference between satisfaction and contentment will move us a long way in the direction of peace:

The body is prone to keep self and self's activities— whether of the mental, physical, or spiritual side of life—in such a position as to be able to conscientiously shift the blame of *whatever* may happen to another. This is not correct. Let the body learn that, he that would have harmony must be harmonious first within his own self, and such radiation from self will bring to the home, to business, to friends, such a peace that brings harmonious contentment—though not necessarily *satisfied;* but be *content* with that *in* hand, and so act, so live, and so manifest harmony through self's action as to bring that to pass; for what is sown one also reaps. 4733-1

Put self rather, then, in the hands, in the mind, of the *divine* from within, and not attempting, not *trying* to be good... but just *be,* and *consecrate* self to the service of others. This peace, this quietness that will come within self from such, will find a ready answer in the mind, in the heart, in the life, in the expression of those—every one—whom the body contacts.

This is *living* consecration... 5563-1

21

Applied Spirituality:
Changing Old Patterns and Lifestyles

As I worked with the *Search for God* material to try to make some positive changes in my life, I learned at least two things. First, changes in behavior are seldom permanent unless they are accompanied by some real, long-term changes in lifestyles and habits. Next, I learned that one of the most difficult things in this world to do is to persuade family and friends to go along with lifestyle changes. Sociologists tell us that folkways and mores are difficult to change. Patterns that we have built over many lifetimes may be even more inertial.

Spiritualizing Desires

In study group reading 262-64, members asked if physical desires were spiritual in essence, and if it was necessary to give them up to attain spiritual growth. They were told that the physical desires should be spiritualized just as Jesus did when He prayed in the garden. This reading then offered the following prayer to go with the lesson on desire: *"I cannot bear this alone, my Savior, my Christ. I seek Thy aid."* It added, "...such a cry has never, no never, been denied—the believing and *acting* heart."

The next study group reading, 262-65, further defined the idea of spiritualizing desires by referring to the Master's teaching in the sermon on the mount, about turning the other cheek. Cayce said that when we have a tendency to feel antagonism toward those who have treated us unkindly, we should remember that any wrong done to us is actually done to our Maker, and He will deal with them appropriately. Then he added:

> What is spiritualizing desire? Desire that the Lord may use thee as a channel of blessings to all whom ye may contact day by day; that there may come in thine experience whatever is necessary that thou be cleansed every whit. For, when the soul shines forth in thine daily walks, in thine conversation, in thine thoughts, in thine

meditation, and it is in that realm where the spirit of truth and life may commune with same day by day, *then* indeed do ye spiritualize desire in the earth.

Diet and Exercise

When I first became interested in the health aspects of the readings, I was still in the Air Force. At that time, I was about twenty-five pounds overweight and right on the limit of what was acceptable by the Air Force. I was impressed by the health advice that Cayce gave to various people and wanted to try some of the suggestions that were given. My wife was pregnant with our third child, so I took the opportunity to do most of the grocery shopping. She very graciously helped me learn how to cook various kinds of vegetables and tolerated most of my new ideas. I lost the weight I wanted to lose and corrected several minor health problems by following the suggestions given in the readings. My wife and I also developed an exercise routine, based on the readings, that was helpful, and our children got a good start in life by adhering to improved dietary standards. Over the years, however, we experienced some relapses into old patterns. Our children grew older and were exposed to other influences, and we took in three other children who had different tastes. The world around us exerted some influences that eroded our dietary standards and often made us feel too busy to exercise.

Reading 305-2, speaking of diet and other applications, said:

...not doing it today and then neglecting it tomorrow—or putting it off because it's too late, or because you are going somewhere else or want to do some other way! Be consistent, be persistent, if you would give this body health!

When I first read this, it only seemed to add to my sense of failure, but over time, science has proved the readings to be essentially correct about many health-related issues. It is becoming a bit easier to follow good nutritional practices now that health experts regularly reinforce these standards. I know there is hope for the world when my grown children come home and chide me for eating the wrong foods.

Farming and Gardening

It is not easy to find time for gardening within the typical modern lifestyle, but those who care about their diet know that it is also difficult to buy foods that are grown properly. The term "organic gardening" was not used in the readings, but the principles suggested were similar. People were often encouraged to produce some of their own food.

> [In response to a question which asked if it would be advisable to own a farm] This should be the aim, the desire of every soul; to be at least to some extent *self*-sustaining; or owning and creating that as ye consume—from *God's* storehouse and soil! 2345-1

> ...for, as has been given, in every clime where the atmospheric reactions are for a body, those vegetables grown in the immediate vicinity are much better than those grown in other places... 264-23

Sexuality

It is difficult to say anything about sexuality without someone taking it the wrong way or being offended. I believe, however, that the philosophy expressed in the readings about sexuality is crucial for most sincere Christians who would try to evaluate the spiritual aspects of Cayce's work.

In 1935, two people asked Cayce for a reading (5747-3) about sexuality for teens and younger ages, and their relationship to delinquency. Here is the advice that they received:

> ...train *them* rather in the sacredness of that which has come to them as a privilege, which has come to them as a heritage; from a falling away, to be sure, but through the purifying of the body in thought, in act, in certainty, it may make for a peoples, a state, a nation, that may indeed herald the coming of the Lord. For this is the problem, that ye keep the law and present same as holy to those who seek. Who seeks? *every* child born into the earth, from the age of 2½ to 3 years begins to find there is something that takes place within its *body*—and that it is *different;* not as animals, though the *animal* instinct is there, of the biological urge, that is a law! For that is the source of

man's undoing. But ye who set yourselves as examples in the order of society, education, Christian principles, religious thought, religious ideals, hold rather than to anything else to that *love* which is *un*-sexed! For He hath given that in the heavenly state, in the higher forces, there is neither marriage nor giving in marriage; for they are as *one!* Yet ye say ye are in the earth, ye are born with the urge! The awakening, then must come from within; here a little, there a little. Each soul, each body, that is preserved unto Him as a channel of blessings has received and does receive that within itself which makes for the greater abilities for awakening within the hearts, minds, souls and bodies of the young who question "what will I do with the biological urge that arises?" *Purify* same in service to Him, in expressions of love; in expressions of the fruits of the spirit, which are: Gentleness, kindness, brotherly love, long-suffering. *These* are the fruits, and these as the urge of sex are in the nature of the association of ideas, conditions or positions as related to the various conditions about the body. Then set the activity in motion and these become either that which takes hold on hell or that which builds to the kingdom within.

(Q) Are there any sex practices that should be abolished—

(A) (Interrupting) There are many sex *practices* in the various portions of this land, as in other lands, that should be—*must* be—abolished! *how?* Only through the education of the *young!* Not in their teen age, for *then* they are set! When there are activities or speech not explained within the sound or sight of those in their formative years, they, *too,* must one day satisfy that which causes men to come into body-form—*experience* same *themselves!*

Then, by word and by act keep the life *clean!* The urge is inborn, to be sure; but if the purpose of those who bring individuals into being is only for expressing the beauty and love of the Creative Forces, or God, the urge is different with such individuals. *Why?* It's the law; it's the *law!*

This reading went on to suggest that the ideals given should be the basis of materials that were being prepared by the persons seeking information. Then it added, "For unless it may be sanctioned by the powers that *rule* and influence the God-given forces of man, little may be accomplished." I assume that Cayce was speaking here of the churches.

I admire the brave souls who try to teach young people self-control and the freedom to choose according to one's ideals, but it is difficult when so much in our secular culture suggests that we are nothing more than evolved animals. It might be difficult for the more conservative Christians and those of other faiths to accept the Cayce readings. They might be surprised, however, at how similar the values found in the readings are to their own. I believe that these readings contain much information that could make their sex education programs even more successful if applied. For example, reading 2072-16 says:

> To be sure, if the activities are used in creative, spiritual form, there is the less desire for carnal relationship; or, if there is the lack of use of constructive energies, then there is the desire for more of the carnal, physical reaction.

Recently, a group of students came into my classroom, and one of them said that they had been learning about safe sex. I asked, "Isn't that almost an oxymoron?" Since he didn't know what an oxymoron was, I handed him a dictionary. In the meantime, another student said, "They told us that the only real safe sex is absence." Of course, he meant to say abstinence, and the rest of the class had a good laugh about it, but I told him that he really had a good point. As in the case of the patriarch, Joseph, who fled from Potiphar's wife, a hasty retreat might be the only safe response to some situations.

Rather than condemning all sexual thought and activity, as some in the early Christian sects did, or glorifying sexuality as many others have done, Cayce said that we should spiritualize these desires like all other desires. He was hesitant to give people answers that they should be learning to receive directly from the Holy Spirit within. The following two readings, one for a thirty-three-year-old man and the other for a twenty-four-year-old woman, are good examples of how a reading could refer one back to one's own relationship with God while, at the same time, giving a very powerful suggestion in favor of morality:

As ye would have men do to you, do ye even so to them. In the light of thine own understanding, keep thy body pure, as thou would have others keep their bodies pure. For thy body is the temple of the living God. Do not desecrate same in thine own consciousness. 826-2

(Q) Is it desirable for this body to have sex relationships other than that obtainable through a marriage, if it has its inception in the spiritual mind?

(A) The relationships that come from that which is of the highest vibrations that are experienced in the material world are those that may be found in such relations, and are the basis of that which is termed the original sin; and hence may be easily misunderstood, misconstrued, mis-interpreted in the experience of *every* individual; but these should be known—that the control of such, rather than being controlled *by* such, gives that which makes for the awareness of *spiritual* intent and purpose. To overstep those conditions created by those environs in social relations and atmospheres that are brought about by such, however, is to take those leaves with self that may not be *easily* retained. Take not, give not, that that cannot be taken and given in the spirit of "*His* will, not mine, be done!" Each must judge such for themselves, in the light of *their* understanding. 911-5

The readings contain numerous suggestions that can put sexual terms in a more spiritual context. For example, reading 3545-1 says, "Do not confuse affection with love. Do not confuse passion with love." Reading 826-6 says:

For *life* is of, and is, the Creative Force; it is that ye worship as God.

Those then that besmirch same by overindulgence besmirch that which is best within themselves. And that should be the key to birth control or sex relations, or every phase of the relationships between the sons and the daughters of men—that would become the sons and daughters of God.

Marriage

Many questions were asked of Edgar Cayce about marriage. Perhaps the most important questions dealt with whether a person should get married and to whom. People were often given some guidelines and told to choose for themselves. A twenty-nine-year-old man who asked for a general standard by which to measure one's motives for marriage was told:

> There should be sought as to whether the relationships between those of opposite sex are for a united, cooperative service to a living God and of a spiritual prompting, or are they prompted by material desires?
>
> If they are prompted by that which has so oft been true—as of convenience, or for only the beauty of the body or of the companionship physical—these must become palls one upon the other.
>
> Then the standard would be as He hath given: There must be the *answering* within each that their *spiritual* and *mental* desires are *one!* 1173-11

Working toward that kind of unity of purpose was probably the most common general advice given for married couples. They were often told to make a conscious effort to be companionable and agreeable with each other.

> ...Individuals should, as this couple, work towards a oneness of purpose. This is indeed a couple where in purpose, in ideal they are one. Hold to this above everything, grow together, unfold in thy study of spirituality, of spiritual things, of God, of God's relationship to man...
>
> ...that which is the ideal as set by the Maker Himself is in those means in which there would be two manifesting as one in their hopes, in their fears, in their desires, in their aspirations. 2072-15

> (Q) If they marry, will there be issue; and if so, how many boys and girls?
>
> (A) This would depend, to be sure, upon their activity in these relationships. This should be kept inviolate. But let rather this be answered from the Giver of those

opportunities, those privileges that are in the experience of father and mother. For those that may be lent them are of the Lord. Let such associations, let such desires be, "Not my will but Thine, O Lord, be done *in* and through me." 939-1

...For the lack of such agreement [concerning physical relations] brings more discordant notes between individuals than any portion of relationships with the opposite sex. The disagreements may be very slight at times, but they grow. For these relationships are the channels for the activity of creative forces and not by mere chance. 4082-1

Then let each—in thy daily activities—think not on that which satisfies thyself alone, nor yet that which would be indulgence of the other; but rather as to how ye may each become the greater, the better channel for the glory of *life,* of God, of His gifts, of His promises, of His peace, of His harmonies—that they may manifest in thy cooperation one with another. 1523-6

...Remember, the union of body, mind and spirit in such as marriage should ever be not for the desire of self but as *one.* Love grows; love endures; love forgiveth; love understands; love keeps those things rather as opportunities that to others would become hardships.
Then, do not sit *still* and expect the other to do all the giving, nor all the forgiving; but make it rather as the unison and the purpose of each to be that which is a *complement* one to the other, ever. 939-1

And in *love* show the *preference* for that *companionship,* in the *little things* that make the larger life the bigger and the better! And *ever* keep this in the inmost recesses of the heart—that in love the world was saved and made; in hate and indifference the world may be destroyed. 903-3

Sow seeds of confidence, even though they are trampled upon. But don't sow them and expect them to be trampled upon! Be hurt whenever they are, yes—but do it again and again!

Was He not buffeted for thee? Are ye not in association and companionship with thy sister, then, that ye may—as He—give and give again of those hopes, of those helps, of those confidences, of that love which bringeth harmony and peace to all? 1523-11

When a woman who ran a business with her husband asked, "Would it be best for me or Mr. [2273] to make business decisions?" the response was, "How has been the counsel? That ye must be as helpmeets one for the other. Counsel together; but oft let the Lord have *His* way,—not Mr. [2273]'s nor your way either!" (2272-1)

A fifty-three-year-old woman asked, "How may we, my husband and I, better unite our soul-forces for the betterment of humanity?" The answer included one of my favorite affirmations:

Be of one mind, of one purpose, or one desire—by that constancy in prayer; in thy own words, but:
Lord, here am I. Use me as Thou seest fit. Be thou the guide, o God, every step of the way; that we may glorify the Christ among men. 2574-1

Several readings gave advice for those who struggled for control or felt a lack of freedom:

So oft is the ego so enrapt in self that it feels it will lose its importance, its place, its freedom. Yet to have freedom in self, give it. To have peace in self, *make* it—give it! 1650-1

But "Vengeance is mine, saith the Lord."
Hence those who attempt to "get even" or those who would stand for their rights irrespective of what may be brought for others will find disturbing forces in their experience in the material sojourns. 1539-2

Then be guided by that which speaks from within, and not by every word of others that would have thee defy this, or demand that, or to feel thou art being mistreated in this or that manner. 1326-1

Divorce

The readings had the greatest respect for the sanctity of marriage. Even so, there were a few cases in which one or the other of the parties involved refused all help, where they were told that divorce was inevitable. In most cases, however, the readings were quite direct in challenging the person asking for the reading to make every effort to make the marriage work. The following reading was one of those difficult cases:

(Q) Considering that I still love my husband and want to win him back, please advise me just what is best.
(A) Then *act that way*. Not in any manner condoning those unhappy happenings, but forgetting self. How hath He put it? Love knoweth no evil; love thinketh no evil; love beareth all things, endureth all things—without question.
Then if that is thy purpose, take it to Jesus—and He will direct thee, He will guide thee.
If thy mate then chooses to flaunt it all and to abuse, mistrust and leave all those things—bear it without question; trusting in God and the promises in Jesus, and ye will find peace and harmony and glorious happiness in service to others. 1326-1

In another reading Cayce not only reminded a couple of their marriage vows, but also that God had a plan for their marriage:

...Each can think for self, but before God and man there was the promise taken "Until death do us part!" This is not idle; these were brought together because there are those conditions wherein each can be a complement to the other. Are these to be denied?
...This ye know, ye will never find harmony by finding fault with what the other does. Neither will the other find harmony without considering what the other will think, or be, or care for.
Know ye this, each of you: The law of the Lord is perfect, ye cannot get around it. Ye may for the moment submerge it, but thy conscience will smite thee. Try it! For a period of six months, never leave the home, either of you, without offering a prayer together: "Thy will, O God, be done in me this day." This is not sissy; this is not weak; this is strong.

289

For God hath a purpose with thee, else ye would not be conscious of thyself as being a living human being this day. 2811-3

Sometimes, in spite of the best advice in the world and the best efforts of the parties involved, divorce will occur. The readings recognized that, in such cases, forgiveness, kindness, and understanding were in order.

Home
Anyone who has been in the military knows that, during combat, the focus of the whole organization is on those who are on the front lines. The rest of the people, from administration to supply, are support troops. Cayce's comments about homes made it clear that homes are on the front lines of spirituality. Governments, schools, health care systems, industries, entertainment, and even churches are all support organizations for the final product—homes:

When the necessities are such as to require waiting and patience even, in those things that may at the time appear to be as negligence on the part of the one or the other, do not rail at such times or allow these things to become stumbling blocks; but always *reason* well together...

(Q) As my Life Reading [480-1] gave that I might attain to the best in this experience thru music or the play, how may I coordinate same with marriage and express the highest in both?

(A) For in the home is the music of what? As indicated, it is an emblem of the heavenly home. And as these are made into the harmonious experiences that may come in the associations, they may bring indeed the music of the spheres in the activities as one with another, and those that must be contacted in the highest of man's achievement in the earth—the *home!* 480-20

The home is the nearest pattern in earth (where there is unity of purpose in the companionship) to man's relationship to his Maker. 3577-1

Hence the greater of all the abilities of an entity is the ability to build an ideal in the home. Rather than so much the ideal home, the ideal in the home; that there may be the seed of the spirit of truth... 1947-1

Dare to do that that is right, and in accord with that ideal chosen as the standard for the home! ...So act, so conduct self *irrespective* of what others may say or others may do. Be rather as he of old, "Others may do as they may, but as for me and my house, *we* will serve the Living God!" 903-17

...For the home is the foundation of the ideals and purposes of the nation. 3241-1

Children

Just as with choosing a mate, the laws of attraction are in operation even in the unseen world of spirit. When one woman asked if it would be wrong to bring a child into such a corrupt world, she was asked what condition the world would be in if Mary, the mother of Jesus, had felt that way. The following readings leave one wishing that we could do more to train young people to prepare themselves for having children:

For this, then is in *every* birth—the possibilities, the glories, the actuating of that influence of that entrance again of god-man into the earth that man might know the way. 262-103

Study as to how Hannah consecrated the life of her son [Samuel] to the service of Jehovah, how that [he was] under the influence of the law in every respect and tutored by one [Eli] who was unable to (or did not, at least) tutor his own. What [was] the difference? The consecration of the body yet unborn! When would one begin, then, to teach or train their children? Many months even before there is the conception, that the influence is *wholly* of the Giver of good and perfect gifts. 5752-2

Here is something each and every mother should know. The manner in which the attitude is kept has much to do with the character of the soul that would choose to enter through those channels at the particular period. This has been indicated as the attitude, "If ye love me and keep my commandments, I will love you—as ye do unto others, ye do unto me –." Does this seem strange, or isn't it consistent with God's plan of creation? That attitude held, then, during these periods, presents the opportunity for the type or character of soul seeking expression. 2803-6

And if such forces [sexual urges] are turned to those channels for the aggrandizement of selfish motives, or for the satisfying of that within the urge for the gratification of *emotions,* they become destructive; not only in the manner of the offspring or also in the very *physical* body of the offspring, as well as in the energies of the bodies so producing same. 826-6

Thus the greater unison of purpose, of desire, at a period of conception brings the more universal consciousness—or being—for a perfect or equalized vibration for that conception. 281-46

There were also many readings that contained sound spiritual advice on raising children. Below are just a few examples:

To deny or to build a barrier between one parent and another in its correction, then this again builds a barrier. And they (the children) cannot love two masters. They (the parents) must be *one!*

Well that the world would learn that given of old, "Know (O Parents) O Israel, the Lord thy God is *one!*

And unless the purpose of all those that aid, all those that guide, all those that direct the developing life of a soul are *one,* they build destructive forces in its (the soul's) experience. 759-13

...Be able, then, of thine own consecration, to be one *with* them in *their* problems, for in the tot that has just begun to think *their* problems to them are as great as thine own, yet how easily are the forgotten—as yours should be!

Train in the way as a child, and when old they will not depart from laying trouble aside. 5747-1

Then, those who would train same,—study to show themselves approved unto God. Not then only by precept but by example teach the entity.
For, the Way was shown by precept and example. 1958-1

Study first in self...to show self approved unto its ideals and *not* to *tradition!* "For of tradition," as the Lord hath given, *"I am done!"* But with purposefulness of knowing and giving the better reaction. 759-12

Music

Many people were told to develop their musical abilities, and a few were told to pursue music as a career. Music is a powerful tool in our lives that helps us attune to spiritual influences, and, like other aspects of our lifestyles, music should be brought into harmony with our ideals. As reading 3179-1 says, "[Music] is that which spans the distance between the sublime and the ridiculous, between the finite and the infinite. Keep the music, for it is oft a help to thee to quell the storms of life." Here are just a few more examples:

Music as color, as tone, is a *destructive* or *creative* force, dependent upon that to which it appeals in the influence of individuals. 3509-1

...For music is of the soul, and one may become mind and soul-sick for music, or soul and mind-sick from certain kinds of music. 5401-1

Have an ideal in the music as well as in the morals, as well as in the spiritual associations, as well as in material aspects. 2011-1

Let thy *joy* in Him break forth in song, even as when He had given, "It is finished," and sang the song that raised the purposes in the minds and hearts of those that were gathered about Him... 827-1

...in thy music, as ye practice even, see in each note a voice, a song, a note of praise raised to *Him,* who is the giver of all good and perfect gifts, and who is hurt when such gifts are used for indulgence, for gratification, or in any respect not to glorify *Him..* Not that this is selfish, for as it glorifies *Him* it is ever as he gave, "And I, if I be lifted up, will draw all men unto me." 3053-3

Balancing Work and Recreation

Then budget the time, that there may be a regular period for sustaining the physical being, also for sustaining the mental and spiritual being. As it is necessary for recreation and rest for the physical, so it is necessary that there be recreation and rest for the mental. The spirit is willing, the flesh is weak. Do not court the flesh, but do give voice and heed to keeping the body as the temple of the living God, as indeed it is. 3691-1

PART FIVE

WORLD TRANSFORMATION

22

A Christ-Centered Worldview:
Integrating Science and Religion

...For the time has arisen in the earth when men—
everywhere—seek to know more of the *mysteries* of the
mind, the soul, the *soul's* mind—which man recognizes as
existent, yet has seen little of the *abilities* of same. 254-52

Having been employed in fields dealing with science and
technology most of my life, I have been interested in those who
study and write about the areas where science and spirituality
intersect, or what used to be called metaphysics. I once read P.D.
Ouspensky's *Tertium Organum* because Cayce recommended it for
a person wanting to understand "myself, time and space." I have
also looked at some more recent works ranging from *The Dancing
Wu Li Masters* to *The Holographic Universe*. I have seen how new
ways of understanding the material world, from relativity,
quantum mechanics, and atom splitting to lasers, holograms,
chaos theory, and fractals, can contribute to, rather than detract
from, a spiritual view of reality. For me, however, the Cayce
readings have still been unequaled in suggesting a worldview that
bridges the gap between science and religion.

In reading 3544-1, Cayce told an individual, "It is well to judge
things—it is bad to judge yourself or your fellow man." I hope that
my remarks in this chapter will be taken as commenting on ideas
and not as being judgmental of the people who may have
advanced such ideas.

Positivism/Humanism
My guess is that it was partly because of a narrow literal
interpretation of the Scriptures, and also because of the
perception that some of the clergy were self serving individuals or
political pawns, that some scholars in the last two hundred years
felt the need to distance themselves from religious or spiritual
belief systems. Calling themselves positivists, these scholars
believed that science should limit itself to the study of phenomena
that could be apprehended by the five senses. This approach to

the world is still fairly common, although today it might be called humanism rather than positivism. To some people, humanism might mean simply a revival of the Greek and Roman classics. Some people are called freethinkers, agnostics, or humanists by those who consider them to be nonbelievers. Others call themselves humanists, or even secular humanists, and believe that they are more enlightened than those who live by faith.

Some early religious humanism came from within the Church itself as a reaction to a proliferation of allegorical interpretations of the Bible that stretched the imagination. At times, when these fantasies seemed to have encouraged superstitions and even mass hysteria, there were those who reacted by swinging the pendulum back in the opposite direction. One such movement sought to study the Scriptures from the point of view that they were written by human beings to be read by other human beings. For some, this approach was fruitful, but it sometimes was taken to the extreme of denying all revelation or any action of the Holy Spirit in the world.

Even some of the religious beliefs that came out of the Reformation may have inadvertently contributed to the appeal of humanism. In addition to the reaction against prayer for the deceased, another belief that may have been a factor in the shift of modern thinking toward a more materialistic worldview is the doctrine of predestination. This spiritual determinism of predestination may have created a mindset that paved the way for material determinism in the name of science. Even though it was a reaction to legitimate concerns about certain practices of the church, various versions of the theology of predestination were justified with some creative interpretations of selected Scriptures, while ignoring the overwhelming evidence of other Scriptures that emphasize God's challenges to us to make constructive choices. For example, the Cayce readings quoted Revelation 22:17 ("...all who want it may have the water of life, and have it free." (JB)) numerous times to make the point that every soul is offered the opportunity to accept the free gift of salvation.

Just as there are religious zealots, there are also humanistic zealots, and they also have their organizations. One group with which I have had some personal contact broadcasts the idea that their philosophy is based on reason while Christians base their beliefs on blind faith and superstition. Some of them actively seek to replace freedom of religion with "freedom from religion." Their belief seems to be that truth can exist only in a spiritual vacuum.

In *The Future of an Illusion,* Freud assumed that all religious rules are designed to protect civilization by frustrating man's asocial instincts. Freud asserted that ideals are really tools used by the ruling class to induce the masses to conform to their wishes, and that only gratification of "instincts" can give happiness. He predicted that, in just a few years, Christianity would be forgotten. Nietzsche declared God to be dead; Marx called religion the opium of the people; and many people assumed that Darwin's theory of evolution had explained away God's part in creation. Such materialistic philosophies were not new to history, but they added great momentum to modern secularism. Whether these ideas may have been taken out of context or not, they were promulgated so vigorously that it seemed that they would succeed in giving a spiritual lobotomy to the mind of modern mankind.

Fortunately these beliefs are not typical of all humanistic thinkers. Some humanists say that they believe in free will, morality, and personal responsibility, and they even accept that actions have consequences. At the same time, as I see it, materialistic thinking pulls the rug out from under the very moral actions that some humanists advocate by denying the possibility of eternal life and even the existence of God apart from human imagination. Carried to the extreme, this kind of thinking implies total environmental and genetic determinism, leaving no room for free will or moral choices.

Cayce often quoted what has been called the humanism passage from the Bible, "We are not being so bold as to rank ourselves, or invite comparison, with certain people who write their own references. Measuring themselves against themselves, and comparing themselves to themselves, they are simply foolish." II Corinthians 10:12 (JB) In the words of one reading:

> Confusion is often caused, then, and is ever caused unless there is an ideal drawn or accepted by which all of these conditions, all of these experiences—whether physical, mental or spiritual—may be judged; or from which conclusions may be drawn.
>
> Otherwise we are measuring ourselves *by* ourselves, and this becomes unwise. For it again leaves confusions as to what is another's standard...

There then cannot be one measure for you and another for I, but rather is it of such a nature that it takes hold upon all that is, all that was, all that may ever be. For that consciousness is a part of same...

It is because the self has become enmeshed or entangled in the desires of the body, without full consideration of the mind and spirit that knows no *end!* and thus confuses the spiritual, the mental, the physical self.

Then the judgment, then the ideal, is that of the universal love, universal consciousness—that as was and is, and ever will be, manifest in Him, even the Christ—as was shown in the flesh in the *man* called Jesus!   954-5

Objectivity

I once worked on a farm for a man who, in addition to the farm, also owned a pest-control company. One day he commented that it seemed to him that all ministers and preachers just pretended to believe in eternal life because of the good living they made off of the contributions elicited from their parishioners. Then he turned to me and asked if I agreed with him. I replied that he might be right about some of them, but that my guess was that the percentage of ministers who were honest and sincere might be at least equal to the percentage of pest-control people who were altruistic. While I believed my employer to be a person of integrity, his smile indicated to me that he might have seen his share of tricks in that industry also. This discussion might be archetypal of the conflicts and false dichotomies between science and religion. Neither is inherently more or less objective than the other. Lack of intellectual honesty is a human frailty that can sneak into any field of study.

The positivist model of objectivity almost requires that we not see the big picture of how individual phenomena are related to the whole. This can lead to some rather spurious tests of objectivity. The following quote, while perhaps somewhat out of context, is just one example of this problem.

In an interview with several scholars in the July/August 1997 *Biblical Archaeology Review,* [scholar A] was accused by [scholar B], a biblical minimalist, of trying to prove the existence of Solomon's gate. Scholar A replied, "...I'm probably more of a disbeliever than you. I don't really care about the tradition. I don't believe any of the myths." This almost gives the impression that biblical archaeology is only legitimate when it tends to prove the Bible wrong or that only nonbelievers can be objective.

The natural tendency to maintain our status as experts is a constant temptation. In the subject of physics, whom would you trust? In his day, Albert Einstein might have been considered the foremost expert in the field. He devoted much of his life to the study of physics, and most scientists would agree that his theory of relativity was quite brilliant and has proved to be correct. It is now generally accepted, however, that Einstein was dead wrong about quantum mechanics when he said, "God does not play dice with the universe." (To which Niels Bohr responded with something like, "Who is he to tell God what to do?") Einstein knew how planets, stars, and galaxies act, but his assumptions about subatomic particles were not infallible.

Habitual objectivity is a virtue to be cultivated and respected in any study, whether physical, metaphysical, or social. But we must admit our limitations, some of which are self-imposed. In *Tertium Organum,* Ouspensky compared the positivist to a person in a movie theater who is trying to determine the causes of the action on the screen by limiting his analysis to the screen itself. As long as he refuses to turn around and look at the projector, he will never fully understand the source of the events that he is observing.

The Religion of Science

One danger in the modern approach to physical sciences is that we often learn just enough to find out that what used to be a mystery can now be understood. We then assume that science will eventually find physical causes for everything that we experience. As we look more and more to environment and heredity to provide completely deterministic causes for human behavior, we might establish some apparent cause-and-effect relationships, but they are often only true in the short term. This quest can only lead to the old clock theory. This is a belief that everything in the universe was set in motion by some first cause billions of years ago and is just running like a giant clock. It becomes increasingly difficult, however, to find that first cause. In fact our "big bang" approach may be leading us away from it.

It is not difficult to see how materialistic science, with its procedures, double-blind studies, and experiments, has become almost a religion for those who rely on it. Some adherents of this belief system have polarized themselves against a few religionists who insist on a literal interpretation of Genesis. Some geologists, for example, have taken the principles of uniformitarianism—the belief that earth changes have been very gradual for millions of years—to imply that the Biblical account of the flood was nothing more than a myth.

Others have attempted to explain away God's work in creating life forms on Earth with the theory of natural selection. Few would doubt that some natural selection occurs, but it may have been expected to explain too much. In *Tertium Organum,* Ouspensky said, "But we do not realize, do not see the presence of intelligence in the phenomenon and laws of nature... But studying the little finger of a man we cannot see the intelligence of the man. The same refers to nature. We always study the little finger of nature."

Reading 3744-2 alludes to another problem of narrowing our view to the physical world only:

> Hence we would have in the truest sense, *psychic,* meaning the expression to the material world of the latent, or hidden sense of the soul and spirit forces... for without the psychic force in the world the physical would be in that condition of "hit or miss," or that as a ship without a rudder or pilot, for that element that is the building force in each and every condition is the spirit or soul of that condition...

Even though we have only scratched the surface of scientific inquiry, it is becoming increasingly clear to the logical mind that some answers must lie outside of the realm of three-dimensional humanistic existence. While we may find some symbolic truth in our evolving myths of the big bang and evolution, we can-not count on them to give meaning to life or answer the question, "Why?"

The Science of Religion

I think of religion today as being in a stage of development comparable to that of science at the end of the Middle Ages. Aristotle had been proven right about some things and wrong about other things. Much of science was still based on Aristotle's work, and he was even called the father of science. Yet, it was the Aristotelian physicists, even more than the Church, whose apple carts Galileo upset with his new theories of physics and with the idea that the Sun was the center of the Solar System. While Galileo's former associate, the Pope, did still favor the geocentric theory, he had only told Galileo not to publish the heliocentric theory as a fact until he could prove it. Galileo, nevertheless, not only published this theory before he had the mathematical proof, but he did so in a manner that many took to be an insult to his old friend, the Pope.

The Church's action against Galileo cannot be excused by the fact that the writing he did while under house arrest has become part of the foundation of modern physics. The Vatican has subsequently acknowledged its mistake and apologized. Historians, however, have begun to recognize that it was the university professors who pressured the theologians to censure Galileo. Today, one has to hope that it will not be religious or spiritual leaders that will offer the greatest resistance to studying, testing, and learning about spiritual truths.

It was not accidental that the word "research" was included in the name of the A.R.E. The readings often said that the organization should be doing more research. Cayce told those who wanted to market some of the medical products recommended in the readings that they should first do the research to prove the efficacy of these compounds and devices. He also suggested research on spiritual subjects. Several readings address this effort:

(Q) Will psychic phenomena ever, or within say 50 years, be accepted and provable on directly scientific measurements; that is on meters (instruments) and mathematics? If not, why?
(A) When there is the same interest or study given to things or phases of mental and spiritual phenomena as has been and is given to the materialized or material phenomena, then it will become just as practical, as measurable, as meter-able, as any other phase of human experience. 2012-1

Be sure that everything is done in decency and order, and there is not the attempt to measure spiritual things by material standards, nor *material* things by *spiritual* standards; for each to their own place. 254-60

Then, interpret not spiritual things by material affairs, nor material affairs by spiritual alone. True, the motivating force must be the spirit of truth—as is the Holy Spirit the motivating force of man's relationship to God and to the fellow man. 1947-1

Cayce told Ms. [5322], who needed to analyze and think things through for herself, to find at least ten promises of the Master in the Bible. He said that these promises were a direct challenge to her in dealing with moods that were troubling to her. Then he added, "Isn't it a scientific fact that He is the savior of the world? Or have ye thought of it in that manner? It is true." (5322-1)

Life reading 487-17, after explaining how the record that a soul leaves upon "the film of time and space" might be recalled, says:

What then, the entity asks, is a soul? What does it look like? What is its plane of experience or activity? How may ye find one? It may not be separated in a material world from its own place of abode in the body-physical, yet the soul looks through the eyes of the body—it handles with the emotions of the sense of touch—it may be aware through the factors in every sense, and thus add to its body as much as the food of the material world has made for a growing physical body in which the soul may and does indeed dwell in its passage or activity in any individual phase of an experience in the earth...

[Here the reading speaks of a seven year cycle, referring to the idea that all the cells in the body are replaced in that time.] How has the scientist or the biologist arrived at the conclusions, that are glibly given, that a body is altered or renewed in such a space of time? By comparing the activities!

But what has still remained that makes those about the body aware that the same *entity* (not body, but *entity*) is manifesting or inhabiting—if you please—such an altered or changed body? That which shows through the activities of the soul of the body!

A couple of years ago, I did a search for studies on reincarnation in the database of psychology abstracts at a nearby university. I was quite surprised, not only at the number of articles that dealt with reincarnation, but also with the scientific methods that researchers employed to assess the sources of apparent past-life recall by various subjects. They usually tried to rule out multiple personality, role playing, genetic memory, clairvoyance, telepathy, possession, fraud, and various other factors before accepting a case as a possible past-life recall. Nevertheless, there were numerous cases where reincarnation was said to be the most likely explanation. Other studies that try to assess the efficacy of prayer in the process of healing have been widely publicized in recent years. I mention these studies not to imply that spiritual phenomenon have been scientifically proved beyond a shadow of a doubt, but to point out that many scientists no longer fit the positivist mold of ruling out spirituality offhand.

In 1937, a group of people who were impressed by finding documentation that verified some past-life information from their life readings from Cayce, wanted to start a research project to prove the validity of these readings. A reading on this project (5753-2) told the group that they would prove little to those who chose to remain skeptical. It suggested that the more important project would be to study several individuals who had had life readings to see if it had made their lives better. The test was always to look at the good that this information produced in peoples' lives:

> Ye may gain knowledge of same, for incarnations *are* a *fact!*
> How may ye prove it? In thy daily living!
> ...Then, seek and ye shall find—if it is to be constructive, well; if it is for self-glorification, well—provided this does not make thee more humble it is bad.
> ...But determine that it is for a constructive force in the experience, and that it is to make for the study of self in such a manner that there may be in the experience a better mother, a better father, a better neighbor, a better relationship with individuals, and that it is to be used as such and not attempted to be either cast before swine or set up as the pedestal to be worshiped or to be impelled into the minds of others! But self-examination and self-development, by and through the will of Him who giveth life to all!

...And unless it is used in such a manner, *we* wound not give that it is worth thy trouble.

I believe that we have all had our soul warmed somewhere by a person who manifested the fruits of the spirit. That may not seem measurable to some, but I believe that this is a manifestation of spiritual growth that can be observed over a period of years by any patient observer.

Religion and Science Are the Same

Just as the forces that tend to fragment human knowledge are ancient, so are the efforts of scholars who tried to reconcile spiritual and physical truths. Pythagoras, Plato, Clement of Alexandria, St. Albert, Roger Bacon, and many others have demonstrated ways in which science and faith go hand in hand.

Reading 5023-2 was given in 1944 for a forty-five-year-old teacher. Mr. [5023], who was looking for answers to his philosophical questions through a study of science, was told that he must understand why "the spirit of life, the spirit of light, of hope, of desire to know the truth, must be greater than that man has called scientific proof, and yet it is the science of light, of truth, of love, of hope, of desire, of God."

It is interesting that Mr. [5023] was told that, in a former life, he had been an associate of Thomas Paine. The reading praised Paine for bringing to the framers of our government "a realization of the need for a trust to man's seeking to be helpful to his fellow man." Yet, he was told that his association with Paine had contributed to his present periods of disturbance.

A quick look a Paine's works reveals that, while not the atheist that some people accused him of being, Paine called himself a Deist, and some of his writings were decidedly anti-Christian. Paine denied the validity of all "inspired" scriptures, and considered the virgin birth of Christ to be entirely unbelievable and contrary to reason. This may help put in perspective the following excerpt from [5023]'s reading:

> For the entity finds that it is true there is nothing in heaven or hell that may separate the entity from the knowledge or from the love of the Creative Force called God, but self. And that the entity should determine in self to apply, rather than mere knowledge or surmise, but apply

and listen to the still small voice within, and the entity will find that the promises are true which have been made in that which is foolishness to the scientific or wise, the simple story of Jesus of Nazareth. But when or if the entity takes this as its study (and set this as its thought and then read, then study the Book which tells of Him, Jesus born in Bethlehem of the Virgin Mary), know this is the same soul-entity who reasoned with those who returned from captivity in those days when Nehemiah, Ezra, Zerubbabel were factors in the attempts of the reestablishing of the worship of God, and that Jeshua, the scribe, translated the rest of the books written up to that time. Then realize that is the same entity as mentioned who as Joshua was the mouthpiece of Moses, who gave the law, and was the same soul-entity who was born in Bethlehem, the same soul-entity who in those periods of the strength and yet the weakness of Jacob in his love for Rachael was their firstborn Joseph. This is the same entity, and this entity was that one who had manifested to father Abraham as the prince, as the priest of Salem, without father and without mother, without days or years [Melchizedek, Gen. 14:18], but a living human being in flesh made manifest in the earth from the desire of Father-God to prepare an escape for man, as was warned by the same entity as Enoch, and this was also the entity Adam. And this was the spirit of light.

... Science and religion are one when their purposes are one. 5023-2

Many of the world's greatest scientists have made similar statements. In *The World as I See It,* Albert Einstein said, "Science without religion is lame, religion without science is blind." Sir Isaac Newton has been quoted as having said; "No sciences are better attested than the religion of the Bible." Blaise Pascal (considered to be one of the fathers of modern computer science) wrote in *Pensees,* "What reason have atheists for saying that we cannot rise again? Which is more difficult—to be born, or to rise again? That what has never been, should be, or that what has been, should be again?"

When it comes to correlating science and religion, the Cayce readings are uniquely helpful. They offer a broader view of creation that avoids the bickering between evolutionists and creationists. They acknowledge that life forms have changed over the billions of years that the Earth has been here. They also acknowledge the action of God's hand and His purposes in this process every step of the way. The readings stress that matter is a manifestation of spirit, not the other way around. And they even suggest that our own attitudes and actions play a part in the direction that changes will take, making us co-creators with God. The readings do not surrender science, democracy, or the responsibility for taking care of the environment to the secular forces within society.

An Integrated Worldview

Sometimes philosophical and religious writers emphasize something they call a "worldview." This is similar to what scientists might call a cosmology. A worldview is a model of the big picture of why the universe exists, how it works, and what part we play in it. It is recognized that our worldview affects our attitudes and behavior, and, in turn, the future of the planet.

Cayce often spoke of balance in our lives and in our thinking. One individual was told that, as a result of his exposure to the works of Socrates, he found, "the reasoning influences and forces from the material angle becoming at times barriers rather than the greater expression of the spirituality." (538-59) Another person was told, "the *material* may overrun the mental and spiritual. *Coordinate* them; and thus find first thy own ideal spiritually." (718-2)

In our educational systems, we have tended to develop compartments of learning. We have physical sciences, biology, sociology, anthropology, archaeology, political science, economics, religion, psychology, philosophy, history, arts, etc. Some of this specialization is constructive, but scholars in the various fields have often tended to be egocentric. Even though they may recognize that there is much overlap in the various fields, they tend to build their own little worlds with special terminology, jargon, and scenarios—even myths, if you will—that attempt to explain how life works. When taken to extremes this results in a fragmented view of mankind. Perhaps this is part of what motivated thinkers like Descartes and Einstein to look for some kind of unifying system.

When I was in college, I was amused by a running controversy between two of the professors. One of them, a psychology professor, insisted that all behavior is learned, while the other, a biology professor, attempted to persuade us to believe that behavior is completely determined by genetics. If the continuity of life is a fact, then neither of these views makes a lot of sense. We are living souls whose behavior is driven partly by past experiences, which are unseen to either the geneticist or the behaviorist. We are also motivated by our view of the future, which could extend beyond this one appearance in materiality. Heredity and environment do have very powerful influences on our behavior. They may even appear to be the only factors governing our actions when free will is not considered or not applied by the individual. Cayce reading 900-340 deals with this timeless debate between nature and nurture when it says:

> Has the entity in its experience through its will *applied* that of will toward the development, or has it allowed itself to be used by the environment and become subject to environment, or has it developed itself through its will towards its own hereditary position—for *all* are the children of God.

The behaviorist and the geneticist have become polarized at the extremes of their imaginary continuum. Each knows that there is some truth in his or her position. Each is also aware that his or her perspective has not been proved to perfectly account for all behaviors but believes that more research will prove that it does. Even if each one objectively looks at the other extreme, they do not see answers for all types of behavior. Therefore, they conclude that the other perspective is simply wrong. However, they do have much in common. They have both confined themselves to a debate that is tangential to the truth, and they both blindly refuse to consider the obvious spiritual factors governing human behavior. I believe that Cayce reading 416-7 provides a third point of view that is closer to the truth:

> For, as indicated through these channels oft, it is not the world, the earth, the environs about it nor the planetary influences, nor the associations or activities, that *rule* man. *rather* does man—by *his* compliance with divine law—bring

order—out of chaos; or, by his *disregard* of the associations and laws of divine influence, bring chaos and *destructive* forces into his experience.

To the extent that positivism has replaced the spiritual model, the above debate is typical of many controversies that exist in our culture. We take two opposing views, set them at the extremes of an imaginary continuum, and assume that the truth lies somewhere on that continuum. The problem is that actual truth may exist in another dimension completely untouched by our measuring stick.

Sure, it is sometimes fun to solve physics problems and work with machines without having to worry too much about offending anyone's theological sensibilities. It is also edifying to experience the healing power of the Holy Spirit during a church service without having to first prove to a closed-minded skeptic that it works. Even so, it is naive to think that we exist in either realm exclusively. Perhaps some folks simply enjoy arguing about it. The real fun starts, however, when those who can integrate spirituality and science work together to improve the environment, to eliminate poverty and oppression, to heal, to save lives, and to make the Earth more fertile ground for souls to grow toward companionship with a loving Creator.

Once, when I was attempting to explain this kind of integrated worldview to one of my children, I used a two-dimensional coordinate system to represent the reference systems used by the various disciplines. The individual schools of thought (sociology, political science, psychology, religion, biology, physics, anthropology, etc.) were drawn with origin points at various locations on a sheet of paper. Then, making an analogy to the mathematical process whereby axes for different equations can be translated to a common origin to simplify the equations, I began to redraw each of the systems to coincide at a common point. The result was a large cross at the center of the page with arrows pointing to it from all directions. We decided to let that cross represent the Christian perspective—or Christ-centered worldview—as expressed in the Cayce readings, which could unify, in our minds, the divergent schools of thought. The readings often say that our purpose in materiality is to become aware of ourselves as responsible individuals and yet one with God. The cross might also represent the whole law—Love for God (vertical member) and love for fellow man (horizontal member)—which the readings so often stressed.

Evolution vs. Revolution

Cayce often spoke of real positive growth and change as being more evolutionary than revolutionary. The modern mind seems to be most enamored with the idea of revolutionary change. We even refer to the establishment of our country as the American Revolution, while in the broader historical context, it was much more of an evolution. On the great stage of modernism, we typically see the damsel in distress (us) caught in the clutches of the evil villain (classical or orthodox order of things). Then, onto the stage prances the handsome, powerful, young hero (whatever new ism we have devised) who slays the villain so that we, in all our natural goodness and innocence, can live happily ever after. Mighty Mouse wins again!

One problem with extreme revolutionary thinking is that we may tend to focus more on destroying the old order than toward designing a new one. Another danger of revolutionary thinking is that we may tend to focus too much on external conditions and quick fixes, rather than on the positive things within ourselves that we could nurture.

This is not to say that we should not confront the powers of darkness in this world. John the Baptist, and even Jesus, did this; but Jesus had a plan to transform the worldly order into something better, and He knew that it would take much time and sacrifice. Do we not often fail to recognize the evolutionary power of the Christ Spirit coming into our world because we are expecting a quick revolutionary change?

Progress

How much suffering there is! And how happy those should be that have been called to a purposefulness in relieving suffering physically, and most of all in bringing and in giving hope to those who find life's pathway in the material world beset with shadows and doubts and false hopes. 254-79

The thing that struck me in the previous reading was "false hopes." Knowing that all error is based upon selfishness, self-aggrandizement, or self-indulgence, we can analyze our own motives. Is not real hope based on a belief that in Christ we can grow toward being less selfish and more service minded? Do we not often base our dreams on unreasonable hopes of fame and fortune that may never be reached, and that, if they were attained, would be a spiritual disaster for us?

I am convinced that many people, even some who think of themselves as Christians, are afraid that hope in eternal life is a false hope, but materialistic rationalizations do not satisfy the deeper yearnings of the human soul. At the bedside of his dying daughter, Louis Pasteur said, "I know only scientifically determined truth, but I am going to believe what I wish to believe, what I cannot help but believe—I expect to meet this dear child in another world."

The readings, in spite of their difficulties, never fail to offer hope—hope that we will not only have other opportunities to grow here on earth, but that we may someday be made fit for other realms which God has prepared for us in what we call heaven. There is also hope that, through the application of sound principles, we can experience improved physical conditions. This material offers more real hope, mentally, physically, and spiritually, than any other system of thought I have ever experienced. I find that this is confirmed when I listen to the still, small voice within. Or maybe it is the other way around. I receive comfort from the readings because they confirm what the Spirit within has been trying to tell me all along.

We must listen to our reason and common sense as well as to our heart and to God. Reading 440-14 says, "Keep thine feet on the earth, but thine head, thine soul, thine mind, to the whisperings of God!" Let us resolve not to sacrifice spiritual growth for material gain, not to condemn those who lead, not to resist the inevitable flow of change, yet to strive to evolve or grow in a constructive direction toward the pattern set in our ideal, Jesus the Christ. We only have to test God's promises and give God a chance to show what He can do.

23

No Desire to Sin—A New Heaven and a New Earth: Hope for World Peace

If there is sufficient, then, of those that will not only declare this in mind and in purpose but by deed and word of mouth, there may come then an enlightening through that which has been promised of old; that the young men shall dream dreams, the old men shall have visions, the daughters or maidens may know the spirit of truth,—yea, that all may come to the greater knowledge of the indwelling of the Prince of Peace. 3976-26

Both in life readings that tell of ancient civilizations and the in advice given to individuals and groups, the belief that the healing power of the Christ in our lives could spread to others and eventually transform the whole world was a frequent theme of the Cayce readings. Perhaps he was only echoing the same hope that the Holy Spirit had prompted the prophets and bards of old, from Isaiah to Tennyson, to speak. "For now I create new heavens and a new earth, and the past will not be remembered, and will come no more to men's minds. Be glad and rejoice for ever and ever for what I am creating, because I now create Jerusalem, 'Joy' and her people 'Gladness'." (Isaiah 65:17, 18 JB) Alfred, Lord Tennyson's poem, *Ring Out, Wild Bells,* also portrays a vision of a world transformed by those who live a Christian life. Is this just mushy sentimentalism? Must we continue to say that there will always be wars and that nothing can be done about the poverty and depravity that exists in so much of the world?

Civilization
In addition to the evolution of the soul, the Cayce readings also relate to the evolution of what we call civilization. The readings say that spiritual and physical laws apply just as much today as they did in ancient times. Reading 900-70 warns that our present civilization needs more than just the proliferation of human knowledge if we are to survive:

...Many times has the evolution of the earth reached the stage of development as it has to-day and then sank again, to rise again in the next development. Some along one line, some along others, for often we find the higher branches of so-called learning destroys itself in the seed it produces in man's development, as we have in medical forces, as we have astrological forces, as we have in some forms of spiritual forces, as we have in forms of destructive forces of the various natures.

I once heard civilization defined as a group of individuals working together for a common purpose. This is similar to Cayce's definition of civilization as, "...an *attempt* of a local people or peoples to *raise their* individual standards to or toward *an ideal!*" (311-3) In reading 1458-1, the suggested ideal of civilization was given as, "the application of kindness." This reading added that only those who have learned to be kind even to those who would intentionally hurt them are truly civilized. Other readings (520-4 and 374-3) equated civilization to brotherly love and indicated that the finer developments come not only in good relationships with our associates, but also in setting an example before the world.

In our attempts to find the common purposes on which our civilization can grow, it is inevitable that we will have to analyze ourselves as to what gods we serve. Even though we have various international organizations that strive for world peace, the idea of world unity elicits in some the fear that we will lose our freedom and become slaves to some world system. People can not all be forced to agree on ideas. We can, however, demonstrate the benefits of sharing the spiritual belief in one God, one Purpose, one Ideal, or one good for all.

Faith in God as the foundation of world peace is not a new idea, nor is it impossible to achieve. Reading 3581-1 says that, during the time of the exile from Jerusalem, some people from the Holy Land went to the coasts of England, where "altars were set up to tie up the meanings of 'The Lord thy God is one.' The building up of this thought makes no bonds, no slaves among any peoples."

I am ready to move forward with the process of building peace, and I hope you are too. Reading 1742-4 suggests that we are not alone, nor are we without the guidance needed to bring about peace. It says:

The whole of God's creation seeks harmony and peace! So, the desire of the soul for harmony and peace is born of Him that gave, "My peace I give unto thee," not as the *world* gives peace, but as the *spirit* that makes alive that which gives the knowledge of *His* peace—that peace that passeth all understanding!

The Invisible Empire

In reading 3976-4, a group of individuals asked for information on how to form an organization to "control finance, railroads, oil and steel industries, ...news syndicates," around the world for the "upbuilding of mankind by establishing hospitals, churches, schools, farm loans, rural road constructions..." Cayce told them that these goals were constructive but very idealistic for a group of their position and means. They were reminded of Alexander the Great and Kaiser Wilhelm of Germany, both of whom had similar ideals in the beginning. Yet, both were diverted from those ideals by the power that they grasped in the pursuit of their goals.

Surprisingly, however, Cayce advised this group to prepare themselves for leadership and to continue their quest, but added "Only in Him in whom there was found no guile." They were told in reading 3976-7 that they must "...*crucify* the *flesh* that the *light* may shine forth" and that they must live their ideals daily if they did not want to become a "Frankenstein." Reading 3976-4 said that, by living the teachings and example of Jesus, such conditions could be "...brought to the realization of those who would *build* an invisible empire within the hearts of men..." Warnings were given about seeking to dominate others and the dangers of dealing with money, but they were also told that "These [their ideas] are worthy, if they will make themselves one in the purpose as set; for many peoples—in many nations, in many climes—are ready and willing to follow that Light, that Star."

Christian Witness

Some people seem to believe that if we avoid using the name of Jesus then we can be more in unity with those of other faiths who might be offended by the focus on the Christ. It may be true that mindless over-zealousness did not end with the Crusades. Nevertheless, the Christ is the catalyst that can help us to grow toward mutual love and acceptance. Jesus knew that Christians would often find themselves in this difficult situation when He said, "For if anyone in this adulterous and sinful generation is ashamed of me and of my words, the Son of Man will also be ashamed of him when he comes in the glory of his Father with the holy angels." Mark 8:38 (JB)

Being Christian must always be a personal choice, but Christianity also has a world vision—to make the world a better place for all of God's children. We must learn to share that vision in ways that are not coercive. I believe that we can join hands peacefully with all around the world who believe in the One God, with great respect for every person's faith, and yet not being ashamed of our own.

Conspiracism

Someone once said, "If all objections must first be overcome, nothing will ever be done." When we speak of world peace there are many who will provide theories about why it can't be achieved. In the book, *Conspiracy—How the Paranoid Style Flourishes and Where It Comes From*, Daniel Pipes wrote:

> Conspiracy theories have a way of growing on a person, to the point that they become a way of seeing life itself. This is *conspiracism*, the *paranoid style*, or the *hidden-hand mentality*. Conspiracism resembles other "isms" in defining an outlook that can become an all-encompassing concern. It begins with belief in an occasional conspiracy theory— Illuminati organized the French Revolution, Jews the Russian Revolution—and ends with a view of history that dwells largely or exclusively on plots to gain world power or even destroy the human race. In complete form, it takes over the lives of the faithful and becomes a prism through which they see all existence.

Of course, there are real conspiracies in the world against which we should be vigilant. But, conspiracism goes beyond the truth and robs us of a proactive outlook on life. This kind of thinking was prevalent among some of the world leaders in both world wars and was a driving force behind most of the atrocities that were committed. You probably know some people in your own sphere who are infected. Whether the enemy is seen as another race, a religion, a "secret" society, the Council on Foreign

Relations, The United States government, the United Nations, or aliens, conspiracism can blur the line between facts and rationalizations.

On June 16th, 1939 (less than a month before I was born), Edgar Cayce was asked the following question during world affairs reading 3976-24:

> (Q) Is there today in operation an outer organization representative of the anti-Christ forces, which has power to subvert governments as well as institutions? If so, will you explain and give directions for counteracting these forces?
>
> (A) As has been given, there is the need more for the world thought, for every soul turning to the power within, and giving *God* a chance with their lives, their purposes, their desires one with His!
>
> And there *is* that power that is only in the influence for destruction as man himself gives it power. But just as has been given of old, *one* with the strength, the power of the Lord, may put the thousands to flight.

Our faith in God's justice should make us a little less susceptible to conspiracism. Jesus said, "Do not be afraid of those who kill the body but cannot kill the soul; fear him rather who can destroy both body and soul in hell." (Matthew 10:28 JB) Cayce quoted this passage in the world affairs readings and elsewhere.

We can be sure that we will be tempted to see others as a threat to our world and our beliefs, but when we externalize our problems, we are not being proactive. Only that which can cause us to think or act selfishly toward any other soul can separate us from God's love. Ephesians 6:11,12 (JB) says,

> Put God's armour on so as to be able to resist the devil's tactics. For it is not against human enemies that we have to struggle, but against the Sovereignties and the Powers who originate the darkness in this world, the spiritual army of evil in the heavens."

The Fatherhood of God and the Brotherhood of Man

...If there is not the acceptance in America of the closer brotherhood of man, the love of the neighbor as self, civilization must wend its way westward... 3976-15

In the above reading Cayce defined the brotherhood of man as loving our neighbors as ourselves. When asked in reading 3976-24 if the Fascist movement was a danger to the U.S., Cayce replied, "Any *movement* that is other than that of the brotherhood of man and the Fatherhood of God is dangerous!" When he spoke of the Fatherhood of God and the brotherhood of man, Cayce was simply referring to the whole law as Jesus gave it in the Bible. Unfortunately, some sectarian-minded individuals seem to fear that this causes us to include in this "brotherhood" those who have not accepted their Savior or who do not belong to their church. Perhaps even the best of Christians occasionally act like something other than children of God. But all souls have the potential of being God's children and should be treated as such.

The phrase, "The Fatherhood of God and the brotherhood of man," was so common in the early nineteen hundreds that some people now consider it to be passé. To further complicate matters, there have been attempts to associate this phrase with some mythical group that wants to control the world. I believe, however, that this idea of the brotherhood of man goes back even beyond the Essenes to the prophets of the Old Testament:

It is not enough for you to be my servant, to restore the tribes of Jacob and bring back the survivors of Israel; I will make you the light of the nations so that my salvation may reach to the ends of the earth. Isaiah 49:6 (JB)

He will wield authority over many peoples and arbitrate for mighty nations; they will hammer their swords into ploughshares, their spears into sickles. Nation will not lift sword against nation, there will be no more training for war. Each man will sit under his vine and his fig tree, with no one to trouble him. Micah 4:3-4 (JB)

New World Order

This prophesied time of peace has been called by some the new age, the new millennium, or "the new world order." This idea of a "new world order" has also become a catch phrase for some reactionary groups. Cayce gave some advice about the bickering that can result from this kind of thinking:

> ...Each and every individual is attempting to give *their* interpretation, and you may be sure that each is just as sincere as the other.
> ...*Thou shalt love the Lord thy God with all thy heart, thy mind, thy body: thy neighbor as thyself!* Those who conform the nearer to that are correct. Yet, do any? Do you? Does your neighbor? Do those with whom you find fault? Do those to whom you apply the principles? 5142-1

Any positive changes begin with a vision. Cayce said, "That thou hast purposed oft in thy heart, through this experience, that thou dost hold as thy ideal in the spiritual realm, applied in thy daily life, in thy daily associations will be a *new vision*—if ye will but hold to same!" (1562-1) While the readings were full of visions of peace, I found only two readings that contained the phrase "new world order." It is hard to see how anyone could interpret either one as anything other than Christian. Here are excerpts from both readings:

> Individually—know that right, justice, mercy, patience— as was represented and presented by Him, the Prince of Peace—is the basis upon which the new world order *must* eventually be established, before there *is* peace. 416-7

> [In response to a question about the A.R.E.'s role in establishing the new world order] In all groups, all organizations, it is not what this or that name or group may do, but as *one.* For, the Lord thy God is *one!* And the Christ, the Savior, died for all—*not* for one! no sect, no schism, no ism, no cult. For, the first to meet the Lord in peace was he that was also crucified. That should, in each heart, make those who have named the Name, and who claim God as Father, Jesus Christ as the elder brother, know that no sacrifice is too great in order that the glory, the honor of the Lord may be demonstrated, manifested among men. 3976-27

Freedom

For groups as well as for individuals, there is more freedom and creativity in unselfishness than in selfishness. Here are some readings that speak about constructive uses of freedom:

> ...These are the purposes upon which this land were founded; and they are those forces, those self-evident facts of man's existence that are a part and parcel of every soul's expression in the material plane; that freedom of speech, freedom of the purpose for worshipfulness of Creative Forces according to the dictates of one's own conscience, shall never perish from the earth. 2167-1

> ...that they may know that the heart of America is in that purpose of supplying thy brother,—though he be black or white, though he be Gentile or Jew, though he be bond or free. For *all* men *must* be free. 257-250

> ...He (the Christ) has set the example of freedom of speech, freedom of activity; yet bound within that which is ever constructive. He has not given freedom that is licentious, or freedom that is self-indulgent, or freedom that does not consider the needs, the desires, the positions of others... 1352-4

Equality

Many Christians today are concerned with the problem of racism, not just in our country, but in the world. While this is only one form of bigotry, some of the ideals in the readings would apply to other issues as well. Reading 3976-27 makes it clear where the readings stand:

> This [racial hatred] also is answered only in that the Lord is not a respecter of persons. "He that doeth the will of the Father, the same is my brother, my sister, my mother." Those to man, represented the closest relationship,—blood of his own blood, materially.
>
> Then, mentally, spiritually, *do something about* those of the races that are misunderstood, or who have been neglected here or there! 3976-27

Cayce not only denounced racism, he also gave practical ways to deal with it within ourselves:

(Q) Why have I strong racial prejudices—and should they be overcome?

(A) This has been a portion of the experiences as through this very sojourn, as well as in many others; but these may not be so well overcome. Rather let the life and the activities be an *active* service and not a passive. For know that *God* is not a respecter of persons nor of races, but is as has been given of old, "Know the Lord thy God is *one!*"

And if the activities are for an active service in that direction, prejudices are lost sight of in the Love Divine. 1438-1

Technology

In reading 1066-1, a man was told that in an Atlantean experience he had used physical force to fight the "sons of Belial and Beelzebub", or to "fight the devil with his own fire." The reading says that this technical knowledge was later used to provide personal conveniences much as we have today and that these conveniences had turned him away from his original purpose of working for freedom for all souls. He had learned that these conveniences are good "...if they are kept in check. But these running riot for self-indulgence, for self-glorification, for selfish interests, become in the end those things that turn and *rend* the very heart of the body itself."

Technology is a tool that can be used to make physical life better in this experience, if we do not lose our focus on spiritual growth. When we use technology as a palliative to avoid understanding the spiritual causes of our problems, then it can become almost addictive. Communications technology, for example, has driven the world economy to new levels in recent years. We must choose, each day, whether we will use the benefits of this knowledge to share spiritual truths and promote peace, or if we use it for exploitative and self-indulgent purposes.

Environment

Our concern for the Earth says something about our relationship to God. We have all heard of stewardship, but we often abuse the good Earth that God has given us, sometimes even allowing ourselves to be polarized against worthy environmental concerns by political and economic fears. Here is a reading that reflects the spirit of Cayce's philosophy on the subject:

> ...those influences for conservation—that *must* become more and more a part of man's experience...
>
> ...with the activity of nations,—whether it be of fishes in waters, birds of certain caliber or needs for food, or for the varied manners that they give protection to certain portions of the land, or timbers or the better conservation of soil for certain seeds or crops—all of these are the channels as we find in which the entity may find contentment and harmony...
>
> Of course, the land continues to grow—for it is God's footstool. Man's abuse of same gives way to those things such that it becomes no longer productive. But if there is the conservation of its strength—the lands, the timbers, and God's creatures that manifest through same—it is a continuous [sustainable] thing. 1931-1

Leadership

When I was quite young, I overheard my father in a political discussion. He said that, even though he had not voted for the incumbent president, he had been elected fairly by the people and we should give him our respect and support until we could elect someone more to our liking. My father was not against honest, constructive criticism, but was obviously unsympathetic to the constant partisan political posturing that is still so common today.

During Franklin Roosevelt's term in office, Cayce was asked by a banker (261-16), if the impression of some businessmen that the administration's programs had slowed down the economic recovery was accurate. The banker was told that this was "whispering propaganda on the part of those who have *formerly* been in power." Then, when the banker asked if Roosevelt had lost in popularity, Cayce replied, "More due to that said in jest than anything else. This jest has been made the scapegoat; yet it, as anything that may be said and taken up as a chorus, may become very destructive..." This was followed by a question as to whether there was a trend toward "radicalism" in this country. The answer was that this trend was confined to certain groups and not likely to infect the whole country. The advice in the following reading might help us to avoid radicalism:

Put away hate, malice, jealousy, or the taking sides with any that stir up strife.

Be ye rather on the Lord's side—knowing that no man is in any position of power or might save by the will of the Father, that there may be fulfilled that which has been promised of Him, by Him, and through that advent of the man Jesus into the material world.

Then, as ye meditate upon the meaning of the resurrection of this man of God—know that the way is open to thee to approach the throne of God; not as an excuse, not as a justification, but rather in love, in harmony, in that which brings hope for a sin-sick world.

Each individual, then, may act, may live, may pray—in his or her own little sphere of activity—in such a manner as to bring peace and harmony, even among those who *appear* to be at variance to the cause of the Christ in the material world.

Let not thy heart be troubled, then. Ye believe in God; believe also in Him—who came to bring peace, and the way to the Father, exemplifying same in the ability to take away death—that is as sin in the experience of man.

And thus may he (man) indeed love the Lord with all his heart, and his neighbor as himself. 5749-12

After reading this, I began to recognize a tendency in myself to take sides too quickly, even to the point of developing strong emotions that were not consistent with my ideals, and then to rationalize my feelings verbally. This facilitated the possibility of spreading negativity to others. The effect that this realization had on my mind was even more powerful as I began to see how my children were affected by my example. Reading 5747-2, which deals with juvenile delinquency, says:

And if there is the force or influence in the high place that shows or is spoken of as questioning, or if there is a question mark put after the name of the minister, the lawyer, the doctor, the politician, the judge, the jury, the father or the mother, it but creates in the *mind* of the individuals that which impresses and leads and directs.

We are fortunate that we can question our leaders and can hold them to the same standards that everyone else is expected to live up to. However, criticism that appears to be motivated by petty jealousy or political ambitions can lead to a lack of respect for all leaders, and therefore, to a lack of cooperation justified by flimsy rationalizations and excuses for selfish behavior.

In an earlier chapter, the Earth was compared to a school. The time of peace that we are promised is a time when those who lead will know that their purpose is to provide a place for souls to grow toward their eternal home. The following readings suggest to me that we should train and pick our leaders according to spiritual standards:

> ...he that would be great in power, in leading, in directing, will be in self a *servant* and not *master* of all...and building such *in* self will give an understanding and a consciousness of *making* self one *with,* not one *of* God's children... Just as it is to be laughed *at* or laughed *with.* Get that! 270-17

> Look into the hearts of those that apparently are successful in material things, and unless such successes are founded in the spirit of justice, mercy, love and long-suffering and brotherly kindness, they must fade and fall away. Yet, if they are builded in these things that are the fruits of the spirit, they will grow and blossom as the rose of Sharon... 531-3

> Know, in thy forming of policies and attitudes towards others, that there are immutable laws; and that what ye would give out—if ye would have any semblance of success, or a growth within thy own experience—must be constructive in nature.

> Also know that what ye sow, in mental, material and physical relationships, will be measured back to thee again...

Know that there are very, very few individuals who do not by nature respond to constructive thought, constructive application...

Then have that policy to do unto others as ye would have others do to you. *Expect* that! *Live* that in thy dealings! And ye will find that He who is the Giver of all good and perfect gifts will bring to thy experience not only harmony and peace but greater opportunities, with material, social and financial success. 1634-1

Starling of the White House

On August 29, 1943, Edgar Cayce gave a reading (3182-1) for a sixty-seven-year-old retired colonel who had been a personal Secret Service guard for five presidents, from Woodrow Wilson to Franklin D. Roosevelt. Col. Edmund W. Starling asked how he could go about publishing a book about his experiences in the White House. Cayce gave a number of suggestions about how to lay out the book and what kind of human-interest stories would be best to include. He was told to focus on principles and not to laud or belittle any particular individual. The reading contained four different warnings that he should leave out politics.

Starling had been with Wilson at the Paris Peace Conference, and it was suggested this should be the main focus of the book. "Then present the *great opportunity* of the American nation, and missing the boat—in the Peace Conference. These are the great themes." The reading said that this should be a warning to the Roosevelt administration not to make the same mistakes at the end of World War II. It said that it was not important for a peace plan to have a certain number of points as long as it had the one important point, "*I am my brother's keeper!*"

When asked who would be the best publisher for the book, the reading said, "Simon & Schuster," and added that they would be waiting for it. The book, *Starling of the White House,* was written with the help of Thomas Sugrue and published by Simon & Schuster just as had been suggested.

Economics/Poverty/Wealth Distribution

...There will be no want in bread for mankind when mankind eventually realizes he is indeed his brother's keeper. For the earth is the Lord's and the fullness thereof, and the bounty in one land is lent to man to give his brother. Who is his brother? Our Father—then each of every land, of every color, of every creed is brother of those who seek the Father God. This instill as you interpret. 5398-1

In June 1943, Cayce was asked, "Will it be possible to maintain a fair standard of living for our own people while helping to raise economic standards in other parts of the world?" His reply was, "Not only *must* it be possible, it *must be done!* if there will be *any* lasting peace! But it must begin in the hearts and minds of individuals..." (3976-28)

In one of the first economics courses that I took in college, the professor started out by saying that the basis of economics was that there is a scarcity of goods and services for which we all compete. In a management course the basic premise was that the main purpose of a company was to make a profit for the stockholders. The first of these ideas shows a lack of faith that God has provided enough for all of His children. The second idea shows a lack of responsibility for putting service to the community first. These traditional attitudes are quite out of touch with the better management techniques that are being taught today, but those old ideas still plague us in our dealings with one another.

The readings often speak of the need for better wealth distribution. The most common means suggested for accomplishing this is to be our brother's keeper and to provide equal opportunities for all people:

> Principles must carry through to the laboring man, whether it is the one that is selling the log, or the man that is the rough finisher, or he that sweeps up the floor! Don't think that the man at the top can take it off of or out of the lives of the laborers and get away with it! He can't! 257-182

> ...For the earth is the Lord's and the fullness thereof, and they that hoard same—whether it be bread, wood, gold or what—are only cheating themselves in cheating the Lord. For thy brethren are thy obligation. For thou art thy brother's keeper. 3409-1

...and there is the seeking for those channels, ways, means or manners in which all men must share with the products of their labors in a manner commensurate with the efforts applied by each individual. 1151-29

Then if those in position to give of their means, their wealth, their education, their position, *do not* take these things [being concerned about all human conditions] into consideration, there must be that leveling that will come.

...These are the manners in which such things as crime, riots and every nature of disturbance arise—in that those who are in authority are not considering every level, every phase of human activity and experience. 3976-19

Cayce gave advice to several people who were involved in mediation between labor and capital. The following readings are but a sample of these to demonstrate Cayce's application of Christian ideals in the field of economics:

...and that only when Capital considers Labor's position, and Labor considers Capital's position—and that they coordinate—may there be the good for all...

This may be exemplified then when Capital and when Labor love one another as brethren. For indeed it is the same cry, "Thou *art* thy brother's keeper!"...

It, such, the spirit *is* the foundation that made the empire of Rome powerful. Only did it begin to fade and its power begin to lessen when it became overburdened with the desire for self-aggrandizement, self-glorification, and forgot that it was its brother's keeper.

So it is in this land of thine own in the present, that is builded upon that *freedom* of speech, *freedom* from those things that would make men afraid.

But freedom means rather the individuals working in cooperation according to the dictates of their conscience as to the *manner* of worship, but the *worship itself* of Truth, Life, Love, Brotherly Love and Kindness!

And these are the basis of this land; and its union of strength lies in *keeping* such as the motivative forces in the lives and hearts and minds of those as they labor one with another. 1151-12

...Let there be a constant stressing of this fact—do not have labor working *for* you, have it working *with* you! This should be stressed! Let each individual be encouraged in its activities with the feeling that it is "our" purpose, and not for the undertaking. This will create just that as indicated as to the purposes, not as to overlording but the all working *together.* 257-238

For all stand as *one* before Him. For the Lord is *not* a respecter of persons, and these things [class distinctions] *cannot* long exist.
From the conditions in these other lands, then, America—the United States—must take warning.
For to WHOM does the wealth belong? to WHOM do the possibilities of the land belong?
Does it belong to those who have inherited it, to those who have been given the positions by power? or to those who have by their labor, by the sweat of their brow *produced* same? 3976-19

...For those with a million dollars are no more precious in the sight of the heavenly Father than they that are hungry in the street! 254-81

The readings caution us not to blame those with wealth and power for our problems, but to look within our own hearts. They also insist, however, that those with more of the world's goods have a responsibility to help others. There is no formula given in the readings as to how much charity should be facilitated by the government, but the ideals given here should be of great help to all who are concerned with such matters:

...in that same principle that he that labors may eat, he that labors not may not eat. These are principles; and, to be sure, capital labors as well as he that worketh with the hands. But *not* to the detriment of, but to the united effort of all to be a greater channel of service. 3976-24

For as ye have caught a glimpse of here as an individual: the manner in which an individual, a community, a state or nation treats those less fortunate, those ill, those aged and infirm, those mentally possessed, is the manner in which such an individual, community, state or nation serves its Maker. For God so loved the world that He gave His Son. That is a pattern which each individual should emulate, he should so love his fellow man. 3615-1

Capitalism vs. Communism: Let Love Rule

While Cayce saw the dangers of idolizing the free market and accepting greed as the primary motivation in our economy, he nevertheless avoided the opposite extreme to which some have taken the idea of communism. The readings suggest that the benefits of free enterprise can be used constructively if we are guided by love:

...the entity was of that *cult* as would be termed of the capitalistic nature today; hence might made right (in its final analysis).

As a business executive, influences arise in the present from that experience that make for the abilities good in the entity—*for* business. For the expansions,—let love rule; and we may find that these *can* and may be worked together. 2381-1

Not that all would be had in common as in the communistic idea, save as to keep that balance...each soul is by his *own* activity to be given the opportunity of expression, of labor, producing.

But all of these, also, are not to say where or what, but are to seek through their *own* ability, their *own* activity, to give that of themselves that is in keeping with those who labor in the vineyard of the Lord.

Hence these may apply in the national and international relationships. 3976-19

Armageddon

Bishop Fulton J. Sheen, in *Peace of Soul*, wrote:

Unless souls are saved, nothing is saved; there can be no world peace unless there is soul peace. World wars are only projections of the conflicts waged inside the souls of modern men, for nothing happens in the external world that has not first happened within a soul.

This is somewhat parallel to Cayce reading 900-272, given in October of 1926, in which it was said:

> ...The spirituality of the American people will be rather as the criterion of that as is to become the world's forces, for, as has been given in that of the peace table, there sat the Master in the American people, with the brotherhood of the world accepted—war was at an end. Without same there will again come the Armageddon, and in same there will be seen that the Christian forces will *again* move westward. 900-272

Notice that Cayce said that Armageddon would come again, indicating that it could have already occurred. In another reading, it was suggested that World War I could have been followed by the expected time of peace if selfishness and greed had not prevented it. Woodrow Wilson also predicted that there would be another war worse than World War I if we did not concert the means to prevent it. He even saw that the United States might later have conflicts with Japan. It is no consolation that he turned out to be right. Just like the prophets of Israel before the exile, the readings insist that wars do not have to occur if we will only put our trust in God. World affairs reading 3976-23 says:

> So long as ye turn thy thoughts to the manners and means for meeting and overcoming those destructive forces, ye show forth that which can bring the day of the Lord. For the promise is that in the latter days there shall be the purposes in the *hearts* of men everywhere.

Save the World Club

As our family read the Bible together many years ago, we were impressed with the story of Abraham as he negotiated with God, hoping to save Sodom. He talked the angel into saying he would spare that city if Abraham could find only ten good people. There were ten of us in the family, so I suggested that we could start a "Save the World" club. If only we could live according to God's

Word, then perhaps we could prevent some troubles from coming to our part of the world. Our children are now scattered around the country and are busy raising their own families. I hope they remember some of the biblical lessons that we studied.

The readings reflected the biblical lessons that Cayce knew so well and that are just as valid today. If applied, they could make pessimism obsolete.

As has been given, however, that which has prevented and does prevent the whole of civilization becoming a turmoil is the attempt of those who have the ideals of the Prince of Peace at *heart!* And as of old, the prayers of ten may save a city; the prayers of twenty-five may save a nation—as the prayers and activities of *one* may! but in union there is strength. 1598-2

And as ye live, so may the Christian light of *love* encompass the earth; not that of hate, selfishness, money, power, or fame!

Then, all ye who are gathered here—Do not entrust this to someone else, but "I—even I!" Let rather thy cry be: "Lord, here am I! Use me in the way and manner that Thou seest best fit; that we may preserve the faith we have in the Lord, the Savior, Jesus the Christ; that we may still be as one brotherhood; as one knowing Thou art near; as one manifesting Thy power, O God; not of ourselves, but that others may see Thy glory—even the one next to me. Even though he may curse; may swear, may do those things that are unseemly, let thy power be manifested, O God; that Jesus, thy Son, may indeed come into the earth; that all men may know that He is the Lord of my heart, my mind, my body, my home, my county, my state, my nation!" 3976-25

Show due consideration as to how much ye owe the world, rather than as to how much the world owes you! 2172-1

Second Coming

Someone recently told me of a sign that said, "Jesus is coming back. Look busy!" Reading 262-114 says essentially the same thing:

> For that which has a beginning must have an ending. Hence rebellion and hate and selfishness must be wiped away, and *with it* will go sorrow and tears and sadness. For *only* good shall rule. For it is the Spirit of God that will move over the face of the earth, and Lo, His Son—even Jesus, the Christ—has borne in Himself all these things, and has committed unto us the keeping of His sheep, His lambs, till He come to make an accounting with each of us.
> Where—where—where will we be?

The readings say that the Master will come again when we have prepared a place for Him in our hearts and in our lives. Cayce said good things about those who love the coming of the Christ, but we do not have to know the exact time. Why not assume that He is coming soon, and act like it? He has given us an example. We should know what to do. Can we not recognize Him even now in the good that we see around us?

> These changes in the earth will come to pass, for the time and times and half times are at an end, and there begin those periods for the readjustments. For how hath He given? "The righteous shall inherit the earth."
> Hast thou, my brethren, a heritage in the earth? 294-185

> And, as has been indicated, when this period has been accomplished, then the new era, the new age, is to begin. Will ye have a part of it, or will ye let it pass by and be merely a hanger-on, or one on whom your brother—the Lord, thy Christ—may depend? 2780-3

The Promised Time Of Peace

Whether you call it the New Age, the Messianic Age, the Millennium, or the New Jerusalem, it is understood that people hope for the promised time of peace. Josephus called it the "revolution of the ages," songs have called it the Golden Age, and theologians might call it something simple such as the eschatological transformation of the world. The readings also speak of this transformation, which must begin within individuals:

[Speaking of Rev. 21:1-4] ...Can the mind of man comprehend no desire to sin, no purpose but that the glory of the Son may be manifested in his life? Is this not a new heaven, a new earth? For the former things would have passed away. For as the desires, the purposes, the aims are to bring about the whole change physically, so does it create in the experience of each soul a new vision, a new comprehension...

(Q) Please explain 2nd thru 4th verse of Chapter 21—the new Jerusalem and no more death.

(A) Those then that are come into the new life, the new understanding, the new regeneration, there *is* then the new Jerusalem. For as has been given, the place is not as a place alone but as a condition, as an experience of the soul.

Jerusalem has figuratively, symbolically, meant the holy place, the holy city—for there the ark of the covenant, the ark of the covenant in the minds, the hearts, the understandings, the comprehensions of those who have put away earthly desires and become as the *new* purposes in their experience, become the new Jerusalem, the new undertakings, the new desires. 281-37

In a Christmas reading (281-59) that was given in troubled times (December 1941), Cayce commented on "the purpose for which the Christ came into the earth:"

First—that the level of man's consciousness might be such that he, man, would be as aware of God as of himself.

Second—as in each of His promises to man—that love might abound; that there would be a *continued* communion with God through the Son, who offered Himself as a means of man's approach to the Father.

Reading 3615-1 says:

...Think not that ye or any other individual may be the only one serving a living God. For since His entry into the world, and His making it possible for man to find his way back to God, there has been and will continue to be an increase.

As more and more individuals manifest the love of God in their personal lives, they will become better citizens and better leaders. Eventually that love, and the peace that it brings, will reach critical mass and become the rule rather than the exception in all of our affairs:

> Though experiences have arisen in the entity's sojourns when might and power were apparently necessary to meet the evil influences being manifested among men, know that it is ever—as man's development comes—the still small voice within that is the direction, and not pomp or glory, or the ringing of bells or the sounding of trumpets as armies march on. Rather it is here a little, there a little, line upon line, precept upon precept, that man attains his relationships to the Creative Forces. 2167-1

> (Q) What is the meaning of one thousand years that Satan is bound?
> (A) Is banished. That, as there are the activities of the forty and four thousand—in the same manner that the prayer of ten just should save a city, the deeds, the prayers of the faithful will allow that period when the incarnation of those only that are in the Lord shall rule the earth, and the period is as a thousand years.
> Thus is Satan bound, thus is Satan banished from the earth. The desire to do evil is only of him. And when there are—as the symbols— those only whose desire and purpose of their heart is to glorify the Father, these will be those periods when this shall come to pass.
> Be *ye all determined* within thy minds, thy hearts, thy purposes, to be of that number! 3976-14

> Be *glad* you have the opportunity to be alive at this time, and to be a part of that preparation for the coming influences of a spiritual nature that *must* rule the world... Be happy of it, and give thanks daily for it. 2376-3

24

What Will You Do With This Man, Jesus?

How beautiful the face, how lovely the clouds! In His presence abide; ye *every one* of you are before Him just now. His face is turned toward thee, His heart and hand is offered you. Will ye not accept Him just now? How glorious the knowledge of His presence should awaken in the hearts of you, for He is *lonely* without thee; for He has called each of you by name. Will ye fail Him now? 254-96

When considering what the Edgar Cayce readings have to offer to modern-day Christianity, two things come to my mind. The first is a balanced understanding of the life of Jesus and the significance of His mission. The second is the daily application of that understanding in real-life situations.

Cayce was able to emphasize the humanity of Jesus and the lessons He taught, without denying the power of the cross and the Resurrection. He saw Jesus who became the Christ as the Savior of the world and a personal Savior for all who will accept Him. Yet, the readings also affirm that the pattern of the Christ Consciousness dwells within each human soul. The readings teach love, compassion, and forgiveness in every situation without denying the fact of cause and effect in the spiritual world as well as the physical. They reawaken the awareness of the immortal and divine nature of the human soul. And, just as important, the readings stress that we grow spiritually, not just by what we know or what we believe, but by what we apply in our relationships to God and to our fellow human beings.

The Work

The readings, as mentioned earlier, often refer to the teaching and dissemination of the spiritual aspects found in the Cayce information as "the Work." The Association for Research and Enlightenment (A.R.E.), which was formed to carry on that Work, is today a very dynamic and far-reaching organization; but the Work as mentioned in the readings often refers to something even broader than the A.R.E. It suggests a sense of mission to join with the Christ to help all souls find their way back to God. It does not exclude those of any other organization, church, or religion. In its wider sense, the Work is being done by others around the world who have never heard of Edgar Cayce and who might even tend to ignore or reject his contribution. I feel strongly, however, that the Cayce readings have the potential to add some essential understanding and power to the Christian movement in the world.

In addition to the thousands of personal readings, the A.R.E. obtained a series of readings called the "work readings." This series (254-1 through 254-116) provided guidance for Edgar Cayce and his associates from 1911 until 1944. These work readings also suggested the formation of an educational institution, later named Atlantic University, to teach these spiritual concepts to the world. In March 1929, reading 254-48 suggested that the educational phase of the Work could reach millions of people:

> ...Not a sectarian awakening; not a dogmatic awakening—but that of the same truths as is set forth in "The meek shall inherit the earth—The pure in heart shall see God". He that is grounded in the truths as set forth here is grounded indeed in the truths that makes the individual one with, in will and purport, the whole creative energy, and will make for that individual the faith that moves mountains and maketh the pastures green where there was a consternation and trouble before.

The Edgar Cayce Foundation is another organization that is part of the Work of the A.R.E. The purpose of this foundation is to preserve the readings and to carry on some educational aspects of the Work. On August 4, 1928, probably at a time when encouragement was needed, this reading was given:

> ...for into thy hands has been committed the keeping of those records—yes, those conditions that are as records—of the foundation of that upon which the better understanding of man's relation to the all creative energy within self may be made manifest in the earth's plane at this period... Keep that committed unto thy keeping against that day when there will be said, "Well Done", according to that as enacted in this present experience. With the coming of the dawn many will call thee blessed. 254-43

The prediction in reading 254-83, given six years later, has come to pass, and the warning in it is still good advice:

(Q) Would it be properly named *The Cayce Foundation?*
(A) If it is any name, it is through these sources, these channels as a name, that much may come. For the day will arise in thine experience, of those, of this group who seek, of those present, when they will see, will hear, it *sounded* about the earth. *Do not—any of you—*make it as other than a welcome of the glory of a crucified self, a crucified Lord! 254-83

My impression is that this Work begun by Edgar Cayce is consistent with the highest ideals of the Christian faith and the Holy Scriptures. I am personally familiar with the A.R.E., the Edgar Cayce Foundation, and Atlantic University, and have found them all to be involved in some very constructive programs. I cannot, however, assure you that they are now, or that they will always be, perfectly in tune with the purposes indicated in the Work readings. Nor can I vouch for the church that I belong to, or any church or any other human organization, in this respect. The only affiliation that I can unequivocally recommend is a personal relationship with Jesus Christ, and only God Himself can tell you if that is right for you. If you do choose to follow Him, you must then choose the organizations within which you feel called to work. Then it will be your job to work to keep those organizations in tune with the Holy Spirit.

The Bible is one record of a people's response to the inspiration of God's Holy Spirit. That same story of our relationship to God is still being written today. Edgar Cayce was just one person of many who have been willing to be used in the process. St. Paul admonished Christians to seek the gift of prophecy. The readings suggest that others should prepare themselves spiritually to carry on the Work at the A.R.E. or wherever they choose to work.

I have been asked if there are other people today who can give readings like Edgar Cayce did. I have known of many other individuals who have a variety of spiritual gifts, some similar to Cayce's. They come from all kinds of orthodox as well as alternative expressions. No two ministers pastor their church in exactly the same way, however, and it is also unlikely that anyone else would have a gift exactly like Cayce's.

I have not personally searched for anyone who could give me a reading. If I did try to find such a person, I would apply all of the tests discussed in earlier chapters. Cayce often insisted that we could develop gifts similar to his, or other gifts even more appropriate to our situation, simply by pursuing a closer walk with God. For now, I am content to work with what I already know and to depend on God to give me more when I am ready.

This is not to say that I do not feel that it is important to connect with other like-minded souls. I have met many people who have read about this Work and then desperately wanted to find other persons to talk to about it. Often, they want to be a part of the Work, but do not know how to go about it. Many times those closest to them do not understand what they are talking about.

If this happens to you, it might be helpful to contact the A.R.E. to check out any *Search for God* study groups that are near you or to find out about programs that might be offered in your area. If you feel called, you should never feel that there is not a place in the Work for you. Reading 262-6 says, "Whosoever *will* has a part, or parcel, in *His* work. This is *His* work! He that has *called to* thee!" This usually begins by applying the information right where you are. You might find a group that is in accord with your own ideals, or you might start a study group with friends, or you might just begin to apply these principles within the organizations with which you are already affiliated.

We must all exercise discernment in regard to any beliefs that we are asked to embrace or condone, but we should also be careful not to reject other members of the Body of Christ just because we have not made the effort to understand one another. It is my hope that *Give God a Chance* might help to build a bridge to those of other groups who might otherwise be apprehensive about the Cayce Work.

Reading 254-54 says:

> ...Let each join hands with Him, for if the work undertaken be not *His* work, have nothing to do with same, and the judge shall be thine *own* conscience; for conscience *is* that which awakens the mind of the soul; the *soul,* that

of thine self that is the nearest portion of the dwelling place *of* the Holy of Holies Himself—the *spirit* of the Master.

A Final Word

The Edgar Cayce readings have been a tremendous source of comfort and help to me. I hope that you have found something in these readings that answers to some need within your soul, or that you can use this book to share your convictions with a friend. I also hope that someday, somewhere, we can meet and enjoy the fellowship of kindred souls. Until then, I will let the readings have the last word:

What, then, will you do with Jesus?

For He is the Way, He is the Light, He is the Hope, He *is* ready. Will you let Him into thy heart? or will you keep Him afar or apart? Will ye not eat of His body, of the bread of life? Drink from that fountain that He builds in the minds, the hearts, the souls of those that seek to know Him and His purposes with men, with the world!

For having overcome the world, He *indeed* has it—as it were—in the palm of His hand; and has entrusted to you this world, because of His faith, His love for you.

What will you do about Jesus and His trust *in you?* 254-95

Give God a Chance is also available as an e-book from 1st Books Library at www.1stbooks.com. This format could be useful as a tool to search for specific words or topics.